Videogames in the Indian Subcontinent

Development, Culture(s) and Representations

Souvik Mukherjee

B L O O M S B U R Y
NEW DELHI • LONDON • OXFORD • NEW YORK • SYDNEY

BLOOMSBURY INDIA
Bloomsbury Publishing India Pvt. Ltd
Second Floor, LSC Building No. 4, DDA Complex, Pocket C – 6 & 7,
Vasant Kunj, New Delhi, 110070

BLOOMSBURY, BLOOMSBURY ACADEMIC INDIA and the Diana logo are trademarks of Bloomsbury Publishing Plc

First published in India 2022
This edition published 2022

Bloomsbury Academic
An imprint of Bloomsbury Publishing Plc

ISBN: HB: 978-93-54355-24-0; eBook: 978-93-54356-91-9
2 4 6 8 10 9 7 5 3 1

Typeset in Manipal Technologies Limited
Printed & bound in India by Replika Press Pvt. Ltd.

Contents

Acknowledgements

I never thought in my wildest imagination that this book would ever see the light of the day. The day I sent off the signed contract to Mr Chandra Sekhar, Publisher, Bloomsbury India, a nationwide lockdown was imposed due to the Covid-19 pandemic. Gone were my chances of visiting libraries, archives and the countries that I had not yet visited for my fieldwork. As the whole gaming world was writing ecstatically about Tom Nook in *Animal Crossing*, I was trying to make sense of the mass of material that I had collected when I was planning this book, knowing that some of the gaps that remained might not be filled. There were days when I was unsure that I would ever be able to finish this book as the pandemic claimed the lives of family members, and life as a department chair during the times of the pandemic made it almost impossible to work on the book. Thanks, however, to the patience of Mr Chandra Sekhar and the full cooperation of Bloomsbury India that this book is now a reality.

Besides the reviewers, the copyeditor—Arnab Karmakar—the proofreader and the staff of Bloomsbury India, I would like to thank my former students, Isha Lahiri and Sohini Sengupta, for their help with compiling the timelines in Appendix One. I had no idea that they would transform what could potentially be a boring task into something that became a serious research project. It is a matter of pride to see these fine young scholars mature as they prepare to embark on their research journeys.

This is the first book that covers the videogame industry and culture of the entire Indian Subcontinent and as such, I have many people to thank, although it will never be enough. Anando Banerjee of Lakshya Interactive spared his valuable time to allow me to interview him even as the pandemic was raging. Professor Bhabani Prasad Sinha, former professor of the Indian Statistical Institute, was gracious enough to talk to me at length about the early days of computing in India. The depth of knowledge that Rishi Alwani has about Indian videogames (and also about the other countries in the Subcontinent) is unparalleled; to him goes my endless thanks for all his help and guidance. Shailesh Prabhu has been kind enough to respond to all my queries as and when I had them. Rajesh Rao of Dhruva Interactive also spared time from his busy schedule to respond to my email. Leena Kejriwal and Satyajit Chakraborty have always been helpful and forthcoming with data and details. Satyajit and I have had many *adda* sessions in the quintessential Bengali fashion and I have learnt much about game design from him. Yadu Rajiv, I am extremely grateful to you for telling me about your fascinating experience of becoming a game designer. Poornima Seetharaman, I was always your fan, and ever will be so for your championing of women in gaming. Dhruv Jani has matured into this fantastic game designer from the day when I met him at the Khoj workshop in Delhi and got late for my keynote lecture after sitting mesmerised with his wireframe game that has now become the hallmark of Studio Oleomingus. I am grateful to Prabhash Tripathy and Gagun Chhina for sharing their research experience with me. Among the designers from abroad, I would like to thank the corporate communications department of Portbliss in Bangladesh for responding to my interview request and Amani Naseem of the Maldives for her cooperation.

As far as my researcher colleagues are concerned, Padmini Ray Murray has been an important figure for as long as she has been involved with games research and design in India. Dibyadyuti Roy has been another important interlocutor about gaming cultures in the region. Debanjana Nayak played an extremely important role in convening the first-ever international game studies conference, GamesLit, which was held in India, despite many unforeseen challenges. No games research in India can be complete without taking into account the work of Adrienne Shaw, Casey O'Donnell and Xenia Zeiler. I have, towards the last phase of writing this book, been fortunate enough to collaborate with Xenia. I also have to thank Tom Apperley and Tomasz Majkowski for their unstinting support of my work. Emil Hammar has been more than a friend and, recently, Frans Mayra and others at the Centre of Excellence in Game Culture Studies, Tampere, have been very supportive. Espen Aarseth, who was kind enough to visit Kolkata, was a big source of inspiration. Tanya Krzywinska has always been a big support as has Mia Consalvo. I learnt a lot from Phillip Penix-Tadsen and Jaroslav Svelch who have both essayed similar adventures before me in writing their books. Umer Hussain was extremely kind in sharing his thoughts with me and connecting to respondents for the survey. Darshana Jayemanne has also been very helpful in connecting me to other scholars from the Subcontinent.

While this book was being written, I was able to achieve my longtime dream of setting up a DiGRA chapter in India. With the tireless effort of Poonam Chowdhury, Souvik Kar, Sourav Chattopadhyay, Aritro Bhattacharya and Riko Banerjee, we started out as Game Studies India and were soon joined by the wonderful Zahra Rizvi and Geoffrey Fernandez in our endeavour to make DiGRA India a reality. With over 20 talks and an almost equal number of podcasts, DiGRA India is about to get its own footing. It has also enabled me to interact with game designers and researchers across India and the Subcontinent. I am also grateful to all the respondents of the survey.

I have to thank a few others who are not connected to game studies but have inspired me and supported me in the process of writing. Rosinka Chaudhuri, Sumit Chakrabarti, Anupama Mohan, Mousumi Mandal, Anirban Ray, Dickens Leonard and Rajarshi Ghose have all been important sources of support. My friend Koushik Sinha listened to my seemingly crazy ideas from his home in the USA and connected me to his father, whom I was able to interview.

Finally, and most importantly, I would like to thank Amrita Sen and Mira Bella Mukherjee for assisting me and keeping me sane during these difficult times. Once again, I cannot believe that this book has finally happened. If it has, then it is all thanks to Amrita and Ada that I was able to write it.

Videogames in the Indian Subcontinent: An Introduction

I was introduced to the word 'videogame' in the year 1988 when I first laid my hands on a 'water videogame' that was given to me. I would be doing injustice to the word 'videogame' as the word was a misnomer for the toy I had received: behind the plastic screen of the toy, there was water in which little plastic rings floated. On pressing a rubber button, the rings would float up and the player had to guide them into two plastic pillar-like structures present in the toy. The so-called water videogame (nowadays known as the water-ring game) may have received its name because it resembles the handheld videogames that came to very few Indian upper-class families as foreign imports. In the late 1980s and into the early 1990s, computers were a novelty in India, handheld videogames were just becoming available to the middle classes and consoles were rather rare. Coming to the present day, we now have a game called *Battlegrounds Mobile India* (Krafton 2021) that had reached almost 50 million downloads at the time of writing this book. Also, an Indian indie game, *Raji* (Nodding Heads 2020), has garnered much respect and a slew of awards internationally. In neighbouring countries such as Sri Lanka and Bangladesh too this is evident: in the former, a triple-A (the industry term for relatively high budget games made by large or midsized companies) game is being planned on a mythological theme and in the latter, a videogame is celebrating the nation's freedom struggle. At the same time, videogames like PlayerUnknown's Battlegrounds or *PUBG* (PUBG Corporation 2017) and *Garena Freefire* (Garena 2017) have been topics of controversy in some countries while others have included eSports among their official sporting events. I have always wondered whether the story of videogames is similar for people in other countries in the region. This book aims to explore the gaming cultures of one of the most culturally diverse and populous regions of the world—the Indian Subcontinent.

The Indian Subcontinent, referred to as the Subcontinent here onwards, comprises India, Pakistan, Bangladesh, Sri Lanka, Nepal, Bhutan and the Maldives. The region is one of the most populated in the world and is home to multiple religions, languages and cultures. Hinduism, Buddhism and Jainism are three prominent world religions that originated in the region.[1] Hindi and Bengali are spoken by over 600 and 268 million people worldwide, respectively. Geographically, and in terms of natural resources too, the region is one of the most diverse in the world. India is a major of the G8+5 group of nations and is a major centre of trade. India, Pakistan and Bangladesh were part of British India and Sri Lanka (then Ceylon) and the Maldives were part of the British Empire. Nepal and Bhutan were monarchies and have now seen a significant change in their political systems. The Subcontinent, particularly India, Pakistan, Bangladesh and Sri Lanka, has taken major leaps in digital technology, despite being latecomers in the field. It must, however, be kept in mind that the region, although sharing common elements in its culture(s) and history, is nevertheless very diverse and also fraught with conflict and complexities. While there has been considerable research on digital cultures in the region in recent years (for example, Punathambekar and Mohan 2019, Ninan Thomas 2012, Gajjala 2003, Rajan 2007 etc.), digital games have received scant attention although they are a hugely influential yet much neglected emerging technological phenomenon today in the Subcontinent. Games like *PUBG* and its current version, *Battlegrounds Mobile India,* have had a major impact on public policy in India, and globally, India has been perceived as a 'sleeping giant' of the videogame industry with immense untapped potential. Bangladesh, Pakistan, Sri Lanka, Nepal and Bhutan also have developed significant gaming cultures but these have been overshadowed by the general concern with India. With the already huge and constantly burgeoning smartphone access, the Subcontinent potentially has the largest reach for videogames across the world.

1 Statista (2021), 'Most Spoken Languages in the World'

Influences and Rationale: Reviewing Earlier Scholarship and Outlining Current Objectives

Following the works of scholars like Phillip Penix-Tadsen—whose *Cultural Code: Video Games and Latin America* (2016) and *Videogames in the Global South* (2019) have taken forward what Bjarke Liboriussen and Paul Martin call 'regional game studies' (Liboriussen and Martin 2016)—and pathbreaking global studies like *Videogames across the World* edited by Mark J. P. Wolf (2015), where I have also contributed a chapter on India, the importance of such research became evident to me. While it was a daunting task, it seemed extremely necessary and timely to start thinking of a book that attempted to make sense of the gaming cultures of the Subcontinent. Of course, in the Global North, there has been some very inspiring research by Mark Wolf, Jason Schreier (2021), Iain Simons and James Newman (2018) mainly on the USA and Europe. Again, from a somewhat 'othered' perspective on the USA, Carly Kocurek's (2015) work on the arcades of the 1970s and the 1980s presents an intriguing study of a lesser-known aspect of American gaming culture. Juho Kuorikoski's (2015) history of videogames in Finland has provided insights into a very different kind of videogame culture, albeit one where the games industry developed later than the USA and Japan through the efforts of a few individuals. Mia Consalvo (2016) and Rachael Hutchinson (2020) have written path-breaking studies on Japanese gaming cultures that have helped compare and contrast the gaming cultures of the Subcontinent with that of another Asian country with a distinctly developed gaming culture and industry. Besides Penix-Tadsen's research on the Global South, it has, however, been Jaroslav Svelch's *Gaming the Iron Curtain* (2018) that has been particularly helpful for me in showing how the history of gaming cultures can be charted in places with very limited access to home computers and hardware and software markets.

Speaking in terms of digital media in general, Ashwin Punathambekar and Sriram Mohan (2019) have also covered this region in their book, *Global Digital Cultures: Perspectives from South Asia*. Their book also addresses a vaster arena of digital media in general as well as countries beyond the Subcontinent such as Myanmar. The degree of their efforts is indeed praiseworthy. They have stated that their goal is to attempt to 'understand the ongoing digitalization of media, communication, and culture in South Asia as part and parcel of global transformations' (Punathambekar and Mohan 2019: 8). Within its limitations of addressing the digital game industry and gaming cultures, this book will also make a similar attempt. There are, of course, many similarities between other digital media and videogames in South Asia. The authors quote Ravi Sundaram (2001) and Mobina Hashmi (2012) in stating that 'the 1980s and 1990s [...] were marked by a "frenetic media multiplicity" when cassette culture, colour television, VCRs, cable and satellite broadcasting, and the Internet all arrived with hardly any temporal gaps' (Punathambekar and Mohan 2019: 9) in both India and Pakistan, presumably also extending to the rest of South Asia. Somehow videogames were not as 'frenetically' incorporated into the media cultures of the Subcontinent. While there was a scramble for cassette recorders, Walkmans and colour televisions, videogames were less common in the Indian markets and middle-class homes. As will be discussed in Chapters 2 and 3, consoles have taken a while to make an appearance in Indian homes and that too after multiple abortive attempts by manufacturers, both foreign and local. Some of the earlier consoles never made it to Indian markets and even early PC games were late in making an appearance.

The history of gaming in the Subcontinent is, of course, that of latecomers to the medium and how that connects to the development of software industries, and other policy-making and cultural mores of the region have hitherto not been explored. As a majoritarian geopolitical influence in the region, India often finds a place in globally popular videogames; this is, however, not exclusively the case—for example, Nepal is most likely the locale of *Far Cry 4* (Ubisoft 2014). Local games often represent their country's histories or sociocultural issues through the medium of videogames. *Missing* (2016), an indie game addressing India's girl-trafficking problem, has recently won accolades in global forums such as 'Games for Change', but has still not received any academic attention. Despite the growing popularity of videogame, stakeholders in the industry, policymakers, academia and the media have not yet managed to fully comprehend the influence of videogames in the Subcontinent. Game studies, although now a well-established area of academic enquiry for the past three decades globally, is yet to enter the curriculum in this region. Despite the best efforts of the National Association of Software Companies (NASSCOM) in India and independent companies like Unity, the industry still requires a stable source of support and guidance even in India, which has the biggest industry presence compared to the other nations in the region. This book aims to provide governmental and private stakeholders in the videogames industry get a better and more accurate idea of the market, player cultures and the potential for its development in global terms.

Building on the author's earlier and pioneering work on videogames and postcolonialism, this book also addresses issues of how discussions of equality and diversity sit within videogame studies, particularly in connection with the Subcontinent. How issues of gender, race, religion, ethnicity and, uniquely in this context, caste, are addressed in digital game cultures of this region and is an important question that this study tackles, arguably for the very first time. Also, questions regarding videogame violence, keeping in mind the recent *PUBG* controversy and other similar issues, will be analysed within the framework of player cultures. Drawing on a series of player and developer interviews and surveys conducted over the last five years as well as very recent ones, this book will attempt to provide a sense of how games have become a part of the culture of the region, keeping in mind its huge diversity and plurality. This book, while considering that it is not possible to provide a holistic description of such a complex phenomenon, will nevertheless attempt to open up avenues for further study through vignettes and snapshots of the diverse gaming culture. In the process, it also aims to make a connection between the development of games and player cultures thus opening up channels for collaboration between the industry and academic research, both local and global.

This book proposes a threefold strategy to understand and analyse gaming in the Subcontinent. Firstly, there is the need to address the massive lack of knowledge about how the world's fastest-developing entertainment medium is faring in one of the most populous regions. Secondly, gaming as a phenomenon is mostly studied as a Western preserve—at most, some discourses include Japanese gaming. The same cultural parameters cannot be so unquestioningly applied to the Subcontinent. The Subcontinent has, arguably, the largest potential in terms of sheer numbers of gamers and a huge diversity of cultures unique to the region. So far, however, it has remained a largely uncharted area for both academic researchers and the global industry. This book aims to address this gap. Thirdly, the analysis of gaming in the Subcontinent also needs to connect to the larger discussions on digital media cultures and digital humanities globally.

In outlining the plan for his book *Latin America and Videogame Cultures*, Penix-Tadsen lays out a clear plan of what he intends to cover:

> For Latin American cultural studies, the book offers a portrayal of the complex relationship between games and the region's cultures over several decades of development. Latin Americans (like all gamers) approach games first and foremost as players, and this book demonstrates how unique local practices, playing habits, and software and hardware adaptations throughout the region reflect a diverse and expanding population of gamers that crosses all socioeconomic sectors of society. (2016: 2)

A book on the Subcontinent covers a similarly significant area not only in geographic but also in cultural spaces. The varied cultural contexts of gaming often differ in subtler ways from the gaming cultures of the USA, Europe and Japan. The peculiarities of the local games industry and the complex relationship between the regions' cultures and games over the decades are all relevant in the context of the Subcontinent. Anyone researching the Subcontinent, however, faces the hurdle of trying to look back at the early history of gaming in the region. In an early essay on games cultures in India, games scholar Adrienne Shaw (2013) notes that games have historically been 'external' to the Indian culture. Shaw's observation has been discussed at length in Chapters 5 and 6; here, it is being assumed that it applies to videogames and not to all games in general (India's rich ludic culture dates back millennia). She goes on to point out how videogames have been connected to time-wasting, antisocial behaviour and addiction—all issues that are still being raised in present times.

Working in a Scattered Archive: The Struggles and the Rewards

How is it possible to comment on the history of a medium that is external to a culture? Also, were there any parallels to the late entry of videogames that could be used as a point of comparison? Svelch's (2018) work on videogames in Cold War Czechoslovakia can be looked into for this. His comments regarding the need to forget the stereotypical Western arc of history will be an appropriate entry point to such a comparison:

> In the 1980s, Czechoslovakia was a state socialist country without a functioning hardware or software market, where much of the microcomputer activity took place within paramilitary clubs and youth organizations. When faced with such an environment, a historian must forget the stereotypical arcs of game history narratives—the rises and falls of commercial companies, the 'behind the scenes' accounts of famous titles, the development of franchises and intellectual properties. (2018: xxv)

Just as in Czechoslovakia where most computer-related activities took place in the army or youth organisations, in India such activities took place either in the army or in specialised academic institutes. Given the serious nature of such applications, computer games were unthought of. There were interesting exceptions but those stories are told in Chapter 1. While the nature of computing activity in the Subcontinent was quite different from that described in Svelch's account of the hobbyist culture in Czechoslovakia, his comment regarding forgetting the stereotypical arc of history, wherein the milestones of gaming in the USA, Europe and Japan are considered important benchmarks, is very apposite—the usual gaming high and low points do not always apply in the context of the Subcontinent. It was only in the late 1990s that gaming in the Subcontinent started catching up with the rest of the world. However, even then, many aspects of gaming, such as multiplayer games and console games, had to wait much longer. For a medium where the records are not available in archives or museums (unlike the museums of digital games in Berlin, Melbourne, Sheffield and California or those of games in general such as the Strong Museum of Play in Rochester, New York, there is no such entity in the entire Subcontinent[2]), reconstructing such history is a challenge. Oral history accounts and ephemera prove to be important sources as do tangential references in histories of computing.

As far as India is concerned, books such as *Computer Education in India: Past, Present and Future* (1996), edited by Utpal K. Banerjee and published for the Institute of Electronics and Telecommunication Engineers in 1996, or the more recent *The Outsourcer* by Dinesh Sharma (2015) or *Homi Bhabha and the Computer Revolution* by R.K. Shyamsundar and M.A. Pai (2011) have been extremely instructive in providing a picture, albeit hazy, of the early days of computing in India. Also, the *Itihaasa* Research and Digital's (Itihaasa-Research and Digital 2020) very recent project on chronicling the history of Indian IT is a rich resource of oral history and curated print archives that throw new light on the lesser-known aspects.[3] Nikhil Menon's research (see Menon 2018) and the publication of Arun Mohan Sukumar's *Midnight's Machines: A Political History of Technology in India* as recently as 2020 made it possible to attempt to create a context for the otherwise empty sections of the timeline of computer gaming in India, particularly in terms of the sociopolitical events of the period. Sukumar's astute observation that '[t]he counterculture movement began as a resistance against industrialization and ended up creating Silicon Valley. On the other hand, its cousin in India, the "appropriate technology" movement, set back scientific progress by at least a decade' (Sukumar 2019) is an apt appraisal of the scenario of comparison between India and the USA and Europe in the 1970s. At the same time, when the USA was being overwhelmed by the dot-eating Pac-man, the computer had become an object of public hatred as a 'job-eating machine' in India. Perhaps, it is because of this attitude to the computer and the complexities that

2 A museum of sports called the Fanattic Museum of Sports was opened in Kolkata, India, in 2017, but it is now closed. Another such museum in the Subcontinent is the National Institute of Sports Museum in Patiala, Punjab, in India, but it is dedicated to outdoor sports.

3 Despite tracing the history of Indian IT from its early days to the present, or as late as 2020, the project does not list any development in digital games, strangely.

led to the exit of IBM from India in 1977 (see Sharma 2019) that public memory relating to the early days of computers in India is so sketchy. As such, the early memories of videogames that have been used to form an idea of gaming culture as it may have existed have had to be gleaned from surveys, personal experiences and accounts of people who would have played the retro games. There is no computing museum in India; I am reliably informed that the HEC-2M and the URAL computers that were the first computers in the country are in a state of disrepair. Tata Institute of Fundamental Research Automatic Calculator (TIFRAC), the computer designed and built indigenously, was exhibited recently by Google at an online exhibition commemorating it. Anyone visiting the museum of India's former prime minister Rajiv Gandhi in New Delhi cannot fail to notice his Toshiba T5200 laptop; he was instrumental in ushering in India's telecom revolution and was also one of the early adopters of laptop computers. However, not even Rajiv Gandhi's laptop with its 4 MB RAM would have been able to support many computer games. These are a few of the pioneering computers in India that there is a record of—that too, of course, is a rather haphazard way and only if one knows where to look. Most of our computing history is to be found in the flea markets of the big cities. Of the gaming machines, the arcade machines, the handheld Nintendo clones or the early desktop computers that could play games, there is even less formal archiving; most of the old arcade machines can be found in the erstwhile videogame parlours or the flea markets. There is also hardly any trace of the 5 and 1/4 inch floppy disks that would store games. From the late 1990s onwards, however, the historical trajectory becomes much more analysable and despite some difficulties regarding information about the earliest games and their makers, there is enough to go on to piece together the role of videogames in Indian culture of the times. Today, although the popularity and availability of videogames are much greater, the old disconnect with a mainstream culture still plays an important part in shaping the perceptions around videogames.

Even less has been published on the videogame histories of other countries in the Subcontinent and a similar disconnect is evident. Mustafa Jabbar's book *Digital Bangla* (2005) helps in getting an idea about the computing scenario in Bangladesh. Blogs such as kushal.

net (Kushal 2018) record the early history of computers in Nepal while 'TRT World' or the Indiana University at Bloomington's blog (Reynolds 2013) lays out how computers were first installed in Islamabad, Pakistan. Sri Lanka has an entire website relating its ICT history—https://www.ict-history.lk/en/. This website lists in detail the contributions by individuals who played an important role in setting up the nation's digital infrastructure with special attention to systems such as payment, policy, legal environment, industry, cybersecurity, language and education. Nevertheless, barring a few such well-documented exceptions, in most cases, it is a difficult task to piece together the history of information technology (IT) in the Subcontinent from the scattered sources; a picture of the gaming culture(s) is even harder to construct as organised archives do not exist. Perhaps because of the erroneous cultural association of games being non-serious, digital games have not been archived adequately in the region. India's preponderance over the other countries and gaming industries and culture is also another factor.

In the largely unresearched Subcontinent's gaming culture, India has received the most attention in international academia. Casey O'Donnell (O'Donnell 2008 and 2014) dedicated a large section of his doctoral thesis (and later his book) to the Indian game industry. Adrienne Shaw's (2013) work has been discussed earlier along with my writings. Xenia Zeiler's (Zeiler 2014, 2016, 2020 and 2021) work also concentrates on Indian gaming as does Padmini Ray Murray's (2015). Aditya Desbandhu's *Videogames in India* (2020) also focuses exclusively on India and that too on a few specific aspects of the gaming culture. The Subcontinent as a whole does not get represented. Because even though the primary focus is on India, the first point of comparison is Bollywood, perhaps because of its global popularity as a key cultural marker for India. Such a comparison, however, is not entirely justified. The film industry in India started in 1913 (Hutchinson 2013)[4], close on the heels of the first film in the world. With *Raja Harishchandra* (Phalke 1913), which derived its content from Indian mythology, the

4 Pamela Hutchinson notes that the Lumière brothers screened their short films in India in 1896, almost two decades earlier.

film industry in India was already connected to mainstream Indian cultural discourses. Videogames have not enjoyed such a connection historically and their appearance on the Indian scene was as imports from the USA, Europe and, less so, from Japan. Although there was a market for Hollywood movies among a section of the Indian middle class, for most people, videogames would remain a distant and largely inaccessible medium for a while, especially until the late 1990s.

Transculturation, Glocalisation and Videogames in the Subcontinent

As such, the cultural framework that informs the identity of the videogame in the Subcontinent is not an easy one to define. Shaw titles her article, 'How Do You Say Gamer in Hindi?' and then follows up by asking about other languages spoken in India. Indeed, these are languages spoken in other countries of the Subcontinent as well—whether in Hindi, Bengali, Urdu, Tamil, Nepali, Sinhalese or Dzongkha—the term 'gamer' does not have a different local equivalent. It is a 'transcultural' term one might argue. 'Gamer' retains its sense that is prevalent in the Global North but it also acquires many different connotations. For those wondering how such a global term takes on a different meaning, a starting point would be to consider the medium on which computer games are played. The term in this part of the world would include the thousands who play these games on their mobile phones or PCs with antiquated graphics cards. The term also carries multiple meanings wherein the level of engagement with videogames is also very loosely defined. In a sense then, 'gamer' is acculturation—a cultural import that has been adopted by a group of people in the Indian Subcontinent; it is, however, also a deculturation in the sense that it has lost some of its original meaning of a die-hard videogame player and in the sense that it has acquired a new meaning without losing the original one entirely; it is a neoculturation that one encounters in the millions playing *PUBG* and *Freefire* on their mobile phones. Together, these processes of acculturation, deculturation and neoculturation are described as transculturation, a concept that was first discussed by the Cuban anthropologist Fernando Ortiz in his book *Cuban Counterpoint* (Ortiz 1995). Ortiz was responding to Bronislaw Malinowski's concept of acculturation from a postcolonial perspective. The framework of transculturation has also been employed mainly by the postcolonial theory to identify relationships that show 'how subordinated or marginal groups select and invent from materials transmitted to them by a dominant or metropolitan culture' (Pratt 2007).

While, of course, the colonial connection of videogames is not evident directly, this chapter and this book will keep it in mind when illustrating the process of transculturation. The framework of transculturation also relates usefully to other concepts such as glocalisation that are discussed at various points later in this book. While transculturation is a concept that can apply to anything and even to Bollywood films and other entertainment media, the evidence of it is more direct in the case of videogames, especially as most of the popular titles are imports from studios located in the Global North. At the same time, many of these studios outsource sections of these games to companies in the Subcontinent and that is a fact that should not be ignored. Likewise, the playing patterns of players in the Subcontinent and also how the region and its peoples are portrayed in these games are also part of the process as are the responses to such portrayals. Such a scenario does not just denote a West-rest situation or even a Japan-rest situation (see Consalvo 2007) but more complex interplays, pun intended. As mainly a Western cultural product (Japanese games are still not as popular in the Subcontinent unless they are imported via the West as are the popular Japanese cartoons Pokemon and also *manga*), there are doubtless resounding indications of cultural imperialism, especially given that many of these countries were part of the British empire until the middle of the previous century. Cultural imperialism as articulated in the works of Louis Althusser, Antonio Gramsci and Raymond Williams has been applied already in the case of television by commentators such as Herbert Schiller (1971).

For East Asian countries, such as Taiwan and Singapore, similar cultural imperialism by Japan has been observed and is described by the term *hari*, which 'connotes irrational admiration for a specific nationality: Japan' (Chen 2013: 411). It is in this context that transculturation has been used in connection to videogames in Asia in prior research (see Wang 2019). Hui Wang comments on how the videogame, despite being a Western invention and 'the RPG game was born from tabletop war games, sandbox, and card games that have long traditions in Europe and later the United States as hobby activities [...] the arena of video gaming was not unfamiliar to East Asia—after the 1983's North American video game crash, Nintendo (Japan) has singlehandedly revived home console game market and since then dominated in both the East and the West' (Wang 2019: 42). It is in this context that he wishes to use the framework of transculturation to analyse videogames because '[t]he mass commodity and participatory nature means that gaming is not a predetermined product, but results of continuous cultural negotiation based on complex power relations of various forces and actors that range from technology, business, culture, and social factors' (Wang 2019: 45).

Wang also invokes Arjun Appadurai's five dimensions of global cultural flow: ethnoscapes, mediascapes, technoscapes, finanscapes and ideoscapes. The scenario of videogames is fruitfully examined based on global technoscapes and mediascapes instead of being looked at as a single cultural entity; these again are influenced by the other dimensions that Appadurai lays out. As Wang further comments to illustrate his point:

> [t]he rapid development of information technology, computer using, Internet literacy, and imported American games such as *StarCraft* (1998) all contributed to the vibrant and unique culture of Internet Café (or PC *baang*) and its social gaming communities, which nurtured the special leisure-sport form of competitive gaming (2019: 46).

Similarly, transculturation within a global media and technoscape is also applicable in the Indian Subcontinent, albeit with different parameters and characteristics. It is intriguing, however, that prior commentators on the gamescape in Asia did not include the Subcontinent in their analyses.

While this is not the space to theorise on why such a lacuna exists, it is important to note that given the question of cultural imperialism of the West and then the framework of transculturation that makes the scenario far more complex than mere cultural imperialism could describe, another important lens through which gaming culture in both South East Asia and South Asia (including the Subcontinent) has presented itself is that of *glocalisation*. Glocalisation (Japanese: *dochakuka*) is a concept that involves adapting global outlooks after taking into account local considerations. Japanese media theorist, Koichi Iwabuchi (2002) describes the process as rendering 'culturally odourless' Japanese products and he uses Mario as an example. While Mario does not have any Japanese characters, Iwabuchi's examples of Pokemon characters and the numerous manga and anime characters such as Naruto that are popular in global contexts are illustrative of his point.

In terms of game development, game designers from the Subcontinent are increasingly engaging in building games that have a local flavour and connect to local history and mythology while also wanting to compete on the global markets and be relevant in other cultures. For example, the Indian game *Raji* has been acclaimed worldwide and has adapted to the Nintendo Switch, which is prohibitively expensive in India and as such does not have a large user base (see Alwani 2020). The game itself is quite a mix in terms of its gameplay, which draws on hack-and-slash and platforming mechanics. Its art, which is a mix of Rajasthani and Mughal architecture with Balinese puppetry, and storyline too draws on Indian mythology. In its attempt to remain relevant to international audiences, the game is localised in multiple languages (the default being English), and it also has sections of conversations between Hindu gods which serve as a tool for narration/exposition. More will be said of *Raji* and other games from the Subcontinent like *Threta* (Prodigi Interactive), which is under development in Sri Lanka, that employ glocalisation strategies in the later chapters.

Even with or without any ostensible intention, the very process of transculturation that informs play cultures in the Subcontinent often also affects glocalisation of sorts. Such a process is not necessarily driven by the industry or the exporters of culture (or cultural imperialism) as in the original description of the concept. Consider the case of a game that is commonly referred to as *Mustapha* or *Mustafa* in

India, Pakistan and Bangladesh. The actual name of the game is *Cadillacs and Dinosaurs* (1993) and it was released in Japan as Cadillacs Kyouryuu Shinseiki (キャディラックス 恐竜新世紀, *Kyadirakkusu Kyōryū Shinseiki*). Made by the Japanese company Capcom and based on the *Xenozoic Tales* series written by Mark Schulz (1987–1996) and published by Wisconsin-based Kitchen Sink Press, the game spans multiple cultures. The protagonists of the game are the mechanic and shaman, Jack Tenrec, diplomat and explorer, Hannah Dundee, engineer Mustapha Cairo and the mysterious Mess O'Bradovich, again representing different parts of the world. In the Subcontinent, the game was called *Mustapha* by most players, after its eponymous protagonist. Although the game features four protagonists, it is known all around India, Pakistan and Bangladesh by the one name that people in the region were more familiar with and the hero they could most identify with. The game takes on a new identity and a title that its fans in the Subcontinent prefer. The Bangladeshi game streamer NoBossGaming (*Cholun Ghure Ashi Mostafar Jogot Theke* n.d.) has a YouTube video that takes the viewers to the world of Mostapha: "চলুন ঘুরে আসি মোস্তফার জগত থেকে' (Let us visit the world of Mostapha). There is Bengali commentary before and during the gameplay and the comments on YouTube are mostly about local experiences where people remember having stolen money or playing truant at school to play the game. Blogger Ishaq Ali (2020) reminisces about his time playing Mustafa in Delhi:

> [B]ut back in the mid-90s, Cadillacs and Dinosaurs was a huge deal in the various gaming arcades of Delhi. Lovingly referred to as Mustapha, who happens to be the fan favourite out of the four selectable characters, this game was a staple for any arcade owner and the go-to game for arcade dwelling kids. [...] No other game offered this much playtime for a single coin at the time.

The predicament of the cash-strapped middle-class Indian youth is also reflected in the playtime that is available per coin. A Japanese-made game that is based on an American comic, therefore, took on a new form in the Subcontinent. There are many other such examples and if one wished to look for even more direct and obvious examples of transculturation, *Grand Theft Auto: Punjab* would be an obvious choice as a modification of *GTA: Vice City*, which is set in the Indian state of Punjab rather than its original American setting.

Such examples are merely indicative of the distinct flavour of gaming in the Subcontinent, with all its diversity and its rich play culture, sports and media cultures that influence the way digital games are perceived and experienced in the region. The somewhat delayed and uneven exposure to digital technology, as has been indicated earlier and will be discussed at length in the following chapter, has also been a crucial factor in shaping the videogame culture in the region. In the face of such diversity, there has also been a resounding archival silence in terms of videogame history or even discussions on gaming cultures. Gaming magazines and websites are also fairly limited; India has had gaming magazines such as '*Skoar!*', which has been revived after having gone defunct, and websites such as the 'themakoreactor'.com and indianvideogamer.com—but this is not true of the other countries in the region. Often, social media groups, such as 'Gamers of Bangladesh', have been important sources of information. Surveys conducted among members of such groups have been helpful. Then again, often online sources tend to be ephemeral. For example, the NASSCOM Game Development Forum's group on Facebook has now disappeared after going strong for many years and has been reconceived to the India Gaming Forum. Documentation has been patchy at best if it has existed, and while organisations such as PricewaterhouseCoopers, Statista.com and others bring out prognostications for the industry and other such statistics, it is an uphill task to collate and compare such reports. Often field trips to some of the countries have been required to get a better first-hand picture of the gaming cultures there; however, the outbreak of the COVID-19 pandemic for the entire period of writing this book has meant that it has not been possible to organise visits to most of the countries in the Subcontinent and the information that has been collected has been obtained via online surveys and interviews. This leaves a lacuna in this study and the gap keeps shape-shifting as videogames, play cultures and national policies towards videogames keep changing. Even at the time of writing this book, the Bangladesh High Court has just banned *PUBG* and *Freefire* as being dangerous games, much to the chagrin of thousands of fans in the country. India banned *PUBG* and then brought it back as *Battlegrounds India*. Pakistan and Nepal have also banned the game at some point. The limitations imposed by COVID-19 have had a two-fold effect. It has not been possible to conduct onsite interviews in any of these countries and, secondly, without access to physical records in libraries, that aspect of archival research has been foreclosed. Many key books on videogame cultures have been published during this period. Some major games have been released in this period. The much-awaited *Cyberpunk 2077* emerged as a major disappointment; the Playstation 5 gaming console was released globally[5] and India's very own *Raji* has completed one successful year on the Nintendo Switch. During this period, much of the Subcontinent was devastated by the first and second waves of the pandemic and many lives were lost. Gaming saw a huge spurt in popularity and then became the subject of controversy in many countries in the region. As such, this study was undertaken under many constraints and some anomalies. Nevertheless, this book is meant to be a starting point for many more discussions regarding gaming in the Subcontinent and is an attempt to highlight the importance of the region to videogame researchers and, indeed, to media studies scholars and historians.

The Map is Not the Territory: A Brief Chapter-wise Plan

The main argument of the book is divided into three sections. Section One focuses on the development and attempts to chart the history of digital games by first looking at the history of IT in the region. After attempting to chart the trajectory of game development from the arrival of videogames on the cultural scene of the Subcontinent (it is important to remember that this did not happen all at the same time for the different countries) in the first section, Section Two analyses and discusses the ludic culture of the Subcontinent in general and then connects to the

5 The PlayStation 5 launch in India was a disaster initially as the console sold out on the first day and there was no restocking. (Tech2 News 2021)

videogaming culture in current times. In Section Three, the videogame is viewed as a cultural text through which the Subcontinent is represented both in global and local games; serious issues relating to diversity and inclusiveness are also raised in the process. The concluding remarks indicate the need to develop more dialogues between the gaming cultures of the Subcontinent and other gaming cultures, particularly that of the Global North. What follows is a more detailed chapter-wise plan.

Videogames are a newer media in the Indian Subcontinent, especially in comparison to the other geographies where the consoles were available much earlier. In Chapter 1, the historical assessment of the software and gaming industries leads to examining the government policies regarding computing and software in post-independence India and other countries as interesting cases to consider. The late entry of computer games and indeed the virtual absence of the Commodore, Amiga and the early Nintendo systems from the Indian market and the relative newness of the player culture in India are, for example, a much-neglected area of research. The general surge in telecom technology and the large number of smartphones running games on Android, iOS or Windows has altered the picture significantly. Earlier commentators observe that the Indian gaming culture is relatively new and they begin making the connection with the development of the software industry; however, the issue needs to be explored in more depth. As for countries other than India, there is no extant academic research to trace the growth of the industry and gaming cultures. This chapter will engage in such an enquiry.

Chapter 2 revisits the current scenario of game development in the Subcontinent, which is comparatively better documented. From the early FPS games (first-person shooter), such as *Yoddha* (based on the Kargil War with Pakistan) and *Bhagat Singh* (based on India's freedom struggle), the Indian gaming industry has now emerged as a significant player with global companies such as Ubisoft, Zynga and Rockstar setting up studios in Pune and Bengaluru. Besides the outsourced content, there is also a growing local game development industry and the number of independent game developers is on the rise. Development for smartphones and using free or low-cost development platforms (middleware) such as Unity or GameMaker has also made the process much easier. The availability of platforms such as Steam,

Google Playstore and Apple Store have levelled the playing field with designers across the globe. Indian game developers are greenlighting more games on Steam. Games such as *Missing*, *Antariksha Sanchar* and *Raji* have been nominated for international awards; nevertheless, the scenario is not entirely promising as developers say they need more support for what is still a fledgling industry.

One of the key elements that need to be understood to better analyse the workings of the industry is the diversity of the cultures of play in the region. Chapter 3 describes how sports is a huge industry in countries such as India, Pakistan, Bangladesh and Sri Lanka where Cricket dominates the play cultures of these countries. In Nepal, the board game *Bagh Bakri* (tigers and goats) and the gambling game *Langur Burja* dice are immensely popular as are other outdoor sports. These games are connected deeply with the sociocultural lives of people, and Cricket, in particular, has great importance economically and even politically. One has to consider exactly where videogames figure within these older long-standing cultures of play. As entertainment and narrative media, the videogame is a newcomer in the already-established film industry in India and Pakistan as well as within their millennia-old rich narrative traditions, both oral and written.

Whether one is concerned with the effects of *PUBG* or *Pokemon Go* on players, or whether one is recommending a videogame to be taught in the classroom, the ludic cultures of the region are paramount in defining the attitudes of players. The digital medium also, arguably, influences player behaviour and the fuller impact of videogames on the region is yet to be gauged. It might be said, however, that the digital medium and the interactivity have ensured some cultural shifts that need to be studied further. The impact of casual games on the public is also immense but there are few records of this. Through interviews with both hardcore and casual gamers, the key ways in which gaming influences cultures and vice versa are studied. Just as a substantial amount of work is being done for social media cultures, Chapter 4 pursues larger discussions on how videogames relate to discourses on pedagogy, violence and diversity among other things. It also makes the medium more transparent for those non-gamers, such as parents or policymakers, who are indirect but important stakeholders in the game cultures.

When one thinks of stakeholders, it is important to remember that the impression that videogames create is often the result of how they are represented. In turn, videogames themselves also are a major medium for representing the Subcontinent to the rest of the world. For example, Nepal is represented as a fictional country, Kyrat, in the game *Far Cry 4* (Ubisoft Montreal 2014) and is largely shown as backward and violent. There are many more examples that need to be contested and this needs to be done responsibly by both games made by global giants as well as locally in the Subcontinent. Chapter 5 scrutinises such global representations and emphasises the need for more inclusive local representations that are more sensitive to the needs of the people of the region and that will help create a positive impression of the medium in a culture where it is a relatively recent entrant.

The Subcontinent has been producing a steady number of such local videogames that represent the history and the cultures of these countries. For example, in *Heroes of '71* (Portbliss 2017), the independence of Bangladesh is the key theme. In *Raji* and *Antariksha Sanchar*, Indian art and architectural forms are showcased. *Missing* addresses the issue of girl traffic' ing in eastern India while *Unrest* explores a mythical historical Indian city. Chapter 5 continues addressing such representations of the local culture to point out how the medium is very important in creating 'glocalised' (following the earlier discussion of the concept and Iwabuchi's comments) marketable products for the world audience. There are, however, many gaps in what videogame cultures in the Subcontinent represent. The gender bias among gamers and developers is still huge as are other aspects that need a nuanced discussion of diversity. A notable absent discourse is that which addresses non-gamers regarding the appeal and the importance of videogames as a sociocultural phenomenon that is complex and cannot be judged by stereotypes, as is emphasised in Chapter 6 and then in the conclusion.

Of Conclusions and Their Limitations

As mentioned already, there are many differences among the countries here clubbed together as the 'Subcontinent'; their relationship has often been marked by conflict and political upsurges. The desire to develop digital technology as a means of advancement, however, is common in all these polities. There is also a second shared objective for digital development: this is to produce software and data in regional languages. Akin to this, in terms of videogame development too, there is the impetus to develop localised content. In many of these countries, the State, after being an arguably bewildered onlooker at the videogame industry and gaming culture, has begun to engage with the medium, for better or worse. Before the ban on *PUBG*, the game had a download base of 175 million from India alone, making clear the pervasive reach of videogames in the Subcontinent and its potential as a market—a fact that cannot have gone unnoticed by policymakers, some of whom are pushing for similar local content. How the Subcontinent arrived here is a set of long stories that need to be told separately for each country before engaging in a bird's-eye view of the scenario.

The following chapters are written in full cognizance that charting the path of such a comparatively new entertainment medium in the Subcontinent as gaming is and analysing its cultural impact are difficult tasks and that these efforts are not likely to provide a complete picture. It is, however, never too late to make a start and this is exactly what this book aims to do.

Section One

Development

1

Digital Technology and Videogames in the Indian Subcontinent: An Attempted History

The European colonial powers that had occupied the Subcontinent had started gradually ceding their colonies just after the Second World War. The war had brought technological advances and had ushered in the digital era just before the countries in the Subcontinent gained independence. India, as the largest country and the considerably bigger economic power, had been using Hollerith machines for computational purposes. Soon, there was an impetus by the Nehru government and its planners to develop indigenous computing technologies. Thereafter, of course, the story becomes more complicated and while the developed world was investing in advanced computing technologies, India took a relative back seat due to the license-Raj up to the mid-1980s but in the last decade of the 20th century, India became one of the leading names connected to digital technologies. It was during the very end of the 1990s that India started producing her very own digital games. That is, of course, a long story some of which will be told in the subsequent paragraphs. India's immediate neighbour, Pakistan, had long vied with her for scientific excellence and was pursuing its own nuclear programme, for example. Nevertheless, the entry of the digital took its time. In 1967, Pakistan International Airlines or PIA launched its own IBM computer and the country opened up to personal computing in the 1980s. Incidentally, two computer software makers from Lahore took the world by storm by creating the first-ever computer virus. Pakistan, too, started developing its own games around 2000. Further away, in Sri Lanka, the first computers made an appearance in 1967 and, thereafter, developments have been underway in building the digital profile of the country. The first games studios emerged in Sri Lanka around 2007. The Himalayan state of Nepal calculated its second census in 1971 using an IBM computer, thus setting off its own computerisation program. From a mere 2.2% in 2011, its Internet connectivity reached 54% in 2017, thus reflecting the role of the digital and the importance accorded to it by the people of Nepal. Most of these countries identified Information technology (IT) as the means to be at par with the Global North, somewhat in the fashion of South East Asia and drew up their IT policies from the mid-1980s to the early 2000s. They have been revisiting these policies since and the Digital India and Digital Pakistan initiatives in the past decade are indicative of the State-owned agencies showing more interest. India's massive biometric data gathering and the reaction of the populace to this exercise is another example of how the digital acts as a connection between the State and the people in the Subcontinent. As the number of personal computers began to grow, and the rapid and widespread adoption of smartphones proliferated, the digital technologies ceased to be as regulated by the State as they used to be before the 1990s or in some cases, such as in Nepal and Bhutan, before the last decade.

Videogames also were latecomers to the Subcontinent and when they came, it was as imports from the West and far beyond the reach of ordinary citizens for over three decades after they became popular in America and Western Europe. Unlike some countries in Eastern Europe (for example, in 1980s' Czechoslovakia) where videogames had come in through the backdoor or unofficial channels, there was also no homebrew scene either in the Subcontinent that would encourage gaming. Coin-operated machines were a novelty in the 1980s when in the rest of the world, the gaming console or the Commodore Amiga had become a popular platform for gaming. It would take around two decades (or even more for some countries) before videogames would reach middle-class households and almost two more before they would arrive on smartphones and be accessible to a large number of people. This chapter aims to trace the development of games and game cultures from the very beginnings of IT in the region to the 2010s, by when telecommunications had been revolutionised and the region became a major software hub.

Digital Technology in Colonial Times

As most of the region was under British rule or was influenced by it, the colonial history of computing in the Subcontinent is important to consider when providing the context for the development of IT. Computers have had a very long connection with British India if only tangentially. The story can be traced back to the 'father of computers'. Charles Babbage's son, Major Henry Prevost Babbage (1824-1918), who learned the design of the complex Difference Engine and Analytical Engine and constructed parts for both, had served as an officer in Bengal. Whether his computing skills were known in India is unknown. Almost a decade before the Second World War, the colonial government of India brought Hollerith machines to perform the complex calculations at the Defence Accounts Department (DAD) in 1931. In 1941, the census of India was completed with the help of Hollerith machines. The student magazine of Sydenham College, Bombay (now Mumbai), reported a visit to the British Tabulating Machines office and mentions the Hollerith machines. Around the same time as these accounts of the Hollerith machines in India, German computer engineer, Konrad Zuse, constructed the Z3 and Z4 computers and designed the computer language called *Plankalkül.* One of the first programs to be run on *Plankalkül* was a game. There were, however, not many takers for Zuse's program and computers such as the Hollerith machines remained tools for accounting and mathematical operations. In India, any usage of computing machines to play games is not recorded. Nevertheless, it is important to note that the usage of such technology in the colonial period played a crucial part before the independence in tabulating the census (Desai 1910: 738), agricultural statistics and reporting on the Bengal Famine of 1943 (Mahalanobis 1946: 6). These achievements led to further developments in computing technology after independence. India's adoption of computing technology came very early on and it is, therefore, necessary to begin with the account of the early days of Indian computing.

From Punched Cards to Outsourcing: A Brief History of India's Digital Technology

With the departure of the British, the young Indian nation was coming to terms with its scientific and technological needs. Like most other things relating to India and its huge diversity of cultures and populations, any reading of digital India is also complicated. Jawaharlal Nehru, India's first prime minister, was technology-friendly but at the same time wary of introducing technology into Indian lives without it being controlled by the State. As Arun Mohan Sukumar comments:

> [T]his view nevertheless stemmed from Nehru's personal conviction that man, who created machine, should not end up its slave. [...] Although India had won its freedom, he believed technology could endanger the individual freedoms of its citizens by eliminating jobs and limiting economic mobility. What's more, conveniences of modern-day technology could restrict civic engagement at a time when partitioned India needed some form of social adhesive to prevent it from further falling apart. (2019: 27)

In the very same year, 1956, Prashanta Chandra Mahalanobis, the founder of the Indian Statistical Institute, was purchasing the HEC-2M from the United Kingdom and sending his researchers to Birkbeck College to learn how to program and maintain the computer when it arrived in India. Computing technology had arrived in India and it would be used by the Planning Commission to generate statistical data and even perform military calibrations. Mahalanobis had met John von Neumann, the pioneer of computer architecture, and Howard Aiken, who built the Mark I and Mark II computers, when he visited the United States. The Indian Statistical Institute had hosted Norbert Wiener, the founding figure of cybernetics, and computer scientist C.M. Berners-Lee as visiting researchers. Shortly afterwards, Nehru's other favourite scientist, atomic physicist Homi Jehangir Bhabha, would assemble India's first indigenous computer, the TIFRAC; his institute was funded by the billionaire Tatas and would take up the leading role in Indian computing. The rivalry between Bhabha and Mahalanobis resulted in the Tata Institute of Fundamental Research (TIFR) obtaining the powerful CDC-3600 and establishing itself as the main computer research centre in India. In Calcutta, however, the ISI in collaboration with Jadavpur University continued the work of developing indigenous computers and the ISIJU-1 was built. Mahalanobis had also planned to manufacture computers locally and had even started the project by making calculators—his plan was shot down by a commission that was appointed to assess it and computing technology remained the preserve of a small scientific elite. As far as digital technology was concerned, the State retained for itself the moral capacity to judge what was good for the people. This attitude would, by and large, govern the policies around the digital for decades to come.

The infamous 'License Raj' meant that it was extremely cumbersome to start new businesses as one had to cross multiple hoops of bureaucracy. Foreign companies such as IBM, ICL and Honeywell were the major players in the computer market and supplied to its key clients, such as the Indian Railways and the Life Insurance Corporation of India. Importing computers during the License Raj was extremely cumbersome:

> The approval procedure was a nightmare. Every prospective computer user had to approach the DoE with a request, along with justification to import a computer. If it was convinced of the need to import the computer in line with "national priorities" as laid down by the Electronics Commission, in principle approval for the import would be given. (Sharma 2015: 49)

IBM was supplying relatively older models to Indian clients and, by and large, looked after the entire maintenance of the computers onsite. In the early 1970s, IBM looked like it was indispensable and even in the face of strikes and protests against automation and computerisation, it still maintained a relative monopoly of the market. While the number of computers had increased, there was in no way a spirit of development akin to what was going on in the Palo Alto garages. India was left disconnected from the innovations in microcomputers and software that were being developed. Indira Gandhi's government decided on siding with the protestors and against digitisation at the Life Insurance Corporation. Despite the political wariness, IBM was doing well in

India until the Congress government was replaced by the Janata Party and George Fernandes, the industries minister, decided to curtail IBM's operations in India when the company refused to comply with FERA or the Foreign Exchange Regulatory Act. When IBM exited, many local computer companies came into being.

Not many know the full name of Wipro (Western India Palm Refined Oil Ltd.) and its origins in palm oil manufacture or the connection between HCL and the textile industry, but these global players in IT had beginnings in other industries. In the case of the latter, the Delhi Cloth Mills had already started making calculators and, from there, had moved on to the microcomputer business. The competition between the computers division and the textiles division, however, influenced six Delhi Cloth Mills employees led by Shiv Nadar to quit Delhi Cloth Mills and start their own business, later came to be known as HCL. India had its own 'garage start-up' in Nadar's venture. Wipro, started by Azim Premji who wanted to diversify his palm-oil business, brought in American-trained engineers and used the expertise of local academia in the Indian Institute of Science, Bangalore. As Dinesh Sharma states, '[b]ased on input from IISc experts, Wipro decided to build a 16-bit microprocessor-based system, instead of the 8-bit option that HCL and DCM were selling [...] The idea was to design hardware, import components, and manufacture computers, instead of importing kits and assembling computers locally' (Sharma 2015: 125). Wipro was developing modular computing units and the Wipro 86 started being seen as a worthy local replacement for the IBM machines; they could also be easily upgraded and the company was soon writing its own spreadsheet software as well. Of course, the State-run ECIL (Electronics Commission of India Limited) had already started producing its own computers as early as the 1960s and was supplying computers to the Madras Police, the Life Insurance Corporation and other State-owned institutions. The private players, however, were more successful.

The increased focus on IT after Rajiv Gandhi became the prime minister in 1984 and his government's reforms concerning the telecom industry were crucial to the development of the IT industry. The New Computer Policy of 1984 and the policy on software export of 1986 were true game changers in India's IT initiatives. Prime minister Rajiv Gandhi was advised by technocrats and was one of the first Indians to own a Walkman and to use laptops at work. Speaking of one of the architects of his new policy, Narasimhaia Seshagiri, Biswarup Sen points out how Sheshagiri characterised the '1984 NCP as "flood in, flood out"—flood the nation with imports and cause a larger flood of software exports' (Sen 2016). Sen observes that the reduction of the tariffs from 100% to 60% resulted in a 100% growth in computer production and a 50% drop in prices. Sharma also notes how the State that was earlier against digitisation under Indira Gandhi was now playing a major role in bringing computers to India under her son, wherein the State played an important part in creating demand for computers. Banks and schools engaged in widespread computerisation, boosting computer sales further. The Reserve Bank of India purchased 500 minicomputers while Indian Airlines also expanded its computerised ticket checking facilities to six cities. According to Sharma, 'The National Informatics Centre began expanding its network to government offices up to the district level. All this created a huge demand for computers. In 1987–1988, India's computer industry crossed the turnover mark of five billion rupees. The development of local industry since IBM's exit was driven by technology and policy, while demand was mostly spurred by government-led projects' (Sharma 2015: 129).

Under Sheshagiri's supervision, the State also set up data-gathering networks like NICNET to collect data on governance from different states; subsidiary citizen networks like ERNET and INFLIBNET grew out of the NICNET initiative. As Sukumar notes, '[ERNET] was set up in the mould of the US-based ARPANET, to connect researchers and educators across universities in India. The Information Library Network (INFLIBNET) would be a digital repository linking public libraries' (Sukumar 2019: 131). From specialised networks that connected educational institutions and corporates, it would take some more time before the Internet was made available to the general public as a dial-up connection on 15 August 1995 (Moray 2015).

Considering the early impetus to developing the Internet for education, before further huge leaps into the digitisation process in India, the role of computers in educational institutions needs to be discussed first. The collaboration between Wipro and the Indian

Institute of Science has already been mentioned, as has the pivotal role of the Indian Statistical Institute in bringing computers to India. The other major players in the educational sector are the IITs or the Indian Institutes of Technology in Kanpur, Kharagpur, Bombay and Madras. IIT Kanpur acquired one of the first IBM machines to come to India—the IBM 1620—in 1962, and a team of American academics contributed to the early computer education in the IITs. Sharma notes that with some exceptions such as IIT Bombay where Soviet computers such as the Minsk II had been installed, '[d]espite Nehru's intention to make Indian engineering education diversified with varied inputs, the U.S. orientation of the Indian technical elite ensured that the American system pervaded all IITs' (Sharma 2015: 34). Instead of creating an electronics park in the model of Palo Alto around MIT (Massachusetts Institute of Technology), the institutes contributed to accelerating the brain drain, whereby it 'became the norm for IIT graduates to go to the United States for postgraduate and doctoral studies, and then stay on for teaching or industry employment' (34). Computer education books written in 1968–1969 by Vaidyeswaran Rajaraman on FORTRAN programming and digital logic sold in large numbers having addressed a key need in the Indian academia. Full-fledged MTech degrees started in the IITs in 1970 and BTech degrees in 1979.

To return to the development of IT in India post-1984, the development of organisations like PCS (Patni Computer Systems), Infosys and TCS (Tata Consultancy Services) in addition to the existing Wipro and HCL contributed a lot to the IT ecosystem. Around the end of the century, the Y2K compliance issues globally opened up the software market to Indian companies and even before this, the so-called 'body-shopping' wherein Indian programmers were working 'offshore' for American companies but under the employment of these Indian companies (and at Indian salaries) had become common practice. As far as the development of software is concerned, this does tend to pose a problem. As a commentator observes:

> [The] Indian software industry is estimated to be worth $73 billion today, and has a respectable status in the global perspective, but a view of the top 10 software companies in India, as ranked by National

> Association of Software and Services Companies (NASSCOM), shows that all of them are primarily software service providers, with modest presence in the software products sector. (Team YS 2010)

This is an issue that is relevant even a decade later and besides Zoho (the online office suite made by Sridhar Vembu) and Tally, the accounting software developed by Tally Solutions housed in Bengaluru, Indian software companies do not have many major brands to boast of despite having a very well-developed IT industry. In terms of hardware, the PicoPeta Simputer developed by Encore Technologies and IISc Bangalore was a handheld device that used 'graphics and voice output to appeal to users in third-world countries with limited literacy' (PG Mag n.d.) and the ability to use an accelerometer to flick the hand and move the screen (something that mobile gaming benefits from) before the iPhone introduced the feature. Introduced in 2004, the Simputer failed despite its huge promise because of a lack of support from the governments (see ET Bureau 2015). Despite such obvious missed opportunities, the industry itself is now huge in comparison to the 1970s, when the whole notion of 'appropriate technology' (Sukumar 2019: 75) as applied by the State would determine what the citizens had access to; today, with the large-scale globalisation of the IT industry, the latest developments in IT now reach the citizens directly and with minimal delay and the industry is more citizen-focused than State-focused. In the second decade of the 21st century, after the country has launched a nationwide 'Digital India' initiative and carried out a nationwide project of creating identity cards for residents of the country linked to their biometric data, it remains to be seen whether there will be a larger impact on digital entertainment cultures such as videogames.

Videogames Come to India

The condensed introduction to the complicated story of the development of ICT in India, provided in the previous section, was required so as to provide context for what was happening in the fledgling videogames industry and to analyse how digital games and gaming cultures could be said to have developed in India. There is another story that needs to be told as well before arriving at the story of videogames in India and other parts of the Subcontinent. This is the story of the development of the games industry globally. Some early dates need to be taken into consideration. Academia and industry had started taking videogames quite seriously in the 1960s and the 1970s in the Global North. In 1958, Willy Higginbotham developed *Tennis for Two* at the Brookhaven National Laboratory (see World Video Game Hall of Fame 2018) and in 1962, a team of programmers led by Steve Russell developed *Spacewar* on the DEC-PDP 1 minicomputer at the MIT. So effectively, at the same time as the arrival of the first computer in India and the development of the first indigenous computer in India, two of the world's cult videogames were being made; there is no record of these games being popular even among the academic or scientific community who had access to computers. In 1978, Tomohiro Nishikado made the *Space Invaders* game, marketed by Taito in Japan and Midway in the USA. This was the same year when IBM exited India. In between, however, more developments had happened in the videogame industry. Founded in Silicon Valley in 1972 by Ted Dabney and Nolan Bushnell, Atari was to emerge as the leading videogame company and a household name in the West. Atari had marketed the extremely successful *Pong* and the arcade machines were churning out millions of coins. Not many remember that Steve Jobs, the founder of Apple, used to work for Atari and that he was instrumental in getting Steve Wozniak to build the *Breakout* game for the company in 1976 (see Hanson 2015). Incidentally, shortly before this, Jobs visited India to spend time in the ashram of Neemi-Karoli Baba (Gupta 2012). India, of course, was still in the mode of State-owned access to technology and the License Raj, and moving towards the Emergency of 1974. The 1980s saw the development of *Missile Command* by Atari and in the same year, *Puck Man* released in Japan was marketed as *Pac-Man* in the USA by Namco. In 1972, the first home console (Magnavox developed by Ralph Baer) was released and in 1977, Atari 2600, capable of playing multicoloured games, made its presence felt in American homes and then elsewhere in the world. Even across the Iron Curtain, Soviet programmer Alexei Pazhitnov had developed *Tetris* in 1984, which proved to be another videogame blockbuster. Other Eastern European countries were also trying to enter the gaming scene despite State prohibitions, and often, in a provocative way, through an underground homebrew culture as Jaroslav Svelch illustrates so adroitly. FPS games, such as *Wolfenstein 3D* (ID Software 1993) and later *Doom* (ID Software 1993) and *Quake* (ID Software), had started making their way into the videogame culture (which would become synonymous, albeit erroneously, with the medium) in the 1990s as had real-time strategy games such as Microsoft's *Age of Empires* (Ensemble Studios 1997), fighting games such as *Street Fighter II* (Capcom 1993) and sports games such as *EA Sports Cricket 1997* (Beam Software 1997), voiced by none other than the famous cricketers Richie Benaud and Ian Botham. Until the 1990s, these developments seem largely not to have connected with the developments in Indian computing, whether for hardware or software. In gaming culture terms, *Street Fighter II* had an Indian connection, which will be discussed at length in Chapter 6 but it was not commented on at the time. One wonders why there was a total disconnect with a rather lucrative and promising cultural medium. Of course, Sukumaran's thesis on 'appropriate technology' comes in handy here. Even after 1984, one does not hear of Indians exploring the ludic potential of the digital.

Largely unknown in the country even today, Indian entrepreneurs were working outside India in the 1970s and making important contributions to the game industry. For example, take the case of Satish Bhutani:

> Mr. Bhutani got his start right at the origin of arcade video games. Of Indian descent and fresh out of college from Texas University, he joined Atari in 1973 to be their export administrator to both Europe and the soon-important market of Japan (Replay 06/1984). Through the latter efforts he got involved with the infamous Atari Japan operation, forming a lifelong relationship with eventual Atari Games president Hideyuki Nakajima. (historyofhowweplay 2017)

Bhutani changed jobs multiple times and founded his own game companies and also became a key figure in the establishment of the American operations of the Japanese videogame company Namco. Bhutani claims that one of the last things that he did before quitting

Namco was to suggest the renaming of the game *Puck Man* to *Pac-Man* to prevent vandalism of the arcade machines for obvious reasons (see historyofhowweplay 2017). The name, as we know, stuck. Whereas Bhutani was involved with mainstream gaming in the USA, another largely unknown Indian was instrumental in setting up the market for the Nintendo Entertainment System in the European Market in 1987. Ashok Chugani is the CEO of SPACO which still has its operations in Madrid, Spain (see Suarez 2015), and he seemed to be able to use his contacts in Japan to promote the sales of Nintendo in Spain. Clearly, Chugani did not see enough opportunities to market Nintendo in India. Ask Rishi Alwani, a leading games journalist in India, who will point out that Nintendo *did* try to market its consoles in India in collaboration with a local vendor, Samurai (see Ghoshal 2018). Coke and IBM had already left the country and any foreign company needed a local partner now, as mentioned before. Nintendo's price tag was also very high and beyond the reach of an average Indian. Also, even though digital India had started taking shape in 1984, the technocrats do not seem to have had much time for the ludic; the videogame industry did not get much attention or support locally. This is what prompted entrepreneurs such as Bhutani and Chugani to look elsewhere for pioneering roles in the newly developing gaming industry.

The academic establishment, however, had not entirely missed the connection with game programming. Around the same time, Professor Bhabani Prasad Sinha was supervising a student-project that involved a digital football game, the ancestor of many such games like FIFA, Pro Evolution Soccer or Football Manager games. Sinha, who described the game to me in a personal interview (Sinha 2020) also told me how he assembled a microcomputer in the Indian Statistical Institute's computer department. Sadly, the student-project did not get a favourable response from the examiner—it was deemed not to be useful enough. There is, however, one case where videogames were accepted in academia: at IIT Kanpur, an army officer, Captain Gurmit Singh (Singh 1979), wrote his MTech thesis on a simulation game of tank warfare in 1981 where he programmed an entire war game for a

DEC 1090 system. Although quite an important development in terms of gaming history, this was almost entirely forgotten.

In many respects, then, India had missed the bus when it came to the videogame industry. Unlike countries like Czechoslovakia, where despite the government restrictions and the prohibitive price of microcomputers, there was a homebrew culture (see Svelch 2018) that kept up a steady interest in game development and the gaming culture, India had none. As Alwani notes that Nintendo and SEGA had both tried to enter the Indian market after 1983 but had failed to rack up the sales because the price tag was prohibitive for the Indian pocket. Rakesh Dugar, the CEO of Mitashi Edutainment (initially named Maze), together with his partner Hasmukh Gada, decided to join a new venture called Columbus that sold commercial arcade machines (see Zachariah 2011). Dugar and Gada created their venture selling Atari cartridges and marketing SEGA's Megadrive at a cheaper price and with two packaged games—*Sonic* (Sega 1991) and *Michael Jackson* (Sega 1989). These two games were included with the Megadrive but even then, ₹14,000 was forbidding for the Indian market. Dugar got Atari to package *Brian Lara's Cricket* (1994), considering the popularity of Cricket in India, and the plan worked. With the arrival of the Sony Playstation on the global market, it was difficult for cartridge-based gaming consoles to compete and as Risabh Mansur (2019) comments:

> For instance, Sony's introduction of the PlayStation console marked a radical shift from 2D cartridge-based gaming to 3D CD-based gaming. Mitashi, which had invested heavily into game cartridges and consoles, could not mimic Sony. But Mitashi persevered in the Indian market and continued to make video games in the way it knew best.

Nevertheless, not many Indians owned consoles at the time. As the respondent of a survey comments, the console games he played were on an imported console: 'Nintendo. When my dad bought one from Thailand during his UN trip' (Ray Murray and Mukherjee 2013). For most Indian families, it was the home computer that opened the doors to videogames; as another survey respondent commented: 'Dad got home a 386, and I first laid eyes on Prince of Persia and Dave. In final year of school, made a game project. While I was studying engineering, I joined a games dev startup. Never looked back' (2013). From my personal experience, growing up as a teenager in the mid–late 1990s, my father's hand-me-down office Intel 486 and earlier stints in my mother's office were my first exposure to games. In school in the 1990s, I remember playing *Digger* (Windmill Software 1983) or *DigDug* (1982) on the BBC microcomputer and also writing BASIC programs to play games such as *Battleships* and *Hangman*. Another respondent to the survey comments:

> First exposure to video games was through the old coin-operated arcade machines in the 80s, True love though happened in 1995 when I chanced upon *Doom*, and I was hooked! Stumbled into video game design in 1997 (I was probably one of the game designers in India) when I was the offered the role of Game Designer (for no reason other than that "management" thought I could do it) on what was a rather ambitious 3D game development project in 1998. That game never got made … (Ray Murray and Mukherjee 2013)

The coin-operated arcade machines formed the main videogaming exposure for many Indian teenagers during the 1990s and as shopping malls were extremely rare, these machines would be housed in cinema theatres, such as the Globe Cinema in Calcutta (now Kolkata). An account provided by a fairly affluent Delhite mentions videogames parlours in the 1990s:

> My generation saw the emergence of video games, with video game parlours coming up, which also offered bowling and air hockey. I, still, fondly recall going to the parlour in Essex Farms in Delhi, but somehow, I was never addicted to playing video games at home. (Thadani 2016)

In Chapter 6, a discussion of Prabhash Tripathy's dissertation on gaming arcades in Delhi and Mussoorie will address their gaming cultures in more detail and from other perspectives.

The PC-based games were becoming more popular in Indian households and the cybercafes (Delhi got its first cybercafe called 'Cyberclub' in 1996, the year after the Internet went public in the country). This was the time when PC game development also saw its beginnings. Just as academics globally were beginning to engage in serious research on videogames and the so-called ludology and narratology debate in game studies, Indian game developers had started developing the first FPS games. There will be an occasion to address the ludology–narratology question later on but a very quick explanation would be that ludology scholars (mainly based in Scandinavia) advocated that videogames are not about storytelling and that they are mainly about rule-based games while the so-called narratologists (a misnomer linking them with the narratologists in Literary Theory) viewed videogames as a storytelling media. The two Indian games that both claim to be the first 3D videogame to be developed in the country were both based on patriotic stories.

Vishal Gondal and Ninad Chhaya developed the game called *Yoddha* (Gondal and Chhaya 2000), set in the backdrop of the Kargil War that was fought between Pakistan and India between May and July 1999. Gondal and Chhaya released their game as a product of their company Indiagames in 2000. Alwani (2000) explores the history of the game in detail:

> Indiagames was also the developer behind *Yoddha: The Warrior*, India's first 3D game, and possibly also the first commercially sold PC game and the first first-person shooter from India. The game went on sale at retail stores all over the country in 2000 [...] at a time when gaming in India was synonymous with 8-bit and 16-bit knock-offs and game development itself seemed an alien subject.

Gondal had already made a browser-based game on the Kargil War in Shockwave Flash. In his interview with Alwani, Chhaya (2000) describes their work quite perceptively:

> We built that game because it was very topical. It got a lot of eyeballs, lot of traction, and we realised that yes, if the content is Indian and people can relate to it would work. At the end, it was a shooting engine, there was nothing new that we did. We just put an Indian skin to it.

Initially, the pair of them had planned a game based on the Indian classic blockbuster film *Sholay* but they could not afford the licensing fees that were asked of them by the film's copyright owners. The popular villain

Gabbar Singh (whose name has become a byword for villains in India) was conveniently renamed Gaddar Singh ('Gaddar' means 'traitor' in Hindi and Urdu) in the context of Kargil; as Chhaya describes, '[the character] Gabbar Singh became Gaddar Singh, because he's a traitor and he's infiltrated into your country and you have to go into the enemy camp to shoot down the bad guys' (2000). The developers also got Pepsi to brand their game and MTV, which was the cult youth music channel in those days, to feature their music video, which became quite popular. There were significant challenges to releasing the game due to local constraints. Graphics cards were not as readily available in India at the time and the developers had to build the game entirely on built-in graphics.

Another claimant for the honour of the first 3D game in India is *Bhagat Singh*, based on the North Indian freedom fighter from Punjab who fought against the British colonial powers. Around the time it was released, in 2002, there were two biopics of Bhagat Singh. This game was made by the company Lumen Phon and released by Mitashi Edutainment (of whom much has been said earlier). Not really an original game in itself, it features Bhagat Singh as the equivalent of the unnamed space-marine in *Doom* or B.J. Blazkowicz in *Wolfenstein 3D* and British and Indian colonial policemen as the equivalent of the aliens and the Nazis. An article in the *Chandigarh Tribune* reports:

> Priced at ₹395, Bhagat Singh is India's first ever 3D animation game where the player actually plays the role of Bhagat Singh and has to go about completing a mission that involves stopping a Bill from being passed in the Calcutta Assembly. The game opens with a short biography about Bhagat Singh, depicting his valour, leadership and his love for the country. (Prashar 2002)

Not too highly priced, the game was seen to be trying to establish a niche in India's market at that time, being, arguably, the first postcolonial/anti-colonial game to be based in the history of India's freedom movement. We will see a similar trend when we discuss Bangladesh in the subsequent sections. *Bhagat Singh* never managed any popularity among the Indian gamers, for whom games such as *Road Rash*, *Quake* and *Age of Empires* were the major gaming attractions. Neeraj Dikshit not so kindly calls the game 'wonderfully terrible' (Dikshit 2017). Dikshit, however, is quick to note the postcolonial underpinnings of the game; writing in India's popular web magazine, *Scroll.in*, Dikshit gives the almost-forgotten videogame some new limelight:

> The birth of the FPS genre in the West needed seemingly irredeemable villains to justify its gratuitous violence, and so too it would seem in India with *Bhagat Singh: The Game*—the British Raj's hated imperialist apparatus makes for a delicious enemy and who better than the most lionised young revolutionary from the Independence movement to be taking them on in 3D. (2007)

The postcolonial connections of *Bhagat Singh* had, of course, already been pointed out by me earlier in a survey of global videogaming. Nevertheless, despite their patriotic appeal and potential, both *Yoddha* and *Bhagat Singh* disappeared from the gaming scene fairly quickly. As Mukherjee (2019) says:

> There haven't been any globally recognized PC-game bestsellers so far and the industry is a far cry from Bollywood. Piggybacking on Bollywood films continued in games such as *Dhoom* and *Ghajini*, both of which were released after the eponymous movies. Megastar Shahrukh Khan starred in a videogame-themed movie, *Ra.One* and a game-based on the film neither of which had any lasting impact.

Meanwhile Indian gaming had also opened up to the consoles and the Sony Playstation 2 made its official launch in 2003.

With the PS2, the console emerged from the grey markets in Delhi's Palika Bazar or Nehru Place, and with its very first Indian videogame came controversy. Sony's *Hanuman: Boy Warrior* (Sony Computer Entertainment Europe 2009), featuring the mighty monkey-god from the Indian epic *Ramayana*, was the protagonist of the game and a US-based Hindu leader wanted it banned:

> Hanuman is one of the more important figures in Hinduism and the Ramayana, an Indian epic poem. So, putting him into a video game—worse yet, a video game in which he can be manipulated—was bound to rankle someone as trivializing sacred figures and concepts. It turns

> out that someone happens to be the US-based leader of the US-based Universal Society of Hinduism. He wants Sony, the game's publisher (it's for the PS2) to pull the title. (Good 2009)

Keith Stuart (2020) describes the success of the PS2 as follows, twenty years after its first launch:

> [T]he sheer ubiquity of the console and its vast global user base also allowed for a growing pool of experimental titles, which used the power of the Emotion Engine in very different ways. From elegiac adventures Ico and Shadow of the Colossus to psychological horror classic Silent Hill 2 and hallucinogenic joyride *Katamari Damacy*, the PS2 was home to titles that inspired the nascent independent game development scene of the mid-2000s.

Sadly, the PS2, despite its much-vaunted (and somewhat controversial) *Hanuman: Boy Warrior* and *Street Cricket* (Trine 2010), did not do much to influence original content in Indian gaming. Even the controversy did not reach Indian shores and although it attracted the attention of researchers abroad (see Zeiler 2014), in India, despite it being playable, in Hindi as well as English. The reviews in India were poor, to say the least. Much later, Indian companies such as HCL Computers also made its foray into the videogame hardware market in 2010 with its HCL ME handheld gaming consoles (see Joshi 2010). Around the same time, the Brazilian 3G mobile-enabled gaming console, Zeebo, also tried to expand to India after successful operations in Brazil and Mexico. In India, it 'teamed up with Educomp to bring educational content to kids in India' (Kris Graft 2011). None of these ventures had any lasting impact. In fact, even before its launch, there were warnings that the console would not sell in India. As a commentator observed, 'If only they had looked at the Indian gaming market a little more closely, they would realise that the factors that they are banking on the most to move units—price and anti-piracy (through digital distribution)—will actually turn out to be their product's biggest drawbacks' (HundredProofSam 2009). The price was higher than the grey market PS2 consoles of that time and Indians were not yet ready for the online purchases that the console demanded. As for HCL, it exited the PC manufacturing business to focus on services and distribution in 2018 (Singh and Thomas 2018).

Nevertheless, in the early years of the industry, the international game development community saw promise in India's fledgling videogame industry. The NASSCOM Game Development Forum actively promoted videogame development in the country and even organised the NASSCOM Game Development Conference (NGDC), which aimed to be an Indian version of GDC in San Francisco, where many experts of international repute were invited as keynote speakers. One of the key movers behind the NGDC is Rajesh Rao, the founder of Dhruva Interactive. Thomas Friedman writes at length about Rao in his book *The World is Flat* (2005) in glowing terms as a case study for the new globalised world. Ernest Adams, who was invited to the NASSCOM Animation and Gaming Summit 2009, described India as the 'sleeping giant' of the gaming industry in his lecture that is unambiguously titled 'The Promise of India: Ancient Culture, Modern Game Design' (Adams 2009). Whether the sleeping giant has really awoken and if not, then when it is likely to awake is a story to return to in the later chapters.

Videogames are a newer media in the Subcontinent, especially in comparison to the other geographies where the consoles were available much earlier. The government policies regarding computing and software in post-independent India and other countries are interesting cases to consider. The late entry of computer games and indeed the virtual absence of the Commodore, Amiga and the early Nintendo systems from the Indian market and the relative newness of the player culture in India is, for example, a much-neglected area of research. The general surge in telecom technology and the large number of smartphones running games on Android, iOS or Windows has altered the picture significantly. Adrienne Shaw in her essay 'How Do You Say Gamer in Hindi?' (2013) and Casey O'Donnell in *Developer's Dilemma* (2014) both observe that the Indian gaming culture is relatively new and they begin making the connection with the development of the software industry; however, the issue needs to be explored in more depth. As for countries other than India, there is no extant academic research to trace the growth of the industry and gaming cultures. Here, after the unavoidably long introduction to the Indian gaming and game development scenario, a major gap in videogames research needs to be addressed—the gaming scenario in the rest of the countries in the Subcontinent. Very little formal research has been done on gaming in Pakistan, Bangladesh, Sri Lanka, Maldives, Nepal and Bhutan. Before looking at the gaming scenarios, however, the history of IT in these countries needs to be explored, albeit briefly, as it is a full-fledged research area in itself. The following sections will engage in such an enquiry.

Looking Beyond India: IT and Videogames in the Rest of the Subcontinent

Pakistan

Although not as big a market for gaming as its larger neighbour, Pakistan has a fast-developing games industry and fairly vibrant gaming culture. The University of Indiana collaborated with the University of Islamabad in 1968 in setting up a computer centre in the latter. The reason for the choice was as follows:

> The computing centre would create post-graduate level training in computer science for the nation, enhance research at the nearby Pakistan Institute of Nuclear Science and Technology (PINSTEC), create a means for storing and retrieving government data, such as census data, tax records, and economic data, and assist with routine administrative support services for the national government, including payrolls, inventory records, and bookkeeping functions. (Reynolds 2013)

The University of Islamabad housed the computing centre because it would combine both computing and instruction at that location, while other locations could be added later. IBM computers were already in use by banks, airlines and laboratories so recommendations were made for the purchase of the same brand. Shortly before this, either in 1964 or 1967 (there is confusion regarding the date), Pakistan International Airlines (PIA) had computerised its operations via an IBM 1401 machine. Coming around a decade later than the early Indian computers, these computers offered a semi-digital system and government departments, such as the Water and Sanitation Agency (WASA), went digital in 1979 with Systems House, the first IT company providing Oracle-based software. In the 1980s, the Pakistani Army inducted computers and by the 1990s, its departments were being computerised (see NOC Team 2009). In 1990, the Telephone and Telegraph Department was converted into the Pakistan Telecommunications Company (PTCL) which started local dial-up connections in 1995. Email and a private dial-up were introduced by Digicom Pakistan in 1992 and 1994, respectively. In 2000, the Pakistan government drew up the National IT Policy and as part of this, developed the IT Action Plan wherein 5 billion Pakistani rupees were committed to the development of the IT infrastructure in 2000–2001 alone. A full discussion of the IT Policy and its impact is beyond the scope of this book but some of the points of discussion were as follows:

1. HR Development, Training and Education IT in Government and Databases
2. IT Market Development and Support IT Fiscal Issues
3. Telecomm, Convergence and Deregulation Cyber Laws, Legislation and IPR
4. IT and Telecom Manufacture and R&D Internet
5. Software Export
6. E-Commerce
7. Incentivising IT investment (IT & Telecommunications Division 2020)

As Yousaf Haroon Mujahid comments, 'Under the dynamic leadership of the Ministry for Science and Technology, Dr Atta ur Rehman Pakistan has charted out a robust roadmap for ICT policy in the country. Financial concessions were granted to IT companies and the government planned to invest in computer education at the school and higher education levels' (Mujahid 2002: 2). Mujahid identifies the developmental aspect of ICT in the country and points out its 'promise to capitulate the digital divide both for the Pakistan society at large and accelerating the pace of business and industry in particular' (2).

The policy also mooted legislation for telemedicine, computer crimes and intellectual property and copyright. Web portals such as Pakissan.com for agricultural workers, SMEDA for small and medium enterprises and Shadighar.com to enable matrimonial connections are all listed as examples of a developing IT economy. Other Pakistani scholars, nevertheless, lamented that '[a]though Pakistan has made sustained efforts to bring its IT sector up to par with the other leading players, if compared to other countries, there is still a long way to achieve the desired goals' (Kundi et al. 2008: 367). Pakistan's software industry also needs to see more growth and its mobile penetration needs to improve. GSMA (GSM Association) reports in its factsheet that Pakistan is projected to improve its mobile broadband connectivity from 8% in 2015 to 28% in 2020, still not a high percentage but a reasonable growth (GSMA 2016). The IT policy would be later followed by the 'Digital Pakistan Policy' launched by prime minister Imran Khan in 2019.

Most people do not know that two Pakistani programmers were responsible way back in 1986 for developing a piece of code that we know as the computer virus. Amjad and Basit Alvi made history when their program, the self-replicating 'Brain' virus, copied itself into the disks of the Universities of Pittsburgh, Pennsylvania, Delaware and George Washington University (Norman n.d.). Other than this, Pakistani software professionals and multimedia artists have worked in Hollywood and globally in the industry. As per the Pakistani magazine *Mag, the Weekly*, Pakistani VfX designer Mir Zafar Ali 'won an Oscar for Best Visual Effects in 2008' (2018). Ali who designed the visual effects for *Golden Compass* would go on to do so for *The Life of Pi*. It is with this backdrop that the Pakistani game development industry needs to be considered. Information regarding the early days of game development and culture in the Subcontinent is usually hard to come by because of the lack of adequate records. The journalist Wajhi Jafri (2019) traces the growth of the videogame industry and culture in Pakistan as follows:

> The journey of videogame development in Pakistan started sometime around the 2000s—when teenagers who had played and experienced games from what is formally known as the 3rd and 4th generation of videogame development internationally, started to become young adults. This generation, that had grown up on early PCs, NES, Sega, Atari and Commodores, soon found that it wasn't satisfied with being a mere consumer.

Jafri mentions how the concept of game development in Pakistan started with modding existing games when gamers started by modding *Counter-Strike* and *Unreal Tournament* maps on LAN connections.

Unlike in India, Pakistani gamers had access to consoles like Sega and Atari, but the development scenario seems to have come a little later in Pakistan. In the 2000s, the early game development companies, such as Trango Interactive, Wireframe Technologies and Fork Particle, set up their studios in Islamabad and Lahore. These studios also carried out outsourcing contracts from international players, such as Zynga, Sega, Disney and THQ. Mindstorm Studios signed a contract with the British company Codemasters to collaborate on the *Cricket Revolution* game (Mindstorm Studios, 2009) in 2009 that was apparently supported by the Pakistani Cricket star Shoaib Malik. Zafri then goes on to say that competition from India and China in outsourcing had a negative effect and that the small talent pool and limited government support made it difficult for Pakistani companies to meet international demands. As such, the computer science graduates moved toward more stable employment in software development and for graphic artists in animation. Jafri says that the scenario is now changing and this will be addressed in the next chapter. As far as gaming culture is concerned, Pakistani gamers have braved many odds and some like Arslan Siddique (better known as Arslan Ash) have emerged as global eSports champions. Women game developers such as Sadia Bashir, the founder of Pixel Arts Academy, have been setting new trends in the industry; Bashir has received awards at the 'Women Can Do' and the US Embassy at the Women Entrepreneurs Summit in 2016 for her accomplishments (Forbes List 2018). More will be said about Pakistani gaming culture and the industry in the subsequent chapters but now it is necessary to look at the other countries in the region.

Sri Lanka

In Sri Lanka, the universities in Moratuwa and Peradeniya acquired IBM 1130 computers in the early 1970s and used them to teach FORTRAN programming. Later, the computer:

> was used by the engineering undergraduate students in preparing course work on power system load flow studies in Electrical Engineering, structural design in Civil Engineering, machine component design in Mechanical Engineering, etc. The computing system at Moratuwa was also used for administrative purposes when in the late seventies, the university payroll and the University Provident Fund statements for the UGC were computed on this. (Induruwa 1999: 219)

In 1983, the Sri Lankan government framed the COMPOL or the National Computer Policy (Munasinghe 1983) as a result of the combined efforts of the NARESA (Natural Resources Energy and Science Authority of Sri Lanka) and the universities. The main objectives of COMPOL included harnessing computer technology in all its aspects for the benefit of the people of Sri Lanka, furthering the economic development of the nation, improving the quality of life of the people of Sri Lanka and increasing the flexibility and dynamism of Sri Lankan society so as to enable it to keep up with future challenges arising from the global scientific and technological advances. The acceptance of COMPOL gave rise to the establishment of Computer and Information Technology Council (CINTEC) which functioned directly under the President at the time. Following further developments, the e-Sri Lanka project was launched in November 2002, aimed at bridging the digital divide and disseminating ICT to provinces away from Colombo. Sri Lanka launched its Internet among its academic and research community in 1992 using the LEARN network, and the first commercial ISP was launched in 1995 (Induruwa 1999). Currently, there are about eight ISPs in the country and the telecommunications industry has seen a growth in recent years. As far as Internet penetration is concerned, around 34.11% of the population has internet access in 2019 compared to 12% in 2010 (Sri Lanka 2019). This bodes well for the gaming industry as well and according to *The Colombo Telegraph,* '[f]or many people in Sri Lanka, however, eSports is a central part of their day to day lives regardless of the latest Hollywood blockbusters [and] Sri Lanka is looking to capitalize on is mobile gaming' (Sri Lankan Gaming Industry Trends 2019).

Speaking of videogames in Sri Lanka, commentator Andre Howson (2016) observes that although the common impression of Sri Lanka is that it is all about 'tea, Cricket and coconuts':

> Gaming in Sri Lanka has been around for a long time, from those of us playing *Pitfall!* on the Atari in the 80s to sharing a PC keyboard for multiplayer NFS 2 in the 90s, to pretty big online tournaments happening now. Gamers have come together to form a tight community, organising e-sports championships [...] Gamer.lk is the biggest community out there, and visiting their site shows you just how big gaming is here.

Some of the major Sri Lankan gaming companies are Dawn Patrol, Gamos Technology Solutions and Arimac. Gamos Technology Solutions developed Sri Lanka's first mobile games called *The Colombo Ride* series in 2007. Incidentally, there is a connection here between academia and gaming in that W.G.T Fernando who heads Gamos is a former professor at the University of Moratuwa, which had led the way for IT education in the country (see *The Sunday Times* 2010). That same year, Raveen Wijayatilake, a fresh postgraduate diploma-holder from the University of Southampton, founded Gamer.lk, Sri Lanka's only and very popular gaming forum. Wijayatilake was building on his previous success in creating Rock.lk, a rock-music forum. Communication via Internet Relay Chat (IRC) was difficult in Sri Lanka but the Gamer.lk founders had an alternative strategy:

> [They] carried out a series of weekend gaming events. Because there was no DNS software back in early 2000's, multiplayer gaming wasn't really a thing. They hosted a server on a separate PC and used Hamachi to login to that PC to play games. Speaking of games, the game of choice was Counter Strike 1.6, now a classic. (Andrado 2018)

Wijayatilake's gaming passion seems to have been stoked by his supportive mother who 'brought home a black and white laptop from office with a collection of 8-bit video games including *Commander Keen*' (2018). Again, the lack of an established gaming culture is evident across the Subcontinent and in most of the countries, players are trying to come up with innovative workarounds to play videogames.

Using the Unreal Engine, Arimac developed a historical game based on Sri Lankan mythology called *Kanchayudha* in 2017. *Kanchayudha* is supposed to be an episodic game based on Sri Lankan stories. According to the CEO of Arimac, Chamira Jayasinghe, the game is 'like most 3rd person role-playing games like *Assassin's Creed*, *Darksiders*, *Prince of Persia*, *Shadow of Mordor* and *God of War*' (ReadMe 2016) but is set in Sri Lankan archaeological sites such as Anuradhapura, Polonnaruwa and Yapahuwa. The account here is incomplete without mentioning more recent Sri Lankan games such as *Nero* (also made by Arimac and to be released in September 2021) and *Threta* (under development by Prodigi Interactive), which will be addressed in a later chapter but such attempts to incorporate local culture in one the newest narrative media will also be seen in Bangladesh, as described in the next section.

Bangladesh

As the youngest nation in the Subcontinent, Bangladesh has shown significant activity in the IT arena. Although the first computer, an IBM 1620, was brought into the country in 1968 when it was a part of Pakistan, the formal introduction of computers in Bangladesh happened in the 1980s, around a decade after its independence. Mostafa Jabbar, the author of *Digital Bangla* (2005) contends that the plan for a digital Bangladesh was implicit in the Bangladeshi constitution and that digital technologies are necessary to combat poverty in the country. He considers broadband Internet, digital lifestyles and digital governance as the three pillars of the knowledge economy of the Bangladeshi society. Jabbar is the current IT minister in the Bangladesh government and has been the president of the national ICT organisation of Bangladesh, Bangladesh Computer Samity (BCS), for four consecutive terms. He created the Bengali digital keyboard *Bijoy* in 1988, which in itself was quite a feat for the Subcontinent. Jabbar is also a former president of BASIS (Bangladesh Association of Software and Information Services). A BASIS report reveals an 84% mobile penetration in 2016 as compared to a 35% penetration of broadband Internet—a statistic that Jabbar also bemoans. Nevertheless, the number of Internet users in Bangladesh is increasing rapidly with a total of 93.70 million reported at the end of December 2019 (Sohel 2016). Further, the country has 'earned $1 billion in 2018 by exporting ICT products and services' (2016).

Despite the recognition by the government and the growth in Internet usage and software exports, local commentators acknowledge that Bangladesh 'has yet to tap into the vast potential of the gaming industry'. As Mahmudul Islam (2020) comments:

> Bangladesh's game market was worth $62.22 million, said a 2017 Newzoo report, which was based on data available up to December 2016. The report ranked Bangladesh as having the third-largest video game market in South Asia after India and Pakistan, and 61st among 100 countries globally. Despite having such a big market, game development has not flourished in the country.

Nevertheless, game development in the country has seen some notable mentions, especially with the rise of competitive gaming as well as the growth of the market because of the rise in the number of gamers.

Bangladeshi gamers had a relatively early start with gaming as they were playing arcade games such as *Mustapha* and *Street Fighter II* in the 1990s. *Mustapha* was the local name for Capcom's *Cadillacs and Dinosaurs* (one of the characters it featured is called Mustapha) as mentioned earlier. The first game to be developed in the country by two undergraduate students was called *Dhaka Racing* (eSophers 2003) and another early game was Trimatrik Studio's *Arunodayer Agnisikha* (2004) which was followed by others like *Ludu Friends* (Tapstar Interactive 2014) and *Heroes of '71*. *Ludu Friends* is a Ludo game but with a Bangla interface and is aimed at reaching the Bangla-speaking majority among whom Ludo is a popular household game (see Lee 2014). *Heroes of '71*, developed by Mindfisher Games (formerly Portbliss Games) and funded by the Information and Communication Technology Ministry, is a patriotic celebration of Bangladesh's war of independence against Pakistan. In this, it has some elements in common with the early Indian games, as mentioned above, where patriotism and independence are important issues. In what is a well-researched game that draws its material from the archives of the National Liberation War Museum, the developer Masha Mustakim says, 'We didn't want to glorify war. We believe our generation and the next has to know what happened in '71' (Islam 2020). *Heroes* was involved in an online controversy where Pakistani players protested against the violence that was depicted and so the game had to be withdrawn from Pakistan (see Khan 2018). The makers, however, defended the game as being influenced by the need to portray the history and have released a sequel.

The Maldives

The Maldives received its independence from the British as late as 1965 and its first telephone exchange was created as late as 1955 with 1968 seeing the telephone being opened to the public. According to a case study on IT in the archipelago, the 'country's economy has seen rapid growth, especially since the 1980s raising the Maldives from one of the 20 poorest countries in the 1970s to a middle income country today' (International Telecommunication Union 2004). It connected to the Internet on 14 October 1996. Dhivehi Raajjeygé Gulhun or Dhiraagu is the oldest and major telephone and Internet provider. The other companies are Qatar-based Oredoo and Rajje Online. Countries such as the USA and India have contributed to the growth of IT in the country. According to a US Department of State website, 'The United States has directly funded training in airport management and narcotics interdiction and provided desktop computers for Maldivian customs, immigration, and drug-control efforts in recent years' (US Department of State 1996). An Indian Ministry of External Affairs (2014) makes a similar point regarding IT education:

> The Government of India financed a US$5.30 million project for Technology Adoption Programme in Education Sector in Maldives. The project, executed by NIIT and EEEC (India),trained around 3000 Maldivian teachers and youth across islands in Computer skills over a 27-month period (2011–2013).

Whether this has been evinced in the game design courses in the island nation is a moot question although some game development diploma courses are offered locally.

The country has seen a considerable leap in its IT and Internet usage from 2004, when the most common form of connection was the dial-up Internet, to 2021, where according to the Datareportal report (Kemp 2021), the current number of Internet users is 342,500 and the Internet penetration is 62.3% with average download speeds of 43.72 Mbps on mobile connections and 24.86 Mbps on fixed-line connections. The report also indicates a very high percentage of 99.4 accessing the Internet via social media. The largest number of users are mobile-based (71%) while those using laptops or desktops are far less (26.8%) and console users are almost minimal (0.4%). Nevertheless, Maldives has been pursuing its gaming connection, particularly in collaboration with designers from other nations. Researcher Amani Naseem (Naseem et al. 2018) organised the 'Playmakers in the Maldives' event, where ten game designers from different countries 'created new games with and for people in the capital Malé to play and participate' (Playmakers in Maldives 2013). Some of the games created in the program were *The Hunt for the Yellow Banana*, *Dreams in a Bottle* and *Jelly Stomp*; Naseem and her collaborators also introduced augmented reality games. Recently, she published her experience in a game studies publication. A recent game called *Thakuru Wars* (Arcils 2020) features Maldivian characters in a multiplayer action game. The Maldives also featured as a location for the *Star Wars* videogame and *Rogue One Scarif* (2016) where the 'island planet of Maldives is actually called Scarif on the game' (Star Wars Rogue One in the Maldives. The Shooting Location for Planet Scarif in the beautiful Laamu Atoll 2016). Nevertheless, the gaming culture and the industry in the island nation remain mostly obscure despite some attempts by designers and scholars to address these issues.

Nepal and Bhutan

Hardly anything is known of the Himalayan countries of Nepal and Bhutan in the bustling world of game studies. A fictitious Himalayan kingdom called Kyrat, which was modelled after Nepal, in *Far Cry 4* (Ubisoft Montreal 2014) brought these countries to the attention of gamers worldwide. In comparison to their neighbours in the

Subcontinent, their economies are small and their ICT development has started much later than the others. Nepal introduced its first computer in 1971 (see Kushal 2018) to conduct its national census. Thereafter, besides the outsourcing company called DSI, which was run by an American couple in the 1980s and the work of Muni Shakya who developed the Nepali font in 1983 and also the first microcomputer in Nepal in 1979 (see Baidar 2021), there was not much activity in ICT in Nepal. In the 1990s, universities in Nepal started an ICT programme and in 1995, the first email service was started by the private firm, Mercantile Communications. In 1997, the Telecommunications Act was passed by the government and in 2000, an IT Policy was drafted [Laws of Nepal—Information Technology Policy, 2057 (2000)]. Internet usage in 2017 was about 7% as reported by the Nepal Telecommunications Authority. Commentators are critical of the studies that claim rapid development:

> Nepali internet and ICT policies are informed mostly by a self-evident vision of connectivity despite highly uneven economic impact of internet connectivity across geographies and socioeconomic strata. Such a conception hides the underlying socioeconomic inequalities and the barriers they pose to internet adoption and benefits acquired from its use. It also overlooks the centrality of supportive physical infrastructures like roads and electricity for efficient functioning of a 'digital society'. (Pandey and Regmi 2020: 1)

Going by this study, the ICT facilities in Nepal fall far short of global requirements. The scenario in Bhutan, the other landlocked country in the Himalayas, is comparable.

Bhutan, with its very small population and largely mountainous terrain, received its first telecommunication links as late as 1963 and again, it received its national telecommunication network in 1998 with Japanese aid; Thimphu, the capital city, got direct access to the world outside. The state-run ISP, Druknet, was built using Canadian support and has two links—one to London via Phuentsholing in India and the other to Hong Kong. Television and Internet were introduced together (quite a unique event) in 1999 with the passage of the Bhutan Telecommunication Act (Pradhan 2001). The ICT

Whitepaper of 2003 provides a framework for developing computer technology in the country and 'states that Bhutan will harness the benefits of ICT to realize the Millennium Development Goals and enhance Gross National Happiness (GNH)' (Ministry of Information and Communications and Royal Government of Bhutan, Thimphu 2003). Thereafter, the Bhutan Information Communication and Media Act 'was passed in July 2006 to provide for a technology and service sector neutral regulatory mechanism which implements convergence of information, computing, media, communications technologies and facilitates for the provision of a whole range of new services' (Laws of Bhutan—Bhutan Information and Media Act 2006). A subsequent telecommunications and broadband policy was drafted to develop broadband networks in 2014. Bhutan's unique aim of achieving a national happiness index seems to be commensurate with its IT policies. As comparatively newer entrants to ICT, videogame development and gaming cultures in both countries are fairly nascent.

The late entry into the domain of ICT and even telecommunication also means a necessarily late entry of gaming cultures. Nepali game developers such as Sashik Srestha outline the problems they face:

> "How many people in Nepal actually buy games? How many of those actually try new games?" says Shrestha. "I think that digital globalisation makes it harder for any niche/Nepali developers to get their work noticed on international platforms. A console game can cost anywhere between $20–50 and as a customer, you would want games that are worth the price. [...] there are gaming markets like Steam, Google Play and App Store, but it's not easy for Nepali developers to enter these platforms and collect revenue from them when there isn't even an international payment platform to simplify this process." (Rana 2020)

Another developer adds that the Nepali economy cannot sustain or support the building of a triple-A game because no local investor would pay the high costs that would run into millions of US dollars. Further, the developers also point out the lack of local content and the scarcity of game development talent. In a rather different take on Nepali game development from that of the local developers, researcher Gregory Price Grieve contends that is:

> imagined through the fantasy of Shangri-La, a fictional place described in the 1933 novel *Lost Horizon* by British author James Hilton. As an isolated Shangri La, Nepal is posed as an underdeveloped traditional nation, full of picturesque poverty, over-determined with religious culture, and blessed with beautiful Himalayan landscapes. [...] The Fantasy of Shangri-La challenges Nepal game designers, but this myth of isolation has nothing to do with reality. (2018: 53)

In his rather brief essay, Grieve does not provide any other explanation but nevertheless observes that game-development in Nepal 'is not isolated, but rather part of a turbulent vortex of global flows' (53). Important as it is to note this observation, the global connection is also seen by some local developers as a problem rather than an advantage. N.J. Subwdi, CEO of Pokhara-based Yarsa Games is, however, hopeful:

> I think more and more people are going to get into game development because there is an undeniable steep rise in the players' engagement from Nepal. We have some popular game streamers on YouTube, like 4K Gaming, Nero, HypeGurkha, and Mr Hyuzu. Some popular apps like Hamro Patro and Daraz are also enabling users to play games inside their apps. All these things are contributing a little bit towards improving the local gaming market. (Rana 2020)

Streaming of games and the increasing reach of mobile gaming among Nepalis is a reason to raise the hopes of game development and gaming culture in the country.

Bhutan, with its relatively recent entry into the world of the Internet and ICT in general, is another interesting case. Whereas an Indian tourist writing about her trip to Bhutan in 2009 notes that 'there are no ice-cream parlours and videogame cafes', by 2016 eSports is quite popular in the country as the newspaper Kuensel reports that there are over 80 gaming parlours in the capital, Thimphu. As the newspaper article states:

> Planet World, a popular gaming parlour in the heart of the capital, is almost packed throughout the day. *Dota* 2 is the most popular game in the parlour. Apart from Dota, football games like *Winning Eleven* is also preferred by some of the adult players. (Tshedup 2016)

The same article also highlights the growing importance of mobile games and eSports. Bhutan has its own eSports celebrity, Pinda Rika Dorji or PindaPanda, as she styles herself. Dorji is based in Kuala Lumpur in Malaysia and hosts her own television programme, 'The PindaPanda Show', which details her entry into eSports as a *Dota 2* player.

Conclusion

Writing the history of videogame development and culture in the Subcontinent is no easy task; very little information is available regarding the early days of gaming in the region, and of that, almost no academic research has been done on countries other than India. Games journalism is also not very common in these countries and access to structured archives is virtually unavailable. In fact, except for the very recent research being done in India on the country's IT history, even research on how the IT industry and computing culture developed in these countries after they gained independence from colonial rule or emerged as very different nations from what they were in the mid-20th century is rather hard to come by. Of course, India being part of the so-called BRIC countries and the harbinger of technological promise and a huge potential market has intrigued Western scholars, entrepreneurs and programmers. Nevertheless, commentators are often nonplussed by how videogames seem to have emerged in India as well—without a history. As will be discussed at length in Chapter 5, Adrienne Shaw (2013) remarks on the lack of a 'history' of gaming in India and that many people who entered the videogame industry in India did not have any gaming experience, unlike similar professionals in North America and Europe. She points out that there is no word for 'gamer' in Indian languages mainly because it was external to Indian culture(s). Shaw, of course, means videogames when she refers to 'games'; anyone who sees the hype around India's Cricket culture and, especially, the very media-friendly IPL matches, will not say this of games in general. The stark contrast with the newer form of games, i.e. videogames, is of course to be noted. This 'externality' that Shaw points towards has been quite perceptible until the recent popularity of mobile gaming in India. Where the 'history' of videogames in India is such a nebulous affair, in other nations, it is even more difficult to access.

Surprisingly, for one of the most populous regions in the world and indeed, one that has seen much recent prominence as an IT hub and a lucrative market for tech exports, the Subcontinent has remained neglected in videogames research. The extant research on the region often does not take into account the colonial history of many of the countries or the rather fraught post-independence geopolitics in the area as well as the local histories of the nations. At the same time, to imagine the region in neo-Orientalist terms may also be counterproductive. Currently, commentators are beginning to wake up to the possibilities and the culture specificities of India:

> [T]he fact is that the Western companies continue to make game after game based upon the northern European tales of adventure—in short, ripping off Tolkien. It's almost as if the rest of the world didn't exist. We also borrow a little from medieval Japan—the era of the Shoguns—and China. But I haven't heard of a single Western company that is making use of the vast wealth of cultural resources of India. (Adams 2009)

Even such comments, however, are just focused on India and should ideally extend to the rest of the Subcontinent as well. A larger study of the development and the culture of videogames in the region thus has become more relevant in recent times and it is this that shall be addressed in the following chapters.

2

The Videogame Industry in the Indian Subcontinent: The Current Scenario

In a recent interview, Rajesh Rao, the young veteran of the Indian games industry, sounded a confident note for the industry even during the Covid-19 pandemic, when many other industries have been known to have suffered. Rao views the situation as one of promise:

> India's games market is now generating between Rs 7,500 to Rs 10,000 crores in revenues, more than half coming from card-based games, and another quarter coming from fantasy games like *Dream 11*. So clearly, Indians have embraced playing for winning in skill-based games. Casual games are also beginning to make money. (Sharma 2020)

Prime minister Narendra Modi has recently called for more effort to be put into the manufacture of toys and games by local manufacturers (see PTI 2021) and Rao responds with the comment that 'we are in a phase of rapid consumer adoption of games, and game developers are learning quickly by analyzing user behaviour. We will certainly see a lot more local content with Indian social and cultural context, we will see innovative business models' (Sharma 2020.). Although the Indian government's Atmanirbhar Bharat project has begun particularly stressing the development of local content in recent times, the videogame industries in other countries in the Subcontinent have also been developing such content already as has been mentioned in Chapter 1. Ironically, however, both the Indian games industry and Rao's own company, Dhruva Interactive, have been very active in developing outsourced work for videogames built by American studios such as Turn 10 Studios and Activision, besides making games with Indian content such as the *Kaun Banega Crorepati* (Dhurva Interactive 2001), a videogame based on the popular quiz show. The scene across the Subcontinent is often similar for other countries as well and there is a mix of the global outsourcing and local game development (or the 'glocal' as described in the Introduction) as far the fairly young industry is concerned.

Rao is one of the heroes of Thomas L. Friedman's popular book as already mentioned in the previous chapter. There he is quoted as supporting Friedman's thesis of the world being 'flat', i.e. connected and globalised in unthought of ways. He describes to Friedman how his company, Dhruva Interactive:

> sent out our new game demo, *Saloon*, to the world […] None of us had ever seen a real saloon before, but we researched the look and feel [of a saloon] using the Internet and Google. The choice of the theme was deliberate. We wanted potential clients in the U.S.A. and Europe to be convinced that Indians can "get it." The demo was a hit, it landed us a bunch of outsourced business, and we have been a successful company ever since. (Friedman 2018)

Friedman quotes Rao as saying 'India is going to be a superpower and we are going to rule' (2018). The major impact of global involvement that Friedman speaks of, in perhaps a somewhat overstated optimism, is very important in studying the scenario of current game development in India. Some of the biggest game companies operating in India are the big international names such as Rockstar, Ubisoft and Zynga. Rockstar India incidentally acquired Dhruva Interactive, Rao's company, in 2019 for $7.9 million and has been involved in the making of international blockbuster triple-A games such as the Western-themed open-world *Red Dead Redemption 2* (Rockstar North 2018). Indian developers were not merely sending out demo games showing saloons from Western films; they were playing important parts in constructing the entire world of the Wild West adventures. Much of the work in games development in the Subcontinent has been initiated in the games outsourcing industry. According to a 2019 report published by KPMG (Ahaskar 2020), India has 250 game development companies and many global firms are looking to cut costs in the development process and outsourcing to India.

With the increase in online gaming during the Covid-19 crisis (and the subsequent lockdowns imposed by some countries), there has been a significant rise in the need for skilled game developers. Lakshya Digital, the Delhi-based game art creation company, states that 'game development work outsourced to us has grown by almost 25–30% in a span of 2–3 months' (Ahaskar 2020). Lakshya Digital is one of India's largest game art studios and has produced artwork for games such as *Middle Earth: Shadow of War* (Monolith Productions 2017), *State of Decay 2* (Undead Labs 2013), *Sea of Thieves* (Rare 2018) and *Borderlands 3* (Gearbox Software 2019). Their CEO, Manvendra Shukul, is one of the veterans of the gaming industry in India and together with Rao, he too is optimistic especially because new clients, especially from geographies such as Japan have started outsourcing to India. Of course, work-from-home has come to the rescue of many such companies during the Covid-19 crisis; it has also created other problems in terms of Internet access and electricity outages. Shukul describes how they 'were able to ship workstations to almost all of our 500+ employees' homes' (Lakshya 2019) and how many of their employees worked long hours to make up for those who were not able to work from home to reach their annual target of contributing to 90 games. Such a commitment has been in evidence since the very early days of Lakshya Digital. Anando Banerjee, another pioneering stalwart in the Indian videogame industry, recounts that he has been associated with Lakshya since its inception in 2004 when Shukul founded the fledgling company (Banerjee 2020). Banerjee is also similarly optimistic about the industry and in a personal interview with the author, he lists the following as key indicators of development:

1. The interest from VCs in this industry is like never before. More and more studios are getting funded or acquired by bigger companies.
2. Service providers in the gaming industry like Lakshya are establishing themselves as major players in the global market.
3. Major international studios like Ubisoft move key elements of development on some titles to India. (Banerjee 2020)

In what is being called GPO or Games Process Outsourcing, Banerjee charts the growing success of Indian companies and attributes it to their familiarity with English, and their cultural flexibility and adaptability. As someone with an overview of the industry from its very early days, his observations are important in outlining the journey of the industry to its current situation:

> The Indian gaming industry is currently valued at over $890 million (approximately Rs 6000 crore) and accounts for roughly 1% of the global gaming industry and is poised to become one of the world's leading markets in the gaming sector. India got off to a very slow start in the business of outsourcing of game development and got a foothold barely a decade and a half back, around the same time when Lakshya was formed. However, India has done extremely well since then and inched very close to China, which has been the dominant player in this space. The growth potential of GPO industry is much similar to the BPO industry in India, and owes much to the availability of a large trained talent pool in the country at competitive rates. There are additional reasons like familiarity with the English language, inherent cultural flexibility of Indians and their ability to quickly absorb and engage with people of other cultures. (2000)

The comparison with the BPO industry is significant as the latter is seen as a big success story in India. The earlier chapter has briefly outlined the rise of major BPOs such as TIS, Infosys and Wipro; the videogame industry in India, despite the optimism about its growth, has come nowhere near the success of the Indian BPO industry. As mentioned earlier, Pakistani and Sri Lankan companies also engage in games process outsourcing and the business is growing in the other parts of the Subcontinent as well. In Pakistan, besides Mindstorm Studios, which has been already mentioned in Chapter 1, '[c]ompanies such as Tintash, Caramel Tech, Gamestorm, and Gen ITeam were quick to set up shop and focus on building games with global appeal' (Husain 2015) with the shift from PC games to mobile games. Caramel Tech was instrumental in coding the game *Fruit Ninja* (Halfbrick Studios 2010) where the Australian company,Halfbrick Studios partnered with Caramel Tech in coding *Stick Cricket* for Stick Sports Inc. Bangladesh, Nepal and Sri Lanka also have opened opportunities of outsourcing. Strangely though, research on games process outsourcing in the Subcontinent is still not available in any organised resource.

Some Less Optimistic Prognostications

A recent monograph focusing on videogames in India surprisingly does not refer to outsourcing and there is indeed very little academic work from India itself that addresses the peculiarities of the industry in India. In contrast, Casey O'Donnell's *Developer's Dilemma* (O' Donnell 2014), addresses these issues and provides a sober counterpoint to the unbridled note of promise that Friedman and other earlier commentators make about the industry in India. O'Donnell makes a few key observations on the scenario of Indian game development based on his experience as an American doctoral student pursuing his fieldwork at Red Octane Studios, India. Drawing on his prior experience as a game developer in the USA as well as his comparative research on the two countries, he observes:

> More than any other question I received while in India, I heard, 'How does game development practice in India differ from what developers in the United States do?' This relatively simple question frequently led to conversations about a disconnect between what Indian developers are allowed to contribute to game development projects and those tasks that are necessary to produce a videogame from start to finish. Some companies do create games from start to finish, though at a different scale. They create games for mobile (cell-phone-based) game platforms Although at a different scale, these networks are as difficult to access as US development networks are. Mobile game studios tend to fund their development efforts by also offering art asset production outsourcing services. Because of this, the companies become more specialized in one aspect of game development and don't develop their capabilities in others. This disconnect cuts deepest at the companies who become solely identified as locations for outsourcing by US companies. As the majority of these studios' resources become focused on that singular aspect of the development process, the studios become disconnected from game development more broadly. (O' Donnell 2014: 179)

Although O'Donnell's study dates back to 2007, there are some similarities even today after 14 years. He also goes on to say that 'Franchises derived from local markets (Bollywood or Hindu legends, for example) that could potentially be lucrative are too risky for US,

European, or Japanese producers whose limited understanding and low risk tolerance demand that local development and productions remain small and independent' (156). This attitude as well as that of creating small sections of a game has changed over the years with the rise of the indies, which, incidentally, have also been thriving as they create content based on local mythologies and culture. The subsequent section will address this question at greater length.

O'Donnell goes on to comment on how Indian game developers do not get much support from their families when they go into game development. Family involvement in one's career is very common in India; he observes that the perception that 'games are childish significantly impacts the ability of the students to move into these positions' (152). Those who do risk their family's disapproval and join the industry usually prefer to work in established companies to minimise the risk to their careers. Also, India's late entry into IT and its phenomenally rapid ascent in the BPO industry had, on the one hand, created little awareness of videogame culture[1] and, on the other, made Indian giants in the BPO industry, such as TCS, Infosys and Wipro, the coveted employers in the IT industry. It is also quite a common thing to hear game developers say that their primary platform was the PC as it would be bought by parents to help with their children's schoolwork. Of course, one needs to look at the gender distribution and related issues—something that is rarely considered in relation to the Indian gaming industry. Geographical location also is an important factor and, in general, the industry tended to gravitate towards, Pune, Hyderabad, Bangalore and New Delhi. Eastern and Northeastern India were entirely neglected. While this book does not aspire to present an in-depth sociological study of the growth of the Indian videogames industry, it highlights how O'Donnell and other commentators initiate such an enquiry.

Local assessments of the scenario in India are also not always upbeat. Speaking from a designer's perspective, Shailesh Prabhu (2016), who

1 It is important to note that none of the business process outsourcing ventures starting with Patni Computers work with the fast-developing videogame industry in the USA or, at least, there is no evidence so far that they did.

has emigrated to Scandinavia after receiving many accolades for his work in India, writes his candid assessment of the scenario in India:

> Poverty problems aside, there are several cultural and technological barriers to games in India. Most of India's large population lives in over-crowded cities with poor infrastructure. Our traffic jams are so severe that more often than not, we lose mobile internet when stuck in one. Being one of the more popular use cases for mobile games, this is definitely a problem. At the same time, our local trains are so crowded that it is largely impossible to play a game while stuck in a crowded train, yet another popular use case for the mobile game. Hell, a HUGE majority of India uses squatting toilets, ever tried playing candy crush while you have to squat to 'go' and use water to clean up after? Yet another popular use case down the drain.

Prabhu is mainly referring to the problems of developing games in India locally, an issue that will be addressed in the next section; what he says regarding available infrastructure and socio-economic issues, however, is relevant for developers as well as players. Also, as mentioned earlier, discrimination on the basis of caste and gender is routinely overlooked in how the industry presents itself to the world; these questions have been rarely addressed in research but are important ones that should not be overlooked. Poornima Seetharaman, who has been inducted into the 'Women in Gaming Hall of Fame', states that 'casual sexism' is common in the industry in India and that she has often spoken out against the inequality of pay structures (First-Person Encounters #4: Poornima Seetharaman 2021). Padmini Ray Murray has addressed issues of the lack of inclusiveness regarding issues of caste in the videogame industry at various forums such as NASSCOM Games Development Conference and these interventions by Seetharaman and Ray Murray regarding inclusiveness shall be discussed in Chapter 6.

Prabhu also points at the vast diversity of India that makes it difficult to create pan-Indian content in local languages, governmental corruption and the poverty of a large section of the population that is not taken into consideration when projecting the market for mobile games in India. Nevertheless, despite Prabhu's incisive observation, the recent Covid-19 pandemic and the subsequent lockdown showed a somewhat different picture regarding mobile downloads. As per a November 2020 report in the *The Hindu*, Indians 'installed 7.3 billion games, nearly 17% of all worldwide downloads, app intelligence firm Sensor Tower stated' (Ramasubramanian 2020). The large *PUBG* player-base in India, which is largely male, made up 24% of the entire world's lifetime downloads and has since suffered due to India's ban on *PUBG*. Homegrown apps such as *Ludo King* also garnered over 500 million downloads in January 2021 (Sheth 2021), again following the lockdown (Singh 2020). Downloads, of course, do not always translate into income as Prabhu (2016) cautions us. He states that:

> If, after all this, you make a great game, you face additional hurdles trying to get global exposure for it. If you try to get in touch with most store/brand owners, they can mostly only get you visibility in India or Asia, where monetisation is much poorer than in the western world. Gladly, some of that is changing and more developers in recent times are getting exposure in countries like [the] US, thanks to the efforts of some store managers looking for cool content. At the same time ad supported games are tough too as eCPMs in India (due to poor purchasing power) are much lower than in other countries. In such a situation it is probably best as a studio to focus on a more global scale, especially as a small developer.

What he is effectively suggesting is again the model of designing for a global audience and to 'bring a slice of India to games' (2016).

As opposed to the designing of Wild West saloons while sitting in a game's process outsourcing facility in Bengaluru, there is also a body of work that revolves around the portrayal of the local cultures of the Subcontinent. Recently, there has been a focus on developing games with local content all across the Subcontinent. In India, the game development scenario is still growing and the various industry-based meets such as the NASSCOM Game Development Conference and its present avatar, the India Game Development Conference, have been key forums for game developers and other interested stakeholders such as game journalists and researchers. Even in the very early days of Indian gaming, people such as Hrishi Oberoi, who has been in the industry for over two decades, says that he was designing a Cricket game for the mobile phone way back in 2002. Mobile games made up most of the country's revenue in 2010 (over 84%) whereas as far as gaming cultures are concerned, mobile (54%) and PC were almost equal (45%). In 2015, mobile games had by far overtaken PC games as far as gaming cultures were concerned—a larger number of people had started playing on the mobile platform and the trend continues today. Six years down the line, at the time of writing, when mobile games are the most popular and from 210 million users in 2016, the number is projected to grow to 370 million users in 2022, as per the website Statista.com (Statista Research Department 2021). Following the *PUBG* phenomenon and arguably as a response, nCore has launched the game *FAU-G* or *Fearless and United-Guards* (Studio nCore 2021). The word *fauji* in Hindi and Urdu means 'soldier' and the local influence is evident as the content is based on an Indian scenario and has been promoted by the Bollywood film star Akshay Kumar as a part of the government's project. Vishal Gondal, the key promoter of the game, also designed one of the first videogames to be released in India—*Yoddha* (Gondal and Chhaya 2000). Incidentally, it too had a similar context of the border conflict with an external aggressor. Despite its initial hype and comparison with *PUB-G* (based on its similar title, its context and the fact that it was released shortly after *PUB-G* was banned), the game was widely criticised by disappointed players.

Gondal, of course, issued an appeal against adverse reviews requesting support on patriotic grounds but according to some commentators such as Chetan Nayak (2021), the adverse reviews seemed more a result of the gameplay than a lack of support for local games. Nevertheless, the phenomenal number of downloads shows the huge interest in local content among Indian players. In fact, *Ludo King* developer Vikash Jaiswal reported that the monthly active users of the game grew nearly 47% between April and May 2020 (Singh 2020) and crossed 500 million downloads worldwide in December 2020 (Tewari 2021). A simple game like Ludo, with its huge popularity in India, has proven extremely popular when remediated on the mobile platform.[2]

2 'Remediation' is used in the sense in which it is used by Jay David Bolter and Richard Grusin (2000). It connotes how all media borrows and refashions other media, particularly in connection with digital media.

As mentioned in Chapter 1, other games made by Indian studios featured local content ranging from street cricket to mythological and historical episodes as well as adaptations of Bollywood movies. In fact, Indiagames had first planned to make a videogame version of *Sholay* (*Sholay* 1975), the cult Bollywood blockbuster, as mentioned earlier. Some of the Bollywood movies that saw adaptations in videogames are *Ghajini* (FX Labs and Geetha Arts 2008) and *Dhoom 2* (FX Labs 2008). The poor quality of game design is reflected in numerous reviews such as: 'it took a lot of time for me to finish it than it should have mainly because of the many bugs in the game which makes this game a torture to play through' (Pandey 2009). FX-Labs even ported a game designed by none other than Ken Levine, the designer of BioShock, for Indian audiences. The game called *Lost* ended up with 'a bunch of Bollywood actors in it. There was this really well-known Bollywood actress in the lead role, and just to see their spin on the game was a bit of cross-culture shock' (From The Vault 2011). The 'well-known Bollywood actress' was Malaika Arora who was heard singing '*in aakhon ke masti*' in the game which was themed on Dante's *Inferno*! Unsurprisingly, *Lost* did not release to either Indian or global audiences.

There were other games with notable Bollywood connections that ended up as big disappointments. *Ra.One* (Trine 2011), where the title is a play on Ravan, the antagonist of Ram in the Indian epic Ramayana, was based on a film (*Ra.One* 2011) that actually portrayed a videogame character coming alive. It must be mentioned that like *FAU-G*, two of these earlier games were endorsed by Bollywood stars—Aamir Khan for *Ghajini* and Shah Rukh Khan for *Ra.One*. The earlier chapter has already looked at games such as *Hanuman: Boy Warrior* (Aurona Technologies 2009) and how they have used Indian mythology. *Chandragupta: Warrior Prince* (Immersive Games 2009), which released in 2011 for the PS2, is also rather disappointing in its use of what was a deeply significant part of ancient Indian history—the game looks like a very early 1990s hack-and-slash with an Indian setting. Trine Software, one of the early console game makers, shut shop in 2013 after a mixed run that included market failures such as *Ra.One* and the more successful *Street Cricket Champions 2* (Trine 2010). Sony also included the *Move Street Cricket* in its PS3 bundle. Trine, however, had a slew of problems related to mismanagement and employees not being paid, as journalist Rishi Alwani reports (Alwani 2014a).

Perhaps anticipating the huge role that the growing telecom facilities would play in the development of gaming in India, the telecom giant Reliance Industries (Anil Dhirubhai Ambani's group) started the online gaming platform Zapak.com via the Reliance Big Entertainment Ltd. Zapak was the first gaming platform in India to garner 100 million downloads, a record that has been far surpassed recently by *PUBG* and *Ludo King*. Zapak is still active and offers a mix of local and global content. Analysing Zapak's games, researchers Dibyadyuti Roy and Aditya Desbandhu have pointed out how such digital spaces become the sites for gendered hegemonic ideologies about race, gender and colonialism. According to their analysis:

> *Sleeping at the Meeting*, *Zombie Pirate* and *Yoga Teacher*, are representative of games categorized as 'Girl's Games' on Zapak.com: where the ludic engagement is limited to dressing and undressing of white women in a variety of professional or social contexts. The fourth game *Bipasha's Beach Blaze* is a continuation of such reductive stereotyping, albeit in the different but culturally significant site of Bollywood. (2021: 1)

The last game mentioned here features the Bollywood filmstar Bipasha Basu and the portrayal of both women and Bollywood is stereotypical, to say the least, and will be discussed in Chapter 7. When the number of downloads and the revenue generated is considered, simple games such as *Ludo King* or the bigger international companies and the local GPO companies are going to determine what gaming looks like in India in the days to come. As PricewaterhouseCoopers reports, India will see a growth of 1,988 million US dollars from 2017 to 2022 and eSports is also expected to grow at a CAGR of 56.6% (PricewaterhouseCoopers 2021). Looking beyond the numbers and the statistics, however, when one seeks to engage deeper with the Indian cultural milieu as reflected in videogames, one needs to focus on the rising indie games scene.

Indie games, short for independent games, have become a crucial part of India's game development culture and have often championed the use of local content. At the time of writing, the Indian indie game

Raji has acquired global recognition. Such recognition has come after months of struggle and financial challenges. The story is 'an action–adventure storyline, where the human realm is witnessing a demonic invasion. In such a setting, Raji, a young girl, has been chosen as the one to defend humankind and defeat the demons' (Pham 2020). The story draws on Hindu mythology and the two Indian epics. The game has received very positive reviews overall and is a lush feast for the eyes as it uses a backdrop of Indian and Balinese art and architecture. While the backdrop is influenced by Rajasthani architecture, the storytelling is done through the ancient *tholu bommalata* shadow puppetry tradition from Andhra Pradesh. Instead of being a mobile-only game, as it is with most Indian videogames, *Raji* is available for PC and even the Nintendo Switch. Some reviews have even compared it favourably to Ubisoft's *Assassin's Creed* games and Eurogamer has even called it 'a game clearly made from a love of other games' (Donlan 2020) that freshly delivers familiar things and achieves the goal of portraying to the West that there is a lot more to India than the Taj Mahal. The story of *Raji's* development is one of struggle; with no support from the government or indeed any local agencies, the developers had to mortgage property to keep on working on the game and had to rely on support from companies such as Epic Games to be able to finally publish the game. A similar story can be told about the other hack-and-slash game based on Indian mythology, *Asura*. Zainuddin Fahad, the founder of the three-member Ogrehead Studios, states that his three-member team ran into many financial difficulties during the development process, especially when potential sponsors learnt that the game was not free. Fahad, however, makes it clear that his strategy for marketing involves not losing the international player-base due to unfamiliarity with the Indian culture; for him, glocalisation is the apt response to such a problem; in an interview with TechAsia, he states:

> Yes, the game is inspired by Indian mythology but we're not making it as obvious as other games have in the past. The focus is on creating a game which has our own flavor in it. Unlike *Hanuman* that was a literal representation of the mythology, we're not doing anything to make things too obvious. Even though we use the term 'Asura' and the lore

> is inspired from the Indian mythos, our approach is very stylized from a visual design standpoint instead of showing off a traditional Indian demon. (Alwani 2014b)

More needs to be said about the content of *Raji* and *Asura* and the way in which they present a certain angle on India that mainly comprises Hindu mythology. Adesh Thapliyal comments on *Raji* that it finds it 'hard to disentangle this surge of cultural chest-beating with the ascent of Hindu right, which rose to power with an eclectic ideology that pairs neoliberalism with fascist calls for a Hindu-first India' (Thapliyal 2020). While such issues remain to be addressed in-depth, it is important to note both the criticism and praise for these indie games that are emerging as representative of India's young gaming industry.

Besides these *Diablo*-style hack-and-slash games, many other significant titles have emerged in the Indian indie scene. Shailesh Prabhu's Yellow Monkey Studios released games such as *Huebrix* (Prabhu 2012) and *It's Just a Thought* (2011) that were internationally acclaimed at game developers' conferences. As early as 2011, Prabhu had been considering using Indian cultural media in games:

> I believe it doesn't have to stop at Indian narrative though it can be any Indian content, how about making a game using *Katputhli* or maybe Indian shadow puppets as your art style? or what about using some Indian classical/fusion music in your games? I have been dying to use some tabla and flute compositions in my game for some time now.

What Prabhu said to this author a decade ago is now coming to the foreground in games such as *Raji* and *Asura* as well as other games such as *Somewhere* (Studio Oleomingus 2014) and *Antariksha Sanchar* (Quicksand Labs n.d.). Both of these games are rich narrative experiences. *Antariksha Sanchar* is a stylised point-and-click biographical game 'inspired by the dream theorems of prodigious mathematician Srinivasa Ramanujan, and originating from an opera by the classical dancer Jayalakshmi Eshwar' ("Antariksha Sanchar: Transmissions in Space" n.d.). The game takes one through the lush scenery of Southern India with Carnatic music playing in the background. *Antariksha Sanchar* is very different—biographically speaking—consisting of journeys in dream sequences and it 'connects these ancient expressions to our imminent digital culture; retaining them for future generations in an innocent and inspirational form' (Antariksha Sanchar: Transmissions in Space 2021). The lead designer Avinash Kumar has also created a dance opera with the same name, starring his mother, Jayalakshmi Eshwaran, and her troupe of Bharatnatyam dancers. While *Antariksha Sanchar* is still in development, Dhruv Jani and his two-member Studio Oleomingus have completed multiple games in an intriguing series that highlights issues of colonialism and subalternity. As commentator Jess Joho (2014) remarks:

> As a comment on post-colonial nationalism, *Rituals* reveals that fictions construct the reality around us, while its mechanics show that other people's fictions can infect one's own sense of self. Hopping from character to character functions as more than just disorientation. The player is constantly aware of his intrusion as he invades each body, leaving behind a pervasive and disturbing sense of alienation. The concept capitalizes on the language of fracture particular to games. A language that speaks so readily to the occupation of identities, and fragmentation of narrative.

Jani is a talented artist and draws on a multiplicity of influences such as Borges and Calvino to highlight the fragmentariness of narrative and how the videogame medium enables rethinking of how stories are told and also how 'truth' is questioned. Besides Jani's and Kumar's experimental work, others have made games with an Indian setting—Pyrodactyl's *Unrest* (Pyrodactyl Games 2014), which claims to be India's first RPG, is set in a fictional medieval India setting, and Ironcode Games' *Pahelika* (Ironcode Software 2009) is a series of adventure games, also set in an Indian backdrop. Finally, there are collaborative ventures such as the *Durga Puja Mystery* (Flying Robots Studio 2020) where Xenia Zeiler from the University of Helsinki collaborates with the game designer Satyajit Chakraborty to create an adventure game based on the Indian festival Durga Puja. In the game, a Finnish student solves a mystery of a missing Durga idol. The game's blog does not reveal too much but it claims that the game reveals various key themes related to Durga Puja and supports the player in their educational and academic quest.

Chakraborty is better known for the game he co-designed with Leena Kejriwal on girl trafficking in India. *Missing* is described by games researcher Marcus Toftedahl as follows:

> Missing is a game developed with the ultimate purpose to end demand of trafficking for sexual exploitation. To address this problem, Missing lets the players experience the horrors of a trafficking process through the perspective of a young girl who is abducted from her home and put in a red light district. By using an interactive game, the developers intend to let the players "feel the story" through both game mechanics and narrative. With this setup, the developer aims to let players experience trafficking from a victim's perspective and thereby hope to inflict a change in the attitude towards prostitution. With Missing, the developers specifically want to target a male audience (by making the assumption that a large amount(sic) of gamers are men). (2018a: 3)

Missing has received many awards locally and internationally and as Toftedahl points out, its main aim is educative and it aims to reach a primarily male audience. The game has received mixed reviews on the Google Play Store but the content of these reviews shows how varied the responses to such a social problem can be, globally. The responses ranged from utter trauma to harsh criticism regarding moral probity. The game has, however, gained popularity across geographies and particularly in other countries in the Subcontinent like Bangladesh after its localisation in Bengali. Recently, other videogames have been made in India on the same theme: the Satyarthi Children's Foundation (run by the Nobel-laureate Kailash Satyarthi) has recently released its game *(Un)Trafficked* (Kailash Satyarthi Children's Foundation n.d.) and Vaibhav Chavan of UnderDOGS Gaming is currently working on a similar-themed game called *Mukti* (Underdogs TBA).

While originality still remains a serious problem in Indian indie game development, there are some innovative concepts in games—*Two Leaves and a Bud* (Flying Robots Studio 2021), *Venba* (Visai Games TBA) and *Forgotten Fields* (Frostwood Interactive 2021) are all in development at the time of writing this chapter. The tea industry in Eastern India is known across the world, especially for the famed Assam and Darjeeling teas; the industry management and the marketing of the teas is a complex affair involving precise logistics and, therefore, makes for a rather challenging simulation game. The developer Satyajit Chakraborty (of *Missing* fame) informed me in a personal interview that he spent considerable time in discussions with the owner of the Chengmari tea estate regarding the nuances of tea production. For the first time, arguably, an industry that is quite unique to the Subcontinent has been featured in a resource-management game. *Venba* and *Forgotten Fields* have an entirely different albeit very Indian flavour. Both games are about remembering. *Venba's* developer, who goes by the online name Abhi, has made the game to reflect the memory of the homeland that he left when his parents immigrated to Canada from India. *Venba* is a cooking game, where the player has to put together South Indian recipes from memory. As the developer comments in an interview:

> Players will be introduced to a variety of South Indian dishes and will be tasked with following a recipe. The trouble is that in the move over to Canada, Venba's cookbook got damaged and some of the instructions are now unreadable. Players will have to click on different ingredients on the kitchen countertop and experiment with the techniques they've been given to try and fill in the gaps, discovering how to get the recipe right in the process. (Watts 2021)

In another interview (*First Person Encounters #7: Abhi, creator of Venba* 2021), he states that along with remembering the recipe, there is also the concomitant remembering of the culture that he has left behind. *Venba* is an attempt at rethinking memory, loss and the cultures we leave behind. *Forgotten Fields* is a similarly themed game about remembering and the places we leave behind. Armaan Sandhu, the developer, comments that the game was created as part of the process of overcoming his creative block:

> Becoming obsessed and worried by my creative block, I did the obvious thing - I based my story around it. [...] In December, I travelled back home to Goa—a tiny state on the Western coast of India. And something clicked—I realized I didn't want to write a story based in 'the big city'. Not now, at least—I was too new to it to be fully inspired by it. (Dawes 2020)

The game is about recollecting his childhood home and again, is about memory, loss and rebuilding. As with all the other games mentioned in this section, the indie genre has facilitated some very thought-provoking games from this part of the world; with a lack of large-scale infrastructure but no shortage of creativity, 'indie' seems to be doing well in the Subcontinent.

As the videogames industry in India moves towards its second decade, the popularity of the 'indie' genre needs to be accounted for. To the best of this author's knowledge, the FICCI, PricewaterHouseCoopers and other business reports do not contain a separate section for statistics on 'indie' games but as evident from a large number of indie titles, these form an important part of the country's game industry. The NASSCOM Game Developer Conference mentioned earlier started a 'best indie game of the year award' and NASSCOM *India's Game Studio Directory* (NASSCOM 2012), published in 2012, lists the indie studios that existed in India at the time. There have been later attempts via social media to track the number of indie studios in India, but these have fallen by the wayside in the recent past. As this chapter is being written, Steam has offered a special sale for Indian indie games on the occasion of the New Year among various communities in India. Just recording the number of new games that were either released for this event or were slated to be released will help gauge the impact of the indies.

The importance of indies in India is neither unusual nor unexpected. In his introductory chapter on indie games, Paolo Ruffino (2020) observes:

> Independence is no longer a marginal or alternative mode of production (if it ever was); instead it is the most common type of organization within the videogame industry. It appears that almost every game developer is now partially or temporarily 'indie' within their career and the trend is expected to grow consistent with recent developments in cinema, music and fashion industries.

Together with the global trend in indie games, there is also a distinctly local aspect in India that, arguably, serves as a driver for indie game development. Padmini Ray Murray and Chris Hand talk about the 'Indian practice of *jugaad*—an indigenous combination of making-do, hacking, and frugal engineering—against the backdrop of making/DIY culture, and how local circumstances might shape intellectual explorations through critical making' (Ray Murray and Chris Hand 2015).

Ray Murray has been directly involved in the making of an 'indie' Indian videogame that 'does the cultural work of conveying the status of storytelling and storytellers in contemporary India' (2015). Her work on *Meghdoot* was influential in the later game by Quicksand Studios called *Antariksha Sanchar,* which has been described earlier. Although Ray Murray's work in the context of *jugaad* will be discussed at greater length in Chapter 7, a brief excerpt from her article detailing her experience with *jugaad* in videogame development will be illustrative for the present purpose:

> The team was also working within considerable financial constraints and so decisions had to be made regarding how the game could be designed in response to its platform and device affordances. The decision was taken early on to work with Unity, an open-source game-engine, and the Kinect2, which could be hacked easily to create a motion sensitive game, and the team was influenced by the desire to be as agile and cost-effective as possible. (Ray Murray and Chris Hand 2015)

Financial constraints and device affordances all contributed to the degree of *jugaad* that the indie game developers had to take recourse to. *Jugaad* is a management mantra today and is looked upon with mixed feelings by the media as the exact meaning of the term is not clear; while it would be presumptive to compare the process of making indie games in India with the flexibility and make-do characteristics as *jugaad*, it is nevertheless true that indie allows developers ways to work around the financial and other resource-based constraints that are faced in the Global South. Anna Marie-Schleiner also makes a similar point stating that 'while living in Southeast Asia, I encountered culturally inspired approaches to independent game development that could in turn serve as models for game making elsewhere in the global South' (Schleiner 2020: 15); the processes of game development in the Subcontinent are also unique and whether they be described as *jugaad* or by some other name, these are creative and flexible processes that underlie making of games in the region. Adrienne Shaw, in her earlier article on Indian gaming culture, points out how different the Indian gaming industry and culture are from those in the United States.

More is going to be said about the gaming cultures in India and the Subcontinent in the following chapters but before that, it is necessary to discuss the current game development scenario in the rest of the Subcontinent. The previous chapter has laid the wider context of the IT sector and the early days of videogame development; now it remains to be seen how the videogame industry and the market have developed in the other countries in the Subcontinent. It must be reiterated that prior research on videogames seems to have forgotten this region entirely and the commentators who have addressed global gaming in recent times have not even paid passing attention to countries such as Bangladesh, Pakistan or Sri Lanka.

Game Development in the Indian Subcontinent Outside India

Videogames have made a rather important footfall in the whole of the Subcontinent. Even in as remote a country like Bhutan, efforts are being made to start game development. In 2014, the UNDP embarked on a game development project involving external experts and local techies to develop an online game about unemployment that would enable 'sourcing local, short-term project ideas addressing youth unemployment issues in Bhutan' (Dorji 2014). Whether it is such internationally sponsored games such as Youth@WorkBhutan or the locally developed games such as *Polytricks* (Arcube 2016), which has been made by a Nepali studio called Arcube, videogames are fast carving a niche in the cultural life of the Subcontinent. Even in a relatively wealthy economy such as Nepal, there is both enthusiasm and creativity as far as the videogame industry is concerned. Going beyond the exclusive attention that has been paid to their much larger neighbour India by games researchers the world over, it is important not to omit the rest of the Subcontinent from the pages of the gaming history.

Consider the gaming industry in Pakistan, for example. Sadia Bashir, who runs the Pixel Art Games Academy in Islamabad, is an important figure in the local game development scene and more importantly, a clear example of a woman influencing what is otherwise a very male-dominated arena. Bashir states that 'I started making video games from there. My final-year project was to make a game that helps with cancer treatment by mimicking the action of treatments attacking cancer cells in an affected person's body' (Kokab 2018). She started coding for videogames ever since she was 13 and has now started her academy to train aspiring Pakistani game developers. Women game developers have often come up with very interesting and locally relevant concepts in Pakistan: *Trying to Fly* (Zia and Sajid 2020) is a case in point. Anam Sajid and Bisma Zaid had received invitations to be part of the Game Developers Conference in San Francisco in 2020; however, both of their visa applications to visit the USA were rejected. Their response was as follows:

> The two joined and made *Trying to Fly*, a game about repairing what they see as a broken visa system. Zia, 25, said she had 'huge feelings of frustration, annoyance and sadness' that she initially didn't want to explore because they were 'all very raw at the time.' In the end, though, the two felt it would help to funnel those tumultuous feelings into something positive. (Elise Favis 2020)

These voices from the margins of the gaming industry in a country where the IT industry is primarily male-dominated are indicative of the reach of videogames and the impact that they have on culture. Besides the voices from the margins, Pakistan also has well-established game development studios as has already been mentioned in Chapter 1. The industry is relatively small and dominated by companies such as Mindstorm Studios, Caramel Tech and we.R.Play. Mindstorm Studio's Cricket game has been mentioned earlier and its *Whacksy Taxi* (Mindstorm Studios 2010) is another popular title; Caramel Tech worked on the fruit-slicing game *Fruit Ninja* (Halfbrick Studios 2010), which was developed by Brisbane-based Halfbrick Studios and had over a million downloads in 5 years (Haridas 2016). Rematch Studios from Karachi has developed a virtual reality game called *Area of Darkness* and another studio from the city, Wonder Tree, has been making educational games for children. Other developers in Pakistan are TinTash, Mega Particle, Gameview, Kwick Games, Folio3, Quixel, Fork Particle, WRLD3D, Frag Gaming and Optera Digital. According to a survey by PakGamers.com (Pakgamers.com 2019) that had a sample size of 200, the majority of the players come from Punjab and over 63% develop for smartphones and tablets while 43.8% develop for PC, around 16% for VR headsets and around 10% for consoles. Action–adventure games, simulation games and educational games are the main genres that are popular according to the survey. Besides Pixel Arts, there are a number of institutes that cater to game development training. Of course, Pakistan has also had its share of controversies related to videogames and games have often received bad press. For example, the *Pakistan Army Retribution* (Punjab Information Technology Board 2015), jointly commissioned by the Government of Punjab and the Pakistani Army to commemorate the victims of the school shootings of Peshawar in 2014, met with criticism from the local press when a reviewer in *The Dawn* newspaper wrote a harsh review: 'One can understand the emotional attachment to the story but as a game, it falls flat. From visuals to controls, the game just doesn't deliver. Even when taking on such an unlikely subject, the Punjab IT Board is expected to deliver something far superior' (Rahool 2016). Eventually, the game was removed from the Google Play Store. Controversies aside, Pakistan's games industry has been poised towards growth and has received government endorsement whereby eSports has been legitimised as a regular sport recently by the Pakistan Sports Board and the Pakistan Science Foundation. Pakistan's Federal Minister for Science and Technology, Fawad Hussain, recently tweeted, 'If you are interested in video games, get ready and new opportunities are waiting for you' (Reuters 2021).

Other countries in the Subcontinent, such as Bangladesh, the Maldives and Sri Lanka, have also entered the games industry with some promise and, again, virtual anonymity. In Sri Lanka, the software company Arimac designed the first 3D game in the country and they describe the transition from the videogame as a hobby to the recognition of gaming as a professional software development endeavour thus:

> Almost all of them [Sri Lankan videogames] are individual hobby-projects done using ready-made game tools rather than using core game development methods. *Kanchayudha* initiated as a concept combat fighting game including the ancient giants of Sri Lanka. [...] This

> is the first time in Sri Lanka that 3D models were build [sic] from scratch specifically for a game rather than a digital render. (Arimac 2017)

The growing confidence of game developers in Sri Lanka is important to note. Recently, the start-up Prodigi Interactive has published the trailer of what it calls the first triple-A game in the Subcontinent. With *Threta* (Prodigi Interactive n.d), a game based on ancient Indic mythology where the *Treta* is one of the four yugas or the age of the humans, Prodigi promises a game based on Sri Lanka's rich history and millennia-old mythologies. The developers have introduced the *Angampora* combat style that is indigenous to Sri Lanka and as the fighting style is unique to the country with heavy hand movements, the team has invested in its own motion capture for the moves. The studio claims that this is a first in Sri Lankan gaming history. The characters connect across multiple worlds or universes in the style of *The Lord of the Rings* and there is another unique cultural element in the game. The designers have created a new language for the game that is influenced by Sinhala, Tamil, Pali, Thai and Burmese—a medley that is aimed at addressing the cultural diversity of the country. The game is slated for release for both PC and consoles in 2021. The fact that the Sri Lankan gaming industry is investing in a big-budget triple-A game whereas this has not yet been possible in India, despite the latter's economic dominance of the region and the 'Digital India' programme of its government, is indicative of the diverse ways in which the gaming industry in the region can function. The distinctiveness that the Sri Lankan gaming industry wishes to maintain is obvious from what Prithvi Virasinghe, the CEO and co-founder of Sri Lankan mobile game studio Dawn Patrol Games, has to say:

> A lot of people mistake Sri Lanka for being like India - we're both full of brown people I suppose - but we're a lot different. I lived in India for six years prior to moving stateside so I can definitely say the level of education—we have a 92 percent literacy rate, the highest in South Asia—quality of life—our cities are a heck of a lot cleaner and not over populated—and transparency is higher here. And we have better surf! The point is the countries are different and we're different from your typical chop shop. (Jordan 2013)

So far, the focus of the international game research community has almost exclusively been on India but comments such as this one indicate the necessity of looking beyond India to the other countries in the region.

Another country where the game development has reflected its strong cultural and linguistic history is Bangladesh. *Heroes of '71* (Portbliss 2017) has already been discussed at length in the previous chapter and the patriotic influence, particularly that of the *Muktijuddho* (battle for freedom), or the struggle for independence against Pakistan in 1971 is a popular theme for videogames such as Trimatrik Interactive's *Arunodoyer Agnishikha* ('the flame of sunrise'), which is based on the Bangladesh Liberation War. Bangladeshi games often use the Bengali language and this is not surprising given the country's deep commitment to the language. The previous chapter has already mentioned the efforts of Bangladeshi programmers to create Bengali fonts and software. Recently, two Bangladeshi game studios, M7 Productions and Attrito, have released a FPS game called *Zero Hour* and an open-world adventure set in Dhaka (the in-game name is 'Dhacca') is slated for release. The game is called *Agontuk* (Attrito 2019), which means 'the stranger' in Bengali, and has been described as follows: 'this third person action-adventure game's map, based on a fictional version of Bangladesh's capital Dhaka, is called *Dhacca*. This virtual version of the city will feature some of the iconic monuments and locations of Dhaka, including rickshaws and CNGs' (Raihan 2019). Crisis Entertainment is developing the country's first online competitive FPS game called *Annihilation*. The mobile game sector is also looking up according to a news report:

> While PC game developers are facing some negligence in Bangladesh, our mobile gaming industry is showing steady growth over the years, and some developers are even providing world-class games and applications. The Mascoteers have already established a dominance in the smart-phone gaming sector, as well as in television games, Gear VR (a virtual reality headset) games, and on many other platforms in Bangladesh. (Madhurja and Siddique 2020)

Gear VR now has 25 games in the Google Play Store while *Tap-Tap Ants*, one of the most popular games developed by the Bangladeshi company Rise Up Labs, has 15 million downloads. Commentators on the industry, however, lament the lack of opportunities and growth in comparison to India despite having a videogame market that is beginning to look promising. According to a 2017 Newzoo report, Bangladesh's gaming market was worth $62.2 million (see Islam 2020). As Madhurja and Siddique (2020) report:

> There is no official statistic on the number of game development companies in Bangladesh. Company owners say indifference towards this sector is a big reason behind its poor growth here, and ICT Minister Mustafa Jabbar agrees. He says there have been no big initiatives to promote this industry in Bangladesh.

Bangladesh's current ICT minister is, incidentally, also the developer of one of the earliest Bengali language software. He is well aware of the lack of awareness regarding videogames as well as the paucity of trained game developers. A developer, however, complains that the major problem is the lack of education and training for videogame developers. An obvious comparison is, of course, to be made with countries in the Global North:

> They have game studies in universities. We had someone from Finland visit us last year. He has a master's degree in game psychology. He told us there had been studies in his country on what colours should be used on which game screens, what the font sizes should be and what pricing model would attract the highest number of customers. Here we do this arbitrarily. Get the difference? (2020)

It is encouraging that game development is picking up pace in recent times in countries such as Bangladesh and that it is getting more of a local flavour; what lies in the future, however, is the main question.

Conclusion

The Subcontinent has been an active but seriously under-researched hub of game development and has seen rapid growth over the past decade. Consisting of some of the world's most populous nations and now with massively improved mobile connectivity in most of these countries, the Subcontinent presents an extremely promising potential market for videogames. The diversity of the region, however, is immense and that brings quite a few problems to the forefront. While this chapter has focused mainly on game development and the industry, it has not been possible to do so without considering the cultural milieu about which more will be said in the following chapters. Issues relating to class, gender, religion, language, caste and other factors arise when a majoritarian perspective of videogames in the Subcontinent ignores the specificities of issues relating to class, gender, religion, language, caste and other factors. Most of the discussions of the region (Schleiner 2020; Toftedahl et al. 2018; Desbandhu 2020; Mukherjee 2015 and 2019; Shaw 2013; O'Donnell 2014) happen to revolve around India, thus neglecting the rest of the Subcontinent. It has to be also remembered that most countries in the region were formerly colonised by European powers and, therefore, viewing these through a postcolonial and a decolonial lens may be a good starting point. It is important to keep in mind Phillip Penix-Tadsen's observation regarding videogames in the Global South:

> [H]ow much perspective can be gained by understanding games as complex technological and cultural products whose creation, circulation, consumption and meaning are shaped by concerns and practices that are fundamentally local [...] Many geographical locales once considered part of the high-tech 'periphery' are in fact home to longstanding and widespread technocultures with their own unique characteristics, and with their own geometries of power. (2019: 6)

Penix-Tadsen goes on to invoke Walter Mignolo's notion of decoloniality which is about 'the decolonization of knowledge and of being and assumes that the way out is to unlink from the colonial matrix of power' (Mignolo 2011). Unlinking from the colonial matrices of power and reflecting on the unique specificities and diversity of the region is, as this book argues, the key to better understanding videogames in the Subcontinent. For this, a discussion of gaming cultures in the region is of paramount importance.

Section Two

Cultures

3

Diverse Subcontinent, Ludic Cultures: The Non-Digital Game Cultures as Context

In the Indian epic (arguably the oldest) the *Mahabharata,* one of the most important events is a dice game (played not with dice as we know them but with the seeds of the *Vibhitaka* plant) that decides the fate of the two kindred clans of the Pandavas and Kauravas. The sporting spirit of ancient India continues into current times when in the 21st century, perhaps the most popular and controversial activity in the Indian Subcontinent is Cricket, prowess which is often equated to national glory in India, Pakistan, Sri Lanka and Bangladesh. Cricketers today are no less than the epic figures of the ancient past; Pakistan's current prime minister is the former cricketer Imran Khan and India's Sachin Tendulkar or Sri Lanka's Sanath Jayasurya are almost legendary figures today. Cricketing stars and their families usually occupy a column to themselves in the local dailies and are as popular news items as film stars and other Page Three celebrities. Not all the nations in the Subcontinent share the craze for Cricket, though the Himalayan nations of Nepal and Bhutan have other key national sports, which are extremely popular and have a major social presence. For Bhutan it is archery and Nepal's national game is a board game called *Bagh Chal* (translated as 'tigers and goats'), which is also common in India. Of course, a slew of other outdoor sports also occupies the public psyche in all of these countries often sports news makes the headlines in print, television and web journalism in the region. A substantial body of academic work also exists now around the cultures of sports in the Subcontinent, albeit mainly focusing on India. Compared to the huge din around sports and cultures of sports, there is very little awareness regarding the cultures of gaming in the region today; of course, in recent years the popularity of competitive gaming and eSports has grown significantly and videogames are beginning to be considered as serious cultural media that have their own cultures and also influence culture in general.

Before addressing the question of gaming culture in the Subcontinent, some discussion of gaming culture in general (and in the context of global Games Studies) is necessary. Regarding the impact of games on culture, Dutch videogames scholar Joost Raessens talks of the *ludification* of culture:

> [T]he importance of rules, the idea that rules can be changed, the playful nature of cultural domains such as politics and media, the understanding that play is often less open than it looks (it is Mr Wilders's playground), the worldwide popularity of game shows, in other words: the cultural significance of play. To study and understand these features, we need a playful turn in media theory [...] Play is not only characteristic of leisure, but also turns up in those domains that once were considered the opposite of play. (2014: 94)

Raessens sees the playful turn in education, politics and even drone warfare. His notion of ludification is important in that through it epistemologically 'play can be used as a heuristic tool to shed new light on contemporary media culture' (Raessens 2014: 96) what Raessens observes is a ludic turn in media theory. Raessens also critiques Eric Zimmerman and Heather Chaplin's comment that the 21st century will be a century of games in their *Manifesto for a Ludic Century* (Zimmerman and Chaplin 2013) as being too broad but agrees that it certainly indicates the growing influence of academic studies of games on appraisals of and thinking through cultures. Perhaps the most compelling case for games as influencing all aspects of culture, or Western civilisation as being *sub specie ludi* has been made in Dutch historian Johan Huizinga's groundbreaking study *Homo Ludens: A Study of the Play Element in Culture,* which was first published in 1938. Huizinga (1949) presents some of the most widely quoted as well as perhaps ambiguous conclusions on play and games in culture. Incidentally, Huizinga's doctoral dissertation (Huizinga 1897) was on the playful figure of the *vidusaka* or the playful jester-figure in Sanskrit drama and unsurprisingly, therefore, his *Homo Ludens* is replete with examples of games and play from Indian literature and mythology. Even though *Homo Ludens* almost has a cult status in Games Studies[1], Huizinga's engagement with Indian ludic culture and its larger significance for his work has not yet been researched and is perhaps the topic for a separate and entire book in itself. Nevertheless, his key thinking on 'play' as culture and play cultures as well as its connection to the Indian Subcontinent (especially as described in *Homo Ludens*) needs to be introduced in brief, at the very least. The following section initiates the discussion of the importance of play in understanding culture and also how this relates to the Indian Subcontinent.

Before entering that discussion, however, one needs to have an overview of how closely the culture of the Indian Subcontinent has been connected to play and games. In Hindu religious thought, for example, *lila* or divine play is responsible for the functioning of the universe. The famous dice game of the *Mahabharat* has already been mentioned—the entire fate of the Pandav and Kaurav clans revolved around that one dice game, arguably also shaping the future for generations to come. Indeed, even before the arrival of the Aryans in India, there was a considerably rich ludic tradition in the region as Elke Rogersdottir's work on the Indus Valley Civilisation shows. In what can be described as a major cross-cultural ludic exchange, the rules of the ancient Royal Game of Ur were finally pieced together by British Museum curator, Irving Finkel, from 'the anthropological data of the Pardesi Jews of Cochin, sent to the museum by the head of the community, the late Sattoo Koder in the 90s that provided him with the crucial jigsaw piece' (Priyadarshini 2015). Over the centuries, treatises on games were written and there are records of many games that were invented and played.

Moving on from the examples in ancient India to the glorious days of the Mughal empire in the 16th century, the art and culture of the times are replete with references to play and games and any visitor to Fatehpur Sikri near Agra will not miss the giant Parcheesi (Indian: *Pachisi*) board where the emperor Akbar played the game with his

1 This is especially due to the debates around its description of play as happening within a 'magic circle'.

courtiers represent the game-pieces. Four centuries later, in India of the British Raj, Cricket and Football, imported from Europe, became absolutely essential for expressing prowess in terms of culture and nationalism. The victory of the Indian football club, Mohun Bagan, all but one of whose team members played barefoot against the East Yorkshire Regiment in the IFA Shield of 1911 is crucial in the annals of India's struggle for Independence and as commentator Boria Majumder says, 'Mohun Bagan had become synonymous with the national battle cry for Vande Mataram' (Majumdar 2013). Ninety years later, Mohun Bagan's exploits possibly inspired the Bollywood blockbuster on Cricket, *Lagaan* (Gowariker 2002), where a village team defeats the British colonial masters so as to get the government to waive its harsh taxes on the farmers.[2] By then, of course, Cricket was no longer a colonial game in India but something far more—as reflected in theorist Ashish Nandy's comment, 'cricket is an Indian game accidentally discovered by the British'(Nandy 2000). Nandy may have spoken for Indians but his comments ring true across the Subcontinent, where Cricket has cultural implications in all walks of life.

Culture in the Indian Subcontinent: *Sub Specie Ludi*?

Huizinga famously called *western* civilisation *sub specie ludi*. There is, nevertheless, an apparent contradiction in his thinking that many commentators remark on. While play seems to have an all-pervading influence on culture, there is another aspect to play wherein it is supposed to be rule-bound (Roger Caillois brings in the division of *ludus* or rule-bound games versus *paidia* or free play) and outside life. Indeed, there is a school that interprets Huizinga to have postulated that games happen within a 'magic circle' or a specific space thereby implying that there is a disjunct between real life and games. Such a reading has been much contested, especially by Game Studies scholars

2 Mohun Bagan's feat also inspired a later film on the Football match itself called *Egaro*, which is Bengali for 'eleven'.

such as Ian Bogost and Mia Consalvo. Without going into this debate at length, it is nevertheless necessary to briefly outline the Game Studies critiques above. Consalvo contends that Huizinga's notion is dated: 'When Huizinga (1950) wrote about the magic circle, our sense of space and place was radically different from what it is now. In suggesting a place "set apart" from everyday life, that space could be envisioned as geographic space fairly easily—the playground, the boxing ring, the hopscotch outline' (Consalvo 2009: 410). Consalvo is right in that digital games, something Huizinga could not have conceived of, function in different ways than those games that he describes. Bogost says that the magic circle is a porous one and not one that is restrictive to players as other critics of the concept such as T.L.Taylor argues against a model where 'formal rules allow players to operate within a "magic circle" outside the cares of everyday life and the world [and] the player steps through a kind of looking glass and enters a pure game space' (Taylor 2009: 117). Consider, however, what Huizinga himself has stated:

> All play moves and has its being within a play-ground marked off beforehand either materially or ideally, deliberately or as a matter of course. Just as there is no formal difference between play and ritual, so the 'consecrated spot' cannot be formally distinguished from the play-ground. The arena, the card-table, the magic circle, the temple, the stage, the screen, the tennis court, the court of justice, etc., are all in form and function play-grounds, i.e., forbidden spots, isolated, hedged round, hallowed, within which special rules obtain. (1949: 55)

The 'magic circle' is just *one* of the many items that Huizinga mentions and as the space for play; it is mentioned in the same breath as the stage, the temple and the court of justice. How far Huizinga intended the play-space to have been seen as cut off from life is, therefore, a moot question. The fact that Huizinga links all of these other aspects to play is significant and his interest in certain forms of play preceded *The Waning of the Middle Ages* (1954 [1933]), for which he is more famous: as a Sanskrit philologist, he had written on the figure of the *vidusaka* or court jester in ancient Indian drama. Very little research has been done on how Huizinga's notions of play related to his earlier work on the playful *vidusaka* character in Sanskrit drama. Among videogame researchers, only Tara Fickle makes a tangential connection in her chapter on the 'oriental origins of game studies' (Fickle 2019). Although not referring directly to his work on the *vidusaka* or even his discussions of Indian culture, some Indian scholars have already made important philosophical connections between culture and Huizinga.

Two essays particularly come to mind. The first is 'Of Gambling: A Few Lessons from the Mahabharata' by Sibaji Bandopadhyay (Bandyopadhyay 2014) and the second is an essay in Bengali titled 'Ki Brittanto' by Arindam Chakrabarti (Chakrabarti 2008).[3] As a scholar of Oriental culture and games, Huizinga often refers to the *Mahabharata* and the famous dice-game scene in the epic. Bandopadhyay's essay takes up the crucial question of how the dice-game matters in the very thinking of human existence in ancient Indian mythology are determined by play: '[t]he fantastic coincidence of names of Ages and throws of dice is made even more scintillating by Manu just before he begins to set forth the characteristics of the four *yugas*'. He says in I.80: 'The Epochs...are countless, and so are the emissions and re-absorptions (of the universe); as if he were playing, *paramesthil* Supreme Lord/ Brahma does this again and again' (Bandyopadhyay 2014: 5). Extending this thinking in terms of Huizinga's framework, he sees a potentially ominous implication and states that '*Homo Ludens* in his gambler-avatar has the potential to confound man's *Homo Sapiens* self with such completeness as to wreck his *Homo Faber* career with no hope of recovery or retrieval' (Bandyopadhyay 2014: 25). The overarching influence of the ludic on Indian culture is obvious from the way the *Manusmriti* employs the play metaphor and Bandopadhyay picks up on this with his astute and scholarly reading. One may argue, however, with the fact that the *Homo Ludens* necessarily wrecks (and Bandopadhyay only says that it has the potential to) the *Homo Faber.* As has been addressed by earlier research in Game Studies (see Mukherjee 2015), when speaking of the narrative character of videogames, *Homo Ludens* is not separate from *Homo Faber.* Indeed, if one goes back to ancient Indian texts that Bandopadhyay quotes, in the divine realm at least, creation and play go hand-in-hand.

3 Chakrabarti's essay is in Bengali and has been paraphrased and translated by the author.

Indeed, it is in this light that Arindam Chakrabarti's comments on games and culture may be read. Chakrabarti's essay is called 'Ki Brittanto?' '*brittanto*' in Bengali means 'description' but it also means the end or edge of the circle (*brittyo*). Chakrabarti speaks of narrative as being the end or edge of the circle—the moment where the circle of time sees a pause, so 'ki brittanto?' or 'how does one describe it?' is also a pun for 'what is the end of the circle?' It is intriguing that Chakrabarti chooses the circle metaphor because he follows it up by connecting this with Huizinga's *Homo Ludens* and then goes on to make an even more astute observation that the universal play of temporal imagination is the description—the act of storytelling. Picking up the trail from a perspective independent of game studies scholarship, Chakrabarti makes an important philosophical point that, arguably, contributes to the games studies debates regarding games and narratives. The purpose of this chapter, however, is to point out how relevant games are to culture and how leading Indian thinkers have already made such connections via Huizinga and *Homo Ludens* although there is still the need to directly engage with Huizinga's thoughts on Indian culture and play.

Histories of Indigenous Game Cultures in the Indian Subcontinent

Huizinga's focus on games in India was a much-needed intervention in the West but it was not unique and his research was preceded by that of many other orientalists such as Thomas Hyde whose *De Ludis Orientalibus was* published in Oxford in 1694. Hyde recounts in some detail the purported origins of Chess, Chaupar (spelt *tchupur* in his treatise) and many other games. In the Middle East, Chess, called *shatranj* in Persio-Arabic, is known to have been an import from India and possibly a derivative of the four-handed game *Chaturanga*. The 12th-century artist in the Sena court, Sulapani (Sulapani 1936), wrote a treatise on *Chaturanga*. Many games from the Subcontinent, both board games and outdoor games, would end up in Europe and North America during the colonial period—notable examples are board games such as Snakes and Ladders (originally *Gyan Chaupar* in India) and Parcheese or Ludo (originally *Chaupar* in India) as well as games such as Polo (in its modern form, the game is said to have originated in Manipur in India).

Another 12th-century Sanskrit text, *Manasollasa* (Someshwara 1939), which can be loosely translated as the 'desires of the mind', written by the Chalukya king Someshvara III who ruled in present-day Southern India, contains an entire section on games called *krida vimsati*. Before this treatise, however, there were many references to games in Indian culture of the ancient past—in the Indus Valley Civilisation (see for example, Rogersdotter 2012) and also in the Vedic period (the 'Gambling Hymn' in the *Rigveda* 10–24). Rogersdotter states that she 'was astonished by the sheer quantum of play-related materials unearthed' (Jayan 2011). The reference to the dice game in the *Mahabharata* may be the most famous in the Indian epics but both *Ramayana* and the *Mahabharata* contain references to diverse ludic competitions. The Buddha is said to have proscribed the playing of games according to a list provided in the *Brahmajala Sutta*; this, however, is to be viewed in context as his full comment is often ignored. The Buddha is not talking about hating a few games and listing them; he is saying that it is worldly people who praise him for abstaining from these games just as they praise him for not going to dances or boxing matches. The Buddha does not have a special grudge against board games. As the prince Siddhartha in Kapilavastu (in modern Nepal), we know that he did let loose an arrow in an archery contest (something he has purportedly criticised in his list of games). For better or worse, games are an integral part of the culture of the Subcontinent.

In fact, in Sri Lanka, the Buddhist goddess Pattini has special games dedicated to her. According to Rohan Bastin:

> The Sri Lankan deity, Pattini, has a number of games (or keliya) held on her behalf. They include the horn game (ankeliya),2 the stick game (likeliya) and the coconut game (polkeliya). These games share the feature of a competition between two teams, with most commonly one team representing Pattini and the other team representing either her spouse or another male deity. (2001: 120)

The main story of Pattini, is told in the Tamil epic *Silappadikaram* or 'The Anklet' where she is enraged by the unjust execution of her husband and destroys her city in a terrible conflagration and a pestilence. These come to an end only when the goddess is appeased by people playing games.

From Bastin's account, it seems that the Pattini games have a deeper connect in the region and that Tamil Hindus also worship the goddess. In Nepal, the games of *Naga Pasa* (a variant of *Gyan Chaupar;* see Shimkhada 1983) and *Bagh Chal* ('Tigers and Goats') are deeply connected to the quotidian culture. The *Ludii* database comments that 'Baghchal is a game popular in Nepal, observed in the 20th century. This game was played by Buddhist monks in Nepal in 1976, with whom it was said to be particularly popular. It may also be played in India, particularly in places close to Nepal' ('Ludii Portal', n.d.). The game is certainly popular even outside the Buddhist monks' circle and dates back much beyond 1976 and also into current times.[4] In fact, there are many variants of the game that date back to much earlier and are found all over the Subcontinent and even in Iran and Malaysia. There are similar games in India called 'Tigers and Goats' and 'Mughal Pathan' (after the series of wars between Mughals and Pathan sultans in India), in Sri Lanka called 'Cows and Leopards' and 'Sixteen Soldiers' (also called *hewakam Keliya* or 'War Game') and in Bangladesh, where the latter is called 'Sholo Ghuti' (or sixteen pieces).

Games have also been the centre of controversy and it is not just *PUB-G* or Cricket that have come under public scrutiny; the Supreme Court of India had banned the popular sport of bull-taming or *Jallikattu* in the state of Tamil Nadu and the ban was subsequently lifted. Jallikattu is certainly an indigenous sport and arguably dates back to antiquity as a seal found in the Indus Valley Civilisation and cave paintings near Ooty. As a newspaper report describes it as:

> The bull has clearly taken Tamil Nadu by the horns, bringing people out onto the streets to protest against the Supreme Court ban on a favourite sport involving the physical taming of the animal. Jallikattu, a festive

4 The Nepali newspaper *Himalaya Times* mentions a recent tournament that was organised by a local panchayat and also another one that was organised in Switzerland.

> game played in Tamil Nadu for centuries as part of the celebrations of the local festival Pongal involves the release of a bull amongst a crowd of people who are challenged to bring it to a halt by physically overpowering it. (Roychowdhury 2017)

The story of the *Jallikattu* ban (on the recommendation of PETA and other animal rights groups) and its subsequent revoking is an intriguing example of how games are deeply intertwined with quotidian cultural activities in India. A more famous example of games being connected not only to the culture of the region but to the history and to the quotidian lives of the people comes from fiction. Munshi Premchand's (1928) fascinating story 'The Chess Players' (Hindi: *Shatranj ki Khiladi*), which was later adapted into a film by Satyajit Ray, is a good example. Premchand describes how an obsession with Chess that two aristocrats in the state of Oudh have, reflects on their quotidian lives, whether it be in their marital relationships or the political scenario in the state, where the East India Company is about to effect a takeover.

Game Cultures in India: Earlier Commentaries from Colonial Times

Perhaps, the two most famous Indian films about games and play are *Shatranj ki Khiladi* (1977) by Satyajit Ray and *Lagaan* (2002) by Asutosh Gowarikar.[5] Both films in their respective ways serve as important commentaries on Indian culture and the influence of games on it. Besides these popular commentaries, there has been a slew of texts that address ludic culture in the Subcontinent. Many of these texts date back to the colonial period when most of the countries in the Subcontinent were part of the British Raj or were its tributaries. Among some of the older Orientalist commentaries were Sir William Jones and Hiram Cox who wrote on the Indian origins of Chess (see Jones and Cox 1883). Cox's theory was extended by Duncan Forbes and was called the Cox-Forbes theory of the origin of Chess. While the Cox-Forbes theory

5 There are other less known films such as *Striker*, which is about the game of Carrom; however [800, chalo paltai, egaro)

has been long debunked, the efforts of Orientalists such as Jones and Cox illustrate the importance that the ludic had in Europe's idea of the Subcontinent. Complementing and speaking to the studies by the likes of orientalists such as Jones, there were also notable pamphlets written by local scholars from the different parts of the Subcontinent itself: Reverend Lal Behari Day and Thiruvenkatacharya Shastri (1814) are among the earliest to publish on Indian games and pastimes in English and the latter's translated work was the first source of Indian Chess problems for Europeans. One of the most unique works on board games that deserves special mention is that of Mummada Krishnaraja Wodeyar, the young king who ruled Mysore after Tipu Sultan was killed by the British. The British were de facto rulers for fifty years until 1881 and during this time, the king devoted his energies to board games—he developed many board games and also composed a commentary that is now painted on the walls of his palace. Krishnaraja Wodeyar, however, was an exception, albeit one whose contribution should be remembered. In general, however, records and commentaries on games before the early 20th century are difficult to find.

In the late 19th and early 20th century, as Projit Bihari Mukharji and Nirbed Ray (Ray and Mukharji 2005) note, there was a rise in the interest in board games in India as part of a nationalist project. As Ray and Mukharji (2005) point out:

> Professor Hem Chandra Das Gupta, Dr Charu Chandra Das Gupta, Haraprasad Shastri, Jatindra Mohan Datta wrote extensively on the subject. If this interest was indeed merely a derivative interest born out of proximity with the British Orientalists, one would have expected much more writing between 1790, when Jones's piece appeared, and 1895, when Haraprasad Shastri's pieces appeared. Yet there were none, but between Shastri's piece and 1942, there were more than 20 pieces that appeared in the journal of the Asiatic Society and in the *Calcutta Review*.

Given the time when these articles were written, Mukharji and Ray see a connection with the Hindu nationalism that was then on the upsurge. Around the same time, of course, what has now become India's virtual national sport was also gaining popularity.

The Unique Case of Cricket in the Subcontinent

In 1877, the European members of Bombay Gymkhana played a Cricket match against the Zoroastrian Cricket Club. Soon this became the Bombay Triangular and included the Hindus as the third team and this was followed by the Bombay Quadrangular and Pentangular, all of which were created along very communal lines. Ramachandra Guha's *A Corner of A Foreign Field* (2003) describes the growth of Indian Cricket and also the rise of the phenomenal Dalit off-spinner Palwankar Baloo who was the star player in Indian Cricket although due to caste-based discrimination, he was never allowed to be captain.[6] Mihir Bose discusses the pervading influence of Cricket on Indian society, on how it differs from its English forbear and how Cricket as *tamasha* (the North Indian word for 'fun, excitement, spectacle') is now an intrinsic part of Indian culture. As Bose explains, the Cricket fever in India spreads across all walks of life:

> Businessmen have had tax inspectors drop hints that a ticket or two would help with assessments, bank managers have suggested a similar leniency towards borrows and to accommodate the demand for press tickets [the Chairman of the Board of Control for Cricket in India] Dalmiya has had to divide journalists between 'working' and 'non-working'. (2006: 109)

The Indian cricketers vie for celebrity status and stardom with Bollywood actors and politicians—recently, the boundaries have melded as cricketers such as Md Azharuddin and Virat Kohli have married film actresses and others such as Navjyot Sidhu and Gautam Gambhir have joined politics. Sachin Tendulkar, India's most popular cricketer, has been awarded the country's highest award, the Bharat Ratna. A similar scenario is true in Pakistan where defeat in Cricket matches often attracts death threats and where the current prime minister, Imran Khan, was one of the country's most famous fast bowlers of all time. As Burhan Wazir notes, 'In sporting terms, the Pakistani cricket team is unlike any other national side. A more accurate comparison might

6 His brother Vithal, however, would go on to captain the Indian team.

be struck with South American footballing giants such as Brazil and Argentina' (Wazir 2014). Cricketers in the Subcontinent are household names and this is most applicable to India and Pakistan, which in turn often take their rivalry as neighbouring nuclear powers to the cricket ground. Cricket stadiums are also iconic places in these countries—the Eden Gardens Stadium in Kolkata and the recent Narendra Modi Stadium (commonly known as the Motera Stadium) in Ahmedabad are the third-largest and largest Cricket grounds in the world, respectively. Established in 1864, Eden Gardens is the oldest Cricket stadium in the country. Pakistan also boasts of the Gaddafi Stadium in Lahore, and Bangladesh, the Sher-e-Bangla stadium in Dhaka. Indian, Pakistan, Sri Lanka and Bangladesh have cricket grounds in their major cities, testifying to the popularity of the game. The stadiums are packed during Cricket matches and the current avatar of Cricket in the IPL (Indian Premier League) aims to be for international Cricket what the English Premier League is for Football. As Bose points out, there is big money invested by the industrialists from the Subcontinent and abroad in Cricket in the region.

George Orwell had once commented on the nationalism that accompanies competitive sports '[i]f you wanted to add to the vast fund of ill-will existing in the world at this moment, you could hardly do it better than by a series of football matches between Jews and Arabs, Germans and Czechs, Indians and British, Russians and Poles, and Italians and Jugoslavs, each match to be watched by a mixed audience of 100,000 spectators' (1945). The Cricket matches in the Subcontinent often result in similar acrimony between the countries and their teams. This cricketing history is, however, legion and many events continue to be celebrated by the fans from the Subcontinent. India–Pakistan matches have often been quite sensitive and at the same time, nail-biting affairs. As Shahryar Khan says:

> Traditionally a Pakistan–India cricket series has been seen as a rivalry that goes beyond the cricketing arena. It reflects the political relationship between the two neighbours which, since independence in August 1947, has been tense and confrontational. An added complicating factor has been the relatively recent phenomenon of religious extremism and terrorism that has led to most foreign

> cricket teams declining to tour Pakistan because of security concerns. (2013: 35)

Cricket in Pakistan has huge significance and as Khan points out, the discussion of Cricket is always connected to questions such as:

> How does history affect the Pakistani cricketer? […] How does the increasing sway of orthodox Islam in Pakistan affect the make up and outlook of the national team? What factors draw the Pakistani cricketer towards criminality like drug abuse, match-fixing and corruption? Do Pakistani cricketers mirror the country's social make up like the lack of education or a feeling that the world, especially the developed world, is constantly conspiring against Pakistan? (2013: xviii)

These are deep issues with which sporting teams are not usually as directly associated but the Pakistani Cricket team seems to be bearing all of this burden when it goes out to play and it plays a crucial role in shaping society and public opinion.

While matches between India and Pakistan still get the most press, there has also been a complicated relationship between Sri Lanka and its neighbours India and Pakistan. In the colonial period, players from Ceylon would play in the Bombay Pentangular while even afterwards, the 'Tamil Nadu Ranji team played an annual contest against the Ceylon (as Sri Lanka was called earlier) national team for the M.J. Gopalan Trophy. It was an annual contest that was staged regularly till Sri Lanka attained Test status in 1981' (Narayanan 2019). Later on, however, there was some acrimony between the Sri Lankan and Indian teams that resulted in India's withdrawal from the 1986 Asia Cup held in Sri Lanka. Of course, in 1996 and onwards, the cult of Sanath Jayasurya was huge in India and according to author Chandresh Narayanan, '[e] veryone in India yearned for a Sanath prototype in the national team. The fans almost pleaded to replicate the Sanath model' (Ibid.). Ashish Nandy comments, however, that 'the story of Sri Lanka can be easily told as that of an outsider who, exuding exotic charms, wins the heart of a fickle princess, and then bewitched by his own success, tries to hold her by becoming a conventional prince' (xix). Whether or not Nandy's assessment is correct, Sri Lanka, conventional or otherwise, is now a major cricketing nation. As far as diplomatic relations with Pakistan were concerned, the Sri Lankan team did not play in Pakistan from 2009 to 2019 because of a terrorist attack on the team while it was on its way to play at the Gaddafi Stadium in Lahore. As for Bangladesh, a later entrant into the league of test-playing nations, it has now come into its own after gaining the status of a—Zeeshan Mahmud's (Mahmud 2016) racy fifty essays on Bangladeshi Cricket provide a glimpse of the enthusiasm of Bangladeshi cricketing culture and its influence on the general public.

Cricket has taken the centre stage when it comes to game cultures in the Subcontinent and the number of commentaries on the sport and its sociocultural impact is quite phenomenal already. In India, Ashish Nandy (2000), Ramchandra Guha (2003), Boria Majumdar (2018), Mihir Bose (2006), Souvik Naha (2015), Prashant Kidambi (2019) and Kausik Bandopadhyay (2017) have all done seminal work on the game and its influence. Pakistani commentators include Shaharyar Khan (Khan 2013) and Osman Samiuddin while in Sri Lanka, Ajith Perera (1999) and Ranjan Mellawa (2017) are some of the prominent writers. Bangladeshi writers such as Mahmud (2016) with his collection of essays and Debabrata Mukhopadhyay (2016) with his biography of a prominent Bangladeshi cricketer have an increasing list of books on its cricketing culture. Writers from abroad such as James Astill and Peter Oborne, writing about Indian and Pakistani Cricket, have made interesting book-length interventions but starting with Neville Cardus there has been a whole genre of Cricket-writing by commentators from outside the Subcontinent, often professional cricketers, writing about Cricket in the region. Of course, there is also the whole gamut of fiction related to Cricket in English and the local languages of the various regions of the Subcontinent. The hype and attention that Cricket gets in the region makes it by far the most discussed sport and makes national heroes out of the cricketers. Nandy's sobering comment should, however, be kept in mind: '[t]he oddity in South Asia is that it is an unpredictable, uncertain game like cricket that has to cope with the feelings of inadequacy and grandiose ambitions of the citizens. Despite the widespread belied that the ideal cricketer is the ideal citizen and, therefore, should "naturally" win his matches for his country, it continues to be in South Asia, as Mihir Bose puts it, a *tamasha*' (Nandy 2000: xx).

Other Games: Cultures and Current Commentaries

Cricket, however, was not the original game that bred nationalism. When Swami Vivekananda, India's famous 19th-century spiritual leader, declared to the youth of undivided India, 'You will be nearer to Heaven through football than through the study of the Gita' (Vivekananda 2010) he was quite well aware of the potential of football as a sport that could promote national identity. Indeed, the IFA final victory of Mohun Bagan against East Yorkshire happened during the height of the *Swadeshi* movement in colonial India and as Soumen Mitra comments:

> Mohun Bagan represented Bengal with its obsession for physical strength and the yearning to cast aside the stigma of feebleness by beating the colonial power at its own game [...] The 1911 victory reflected the image of the Bengali society surging in anger against colonial rule. While sports became a symbol around which anti-colonial consciousness developed, football became an instrument for establishing 'native' superiority over the 'whites'. (1991, pp. 56–57)

Majumder and Bandopadhyay are also quite specific regarding the cultural impact of the victory:

> Post 1911, football was looked upon as a cultural idiom and Mohun Bagan as a cultural institution capable of challenging British hegemony. Football, a common language of the Bengali people irrespective of class, caste, creed, community or religion, thus introduced a unique means of cultural self-expression in contemporary society. (2018: 147)

The match became an iconic event and Majumdar and Bandopadhyay capture the impact: '[a]ll other activities had become secondary in this state of euphoria. Offices and shops owned by Indians were closed on the day of the final. Prayers were offered all-round the city in the hope of a native victory' (Ibid.). They go on to observe how the victory of Mohun Bagan started symbolizing the Black resurgence against the White regime and how people even compared to the revenge against Clive's victory at the Battle of Plassey. Although, Football was the major game through which nationalism has expressed itself most often in the colonial period, India's most striking international protest against racism and fascism came from Major Dhyan Chand, India's hockey captain who refused to give the Nazi salute during the Berlin Olympics of 1936 (see Majumdar and Mehta 2021). Dhyan Chand scored a hat-trick in British India's eight-nil victory over Germany. India's prowess in Hockey is legion (they were reigning Olympic champions until 1980) but it gets overshadowed by the celebrity status of Cricket and Football.

Concluding Remarks

It is a truism to say that there is a very rich diversity in India regarding sports and games that goes beyond the oft-celebrated Cricket and Football worship; many indigenous games such as the snake-boat races and the tug of war (*Vadam Valli*) in Kerala, *Kabaddi* and *Kho Kho* in Northern India or *Kori Khel* (playing with cowrie shells) in Assam are some examples (see Sharma and Sonowal 2017). The latter, for example, is linked with the *Bohag Bihu* new year celebrations in Assam and is part of the ritual celebrations as is *Gyan Chaupar* (the Indian predecessor of Snakes and Ladders) in the *Paryushan* festival celebrated by the Jain religion. The stories of these games are often lost to history as the main funding and hype remain around Cricket and to a lesser extent, Football. Among board games, the interest varies from one country to another, Chess and Bagh Chal being popular in India and Nepal, respectively. The one board game that has had phenomenal popularity before the advent of digital games, is Carrom. Carrom-boards were once part of the furniture of public establishments, clubs and staffrooms in offices all over the region. Research on these games is still inadequate and although there have been some key commentaries written on board games in the region and their histories, there are many research gaps to fill.

As digital games become more popular in the Indian Subcontinent, there are fears that earlier ludic cultures will be forgotten. Such fears are unfounded given the recent surge in boardgame cultures and the efforts of organisations like Kreeda Kaushalya in Mysore, India, is commendable in reviving the earlier traditions. Similarly, the contribution of the Rani of Sawantwadi in supporting the *ganjifa* card artisans and enabling them to market these cards internationally or the Kickstarter campaign of Sunit Chabba also has a similar aim are interesting developments. Similarly, recent board games from Europe and North America, such as Settlers of Catan and Risk, are now becoming available in India and have spawned boardgame societies and clubs. As far as outdoor games are concerned, the focus on Cricket to the detriment of other games has now become almost institutional. An article in the popular Sports magazine *The Sportstar* declares, 'cricket is indeed killing other sports in India [...] it is celebrated as a festival, thanks to our Board, Government, sponsors and the media' (Is cricket killing other sports in India? 2004). Many traditional games in different parts of India now remain forgotten and do not get the publicity that they richly deserve. The case remains the same for Pakistan, Bangladesh and Sri Lanka as well. Nepal and Bhutan are notable exceptions, of course. Bhutan's national sport is archery and is quite a serious affair that is connected to festivities and social gatherings. Nepal's Cricketing interests are on the rise but during the *Dashain* festival, the lakeside of Pokhara's Phewa Tal is dotted with numerous groups of people betting on the Nepali *langur burja* or langur dice. In what is a very diverse potpourri of cultural influences, the ludic cultures of the region are, arguably, among the most varied in the world and a mix of the ancient and the modern where much has been appropriated from other cultures and much in other cultures have been transculturated from the games of the region. Digital Games, new as they might be to the region, do not operate in a vacuum. Videogames may be new but ludic culture is not and it is necessary to frame discussions of newer ludic cultures within the older ones.

4

Digital Gaming Cultures in the Indian Subcontinent

On 20 October 2020, Indian mobile gamers bid adieu to the extremely popular *PUB-G Mobile*, following a ban that started taking effect from the previous month. Others said that they would keep playing on PC (where the game incidentally has not been banned). The game is indeed available on Steam at the time of writing, incidentally. Still, others expressed disappointment with *FAU-G*, the similarly named much-touted replacement that has a considerably lower rating of 2.67 as of May 2021. Videogames were, for the space of a few months, almost synonymous with the mobile-based game and in January 2019, even the prime minister of India gave advice on playing videogames at a session on how students should prepare for examinations (*Pariksha pe Charcha*), where he was seen as being clued into youth culture when he asked 'yeh PUBG wala hai kya?' (Is this the PUBG question?) (Education Desk 2019). Two months later, police arrested ten university students for playing *PUB-G* in the prime minister's home-state Gujarat, probably the only case in the world where people have been arrested for playing a videogame. Nevertheless, *PUB-G* continued to be played in India on PC and even on the mobile via VPN (virtual private network) despite the ban and currently has returned officially as *Battlegrounds India*. India is not the only country to have banned *PUBG*, though. Pakistan and Nepal had both banned *PUB-G* but then revoked the ban subsequently. The Pakistan Telecommunication Authority (PTA) had temporarily banned the game based on parents' complaints that the game caused addiction. In Pakistan #ImranKhanPUBGKholo ('Imran Khan open PUBG') emerged as the top twitter hashtag with more than one million tweets (News18 2020). Incidentally, Imran Khan, the current prime minister, is also a renowned cricket-player who was once a role model for Pakistani youth. The Islamabad High Court revoked the ban in less than a month and declared the ban unlawful. The game was banned in Nepal for similar reasons and again lifted by the intervention of the court on the grounds that freedom of expression needed to be safeguarded. India's ban was the consequence of an escalation with China and the threat to the country's security under 'Section 69A of the Information Technology Act. The Government of India said the PUBG Mobile Application was engaged in activities that are prejudicial to sovereignty and integrity, defence and security of the country' (PIB Delhi 2020). A similar ban has been imposed in Bangladesh after a High Court was passed, during the time of writing this book. *The Daily Star* (Star Digital Report 2021) claims that the main reason is that the game affects players psychologically and creates an emotional imbalance while the Bengali daily *Jugantor* (Jugantor 2021) believes that the ban is being considered because of the large amount of currency that is leaving the country. Also, at the time of writing, the Indian company Krafton has also been facing more controversy after launching *Battlegrounds Mobile India,* another version of *PUBG Mobile India.*

The reason for this long exposition is simply that *PUB-G* had become synonymous with the very idea of videogames among the populace of the Subcontinent. Bhutan and Sri Lanka have not considered banning the game at any point. Besides being a popular game among casual gamers, *PUB-G* was also becoming one major forum for the rising and lucrative competitive world of eSports. YouTube contains a series of videos on *Indian Heroes of PUBG* (2019) and *Gamer Girls of India* (2019) in eponymous channels. Paridhi Khullar, featured in the latter, describes how she trained for playing *PUB-G* for a month before beginning to best the other players she competed against. There has been cooperative play across international borders even: when Zeyan Shafiq's eSports team was left three members short after India banned PUBG, he invited Pakistani players to join his team: 'Shafiq, 18, feared reprisals over his move, but none came. It resulted in an unheard-of alliance between Indian and Pakistani gamers, forged in one of the most dangerous regions in the world' (ET Online 2020). Nevertheless, besides the interest, there were also concerns aplenty. From a school principal who picked on *PUB-G* and addiction the moment this author mentioned videogames, to the worried parents in India and

Pakistan who had the game banned, videogame culture is something circumspect. Not so long ago, a mobile app called the *Blue Whale Challenge* claimed the lives of some children in the Subcontinent and the app was, erroneously, described as a videogame. The Blue Whale Challenge was a series of self-destructive tasks that participants would perform, the final one leading to their death. As I have commented on this elsewhere, 'If the Blue Whale Challenge is a digital game, then one could say, for example, that Russian Roulette is a game and by the same logic, indeed, Gabbar Singh was playing a game with his hapless victims in that famous scene in Sholay' (2020).

Nevertheless, it is true that videogames often contain scenes of violence and are often about shooting monsters, zombies and terrorists. The jury, however, is out on whether videogames cause violent behaviour in players with reports claiming that 'video games do not lead to violence or aggression, according to a reanalysis of data gathered from more than 21,000 young people around the world' (Hern 2020) and the American Psychological Association (APA) declared in 2020 that 'Attributing violence to video gaming is not scientifically sound and draws attention away from other factors, such as a history of violence, which we know from the research is a major predictor of future violence' (American Psychological Association 2020). As such, banning videogames because they cause violent behaviour is based not on research but on hearsay. One of the drivers for such erroneous conclusions is the unfamiliarity of parents with videogames as a generation and of course, what O'Donnell (O'Donnell 2014) has rightly identified (when discussing Indian game developers) as the Indian parents' insistence on work-culture versus play-culture and of seeing work as paramount.

This, however, is not the only position that is prevalent in the Subcontinent. The number of gaming communities on Facebook, Instagram and discord from the region is impressive and gaming has made an impact on cultural performances as well, with Game Studies being taught in a Postcolonial context in undergraduate and postgraduate lectures at India's oldest modern higher education institution, Presidency University (formerly Presidency College). Amitesh Grover, eminent theatre professional, has been making mixed-media productions using videogames and there have been over three videogame artists' residencies organised by Khoj, the international artists association in New Delhi. The Goethe-Institut Pakistan has sponsored numerous game jams and there have also been cultural events in the other countries in the Subcontinent. Writing about Sri Lanka, Mazin Hussain (2021) observes:

> Video games have largely been absent from the mainstream consciousness of Sri Lankans. They are often disregarded and lumped together with cartoons as a means of keeping children entertained. It's a traditional perception shared across South Asia. eSports has played a pivotal role in changing these perceptions.

The shift in how videogames are being perceived in cultural terms is becoming obvious albeit gradually. As mentioned in Chapter 2, Pakistan's federal minister for Science and Technology has announced the legitimisation of eSports as a regular sport. The Sri Lankan government has also done the same thing when the National Olympic Committee of Sri Lanka (NOCSL) agreed to make Sri Lanka the eSports hub for South Asia (Palmer 2020). Finally, for many who are not professionals, gaming nevertheless is a way of life. Whether one is concerned with the effects of *PUBG* or *Pokemon Go* (Niantic 2016) on players, or whether one is recommending a videogame to be taught in the classroom, the ludic cultures of the region are paramount in defining the attitudes of players. The digital medium also, arguably, influences player behaviour and the fuller impact of videogames on the region is yet to be gauged. It might be said, however, that the digital medium and the interactivity have ensured some cultural shifts that need to be studied further.

At a Disconnect of Cultures: Gamers in the Subcontinent

In recent years, there has been much work done on Indian gaming cultures, including two book-length studies, book chapters, magazine articles and PhD and MPhil theses. At the very outset, this section will first address the existing volume of research on gaming cultures in India and then move on to explore the links and the differences with the rest of the Subcontinent.

In her essay cited earlier, Adrienne Shaw (Shaw 2013) asked 'How do you say gamer in Hindi?' and the answer she has is that you say 'gamer', using the English word and not *khiladi* or any other Hindi synonyms. In fact, there is no translation for 'videogame', unlike there is for radio (*betar*), film (*chalachitra*), television (*doordarshan*) and telephone (*durabhas*). Gaming culture, therefore, is indeed quite new and also, apparently, at a disconnect with the earlier cultures of entertainment media. As has been stated earlier, Shaw's comments on a lack of history of gaming in India are apposite in this context:

> Perhaps, the use of the English term 'gamer' exemplifies the ways in which history, access, and culture come together to shape how digital games are experienced in India. Games have historically been external to Indian media culture, unlike other media industries, and in turn a marker of globalized progress. The resources video games demand in terms of space, time, and money make them largely unavailable to the majority of Indians. Moreover their characterization as time wasters, antisocial, and addictive frame the experiences of those who play video games. [...] The focus of mobile gaming is a similar negotiation of these factors. This approach drops the resource commitments at the same time it increases the local embeddedness of the game. Cricket and Bollywood-based games are consistently the top-downloaded games in India. Since it requires limited time and is usually played in transit, it sidesteps the antisocial connotations of console and PC gaming. Thus far, it is seen as a 'time-filler' for the lower social strata groups rather than a 'time-waster' for the upwardly mobile. (2013: 197)

Shaw's observations, made over a decade ago, are indeed incisive although with the advent of *PUB-G* and indeed, even *Angry Birds* (Rovio Entertainment 2009) and *Temple Run* (Imangi Studios 2011), mobile games have taken on a different significance than she describes. Indeed, as evinced in the comments by developers in the previous chapters, mobile gaming happens to be the main platform where the majority of Indians, across social strata groups, engage with videogames. In perhaps one of the earliest academic publications on the Indian gaming scenario, I had commented that videogames, 'Due to the wide economic disparity, video games are restricted to the wealthier sections of society although there are ongoing attempts to use games as a teaching medium for mainly children from deprived families' (Mukherjee 2012). Contrary to such a position some commentators have provided divergent, albeit very valid, responses; Shaw has commented on how mobile games were time-fillers for the lower social strata groups and Prabhash Tripathy has commented in MPhil thesis on fighting games in India's arcades that 'that video games are accessible to wealthier sections of the society is also confusing as many of the video game parlours were located in spaces which Mukherjee would agree are not the wealthier sections of the society' (Tripathy 2017: 157). This is an issue that needs to be addressed before commenting on the other aspects of player-culture in the Indian Subcontinent.

Shaw's observation regarding mobile gaming, of course, has lost its currency given the massive surge in the ownership of mobile phones and increased access to internet connectivity: according to a IAMAI report from 2021, 'India has more than 500 million smartphone users today with forecasts to reach 859 million by 2021. Among these, mobile gamers are projected to reach 368 million by 2022' (Ikigai Law 2021: 6). According to the Statistics website, Statista.com (Statista 2021), the penetration of smartphones in India is 42% as of 2020 and the online magazine, *Your Story*, reports that with an 88% 4G penetration in India, rural internet users have outpaced urban users by 10% in 2019 'thus eliminating the digital divide' (Mitter 2020). Tripathy's point is important; he focuses on a segment of gaming culture about which very little research has been done. Gaming 'arcades', especially fighting game parlours, have been described by Tripathy and others as 'from learning a new set of Hindi expletives to making a separate set of friends, shops like these became the OG spot for youngsters to play video games without worrying about getting rebuked by their parents' (Mudgal 2020). Sparsh Mudgal reminisces though that 'From 2 coins for a rupee, we had moved to 50 rupees per session and sometimes even 100 bucks for a couple of FIFA matches. Insane, ain't it?' (2020).

Mudgal brings up an important concern in what seems a casual observation. The affordability of videogames is a concern today. Before addressing this further, it must be noted that the arcade cultures in such a large and diverse country like India differed from city to city and Tripathy's experience in northern India (the cities of New Delhi and Mussoorie) would have differed from that of my own in Calcutta (now Kolkata) or from that of someone in Kerala. Nevertheless, the breaking of class barriers in the fighting game arcade where people played *Tekken 3* (Namco 1997) or *Mustapha* (the name for *Cadillacs and Dinosaurs* in India and Bangladesh) is noteworthy and more research needs to be done here. Even so, based on Mudgal's comment, it is evident that videogames have remained a luxury of the wealthier sections—especially when one looks at defining the poor in India by the government's own designated poverty line. The current poverty line in India is ₹1,059.42 (62 PPP USD) per month in rural areas and ₹1,286 (75 PPP USD) per month in urban areas (Drishti 2019). According to the same report, the poverty line in the 1990s was set at ₹49.09 (rural) and ₹56.64 (urban) per capita per month at 1973–1974 prices. It would have been difficult to imagine people from such low income-groups to be paying to play videogames.

Regarding the burgeoning rates of mobile phone usage, often attributed to the availability of the low-cost data provided via the Jio sim sold by the telecom giant Reliance, there is nevertheless a caveat to be heeded before dismissing the digital divide. Although India may have 42% smartphone users, in rural India the scenario may be different. Often the Internet usage may be concentrated among a few:

> Even though internet users in rural areas are more than those in urban areas, there is immense headroom for rural growth. Close to 70 percent of the rural population does not access the internet. This will further contribute to an increase in the overall internet population over the next few years. (IAMAI-Nielsen 2019)

While the IAMAI-Nielsen report flags this as an opportunity, it is evident that there is a large section of rural India that cannot access the Internet. Perhaps, the digital divide should be looked at from other perspectives and should consider access, linguistic skills, education among others as possible areas to note. In this context, game developer Shailesh Prabhu's (2016) cautionary note regarding the disparity in India, needs to be considered seriously:

> The first point to consider is that a large part of India lives below the Poverty Line: about 30% of India falls in this category. That still leaves 750+ million people right? Well, India's last definition of poverty line was ₹ 32 per day (USD 0.48 per day) in rural areas and ₹ 47 per day (USD 0.7 per day) in urban areas. I can vouch for the fact that those poverty limits are not really indicative of a decent life. These people definitely can't really consume games. Similarly, how much of India is clumped around or just above those poverty lines? How many can even think of spending on games? Is anyone even considering how much of India can afford games at all?

As such, conclusions such as Tripathy's, albeit made about a hitherto neglected area of gaming culture, nevertheless, do not alter the fact that videogames are, in the main, not accessible to the poorer sections of Indian society.

In this context, perhaps, the rest of the Subcontinent could also be compared to the Indian situation. Stating somewhat higher figures for India's smartphone penetration, the Bangladeshi newspaper, *The Daily Star*, reports that Bangladesh lags behind its neighbours in terms of smartphone usage as it has 41% smartphone users as compared to 'India [which] has the highest percentage of smartphone users, at 69 percent, followed by Sri Lanka with 60 percent, Nepal 53 percent and Pakistan 51 percent' (The Daily Star 2021). There are varying figures for smartphone penetration from different organisations; however, the digital divide between the smartphone users (and the range of gaming they have) versus the feature phone users (who have a limited range of games to choose from) is quite stark. The statistics need to be thought through carefully before announcing the end of the digital divide. Perhaps, it was easier to negotiate the bosses in Mustapha in the community gaming parlours where players of diverse income groups, religions, caste (regarding which there is very little research), ethnicity and education could have mingled but these would have been very niche spaces of gaming culture. Tripathy concedes that 'the ones who have access to the latest hardware and play in tournaments get to represent India in EVO, whereas the gamers from the video game parlours turn towards more humble pursuits, the other gamers like chotus [who would work in the parlours and help fix the games], who played well and managed the video game parlours, remain faceless' (Tripathy 2017: 163). Finally, despite the vaunted claims of egalitarianism and the erasure of the digital divide, given the smartphone penetration, the actual ground reality of internet access, language issues and various other factors, mobile gaming is not as seamlessly pervasive across social strata, demographics and the geography of the region.

In all of this, so far, only casual gaming has been considered as it makes up the largest percentage of the gaming population. Before going further into the discussion, maybe the classification that is often used as a shorthand in studies of gaming culture needs some attention. In fact, although this section started with a discussion of Shaw's article on how one says 'gamer' in the languages spoken in the Indian Subcontinent, some of the players discussed here would not call themselves 'gamers' while some (especially the players of fighting games that Tripathy discusses) would certainly wish to do so. Perhaps, at this stage, the industry terms 'hardcore', 'midcore' and 'casual' should be introduced. As commentator Nick Yee describes them, 'Hardcore gamers are most different from Casual gamers in terms of Competition (duels, matches, leaderboard rankings), Challenge (practice, skill improvement, high difficulty), and Excitement (fast-paced, thrills, surprises)—they are looking for fast-paced, skill-based matches against other players. Casual gamers, on the other hand, are looking for calm, non-adversarial games that are easy to learn and play' (Yee 2019). One must also note that hardcore gaming requires access to advanced and sophisticated computing devices—a recent panel discussion in the series *Games Studies India Adda* (*Games Studies Adda Podcast: Adda on Ludonomics* 2021) focused on how the lack of access to expensive graphics cards has affected gaming cultures across India. One must also account for the role played by gender and other social categories in the very definition of 'hardcore' and 'casual' as Yee points out in his article. In addition to these two categories, there are multiple other categories in between, such as 'mid-core', which are often used in the industry.

The digital divide is not restricted to hardware access although that can be an important issue. In a region with such a huge linguistic and cultural diversity as the Subcontinent, it is difficult to localise content. For example, *Raji* (Nodding Heads 2020) has a few complaints from

Indian players that addressed the question of the game not being available in Indian languages. On the Steam feedback page for the game, a user who is called 'Ignite' states '[n]ot complaining but little disappointed to see Indian game develop by Indians and still not a single Indian regional language. I was hoping at least Hindi language to be there' (Steam Community 2021) while another player complained about the lack of representation of the local language. Akhil Arora (2020) in his review of the game in Gadgets 360 makes the same point:

> But in making it accessible, *Raji* loses out on some of its authenticity. The game is largely in English with small parts in Hindi. There are no Indian language options for the subtitles either, even though *Raji* offers the likes of Spanish, French, Korean, Russian, and Mandarin. But that's understandable from a business perspective. The (non-mobile) gaming market is much stronger outside India, which is why it makes sense that *Raji* is aimed at the international audience.

To use a contrasting example, in a recent talk on the indie game *Missing*, Marcus Toftedahl et al. have discussed the effect of the localisation of the game in Bengali: 'The choice of localizing the game into Bengali helped the game to get attraction not only in India but also in the surrounding regions where Bengali is a big language. The game topped the charts on Google Play in Bangladesh and the developers noticed by the player reviews that the game was popular in Bangladesh because of the Bengali localisation, a language in which few games are localized into' (Toftedahl et al. 2018b: 9). The content of *Missing*, child trafficking, is a major social concern in both Bangladesh and West Bengal in India and judging from the feedback on the Google PlayStore, the localisation in Bengali made it accessible to a much larger audience than it would have been, otherwise.

Even in religious terms, there are differences in opinion regarding videogames. A newspaper report in India's *Times of India* quotes a Shia cleric stating that 'though playing videogame will not deprive you of the benefit, it is advised to avoid such activities during the fast' (Agarwal 2013). In quite a contradiction, Ather Ahmed (Ahmed 2017) writing for the Pakistani website, Mangobaaz.com, lists thirteen videogames one can play during *roza*. Similarly, when Nevada-based

Hindu activist, Rajan Zed, objected that 'Lord Hanuman was not meant to be reduced to just a "character" in a video game to solidify [a] company/product's base in the growing economy of India' (Good 2009), there were no protests of the kind in India when Sony released its PS2 game, *Hanuman: Boy Warrior*. As Xenia Zeiler states in her article, 'in this case, a debate on a digital game with a high amount of media attention in primarily the United States was employed to (1) negotiate Hindu authority, (2) establish a characteristic identity marker for one particular Hindu organisation, and (3) construct and present a particular picture of 'Hindu-ness' as approved by the Universal Society of Hinduism' (Zeiler 2014: 67) and that

> the protest against Hanuman: Boy Warrior was almost exclusively restricted to the West. Although some Indian organizations joined the debate once it was opened by Rajan Zed, only diaspora-based Hindu organizations criticized the embedding of Hanuman in a game setting. In India, nobody seemed to care about this issue much. In fact, a large internet audience applauded the inclusion of Hindu mythology and deities in digital gaming. (Zeiler 2014: 77)

There is much diversity regarding how videogames are perceived on religious lines and how restrictions in accessing and playing these games are received in the Subcontinent. The other main issue, especially in India, on which discrimination and access may need to be analysed, both in the playing of the videogames or gaming cultures as well as the development of games (reiterating a point briefly mentioned earlier) is that of caste-based discrimination. Very little research has been done on the topic and it is one that deserves more detailed attention.

Videogames are in themselves a very diverse media and any overarching comments about their reception in an area also as diverse as the Indian Subcontinent are bound to fall short of describing the scenario accurately. The digital divide and the disparities in access notwithstanding, social media groups in Discord and Facebook testify to the camaraderie of gamers as well as to shared culturally specific issues in the different gaming communities. The anecdotes shared in these groups are many and they indicate gaming experiences. When Zain Rajpoot, comments on his experience of playing videogames on a rainy morning, another user of PC Gamers of Pakistan quips that when it rained in Karachi, there was always a power cut. On Gamers of Bangladesh, Shaon Selyse Sarkar, for example, ruminates on the merits of the 2012 game *The Sleeping Dogs* (United Front Games 2012) and starts a conversation that engages over fifty people. Another gamer, Faysal Talukder, comments on the struggles he had to face in getting access to videogames and his first struggle to buy a PS4 as a rural middle-class person. Mostly, however, there are heated discussions regarding graphics cards and hardware. There is indeed a shared vocabulary among gamers in the Subcontinent but there is also a stark digital divide, on the lines of gamer versus non-gamer, hardcore versus casual, the language barrier and various other factors such as class, caste and religion.

Gaming Cultures in India: Prior Case Studies

Despite the neglect, by and large, of the Subcontinent in global Games Studies, there has been prior research on India in multiple edited collections, dissertations, academic papers and finally, in a recently published monograph. As such, it will be necessary to devote an entire section to respond to the research done earlier before moving on to look at the (often scanty) available research on the other countries in the Subcontinent.

My article in the *Encyclopedia of Videogames* (2012) edited by Mark J.P. Wolf was followed by a more detailed chapter for *Videogames across the World* also edited by Wolf and another one (Mukherjee 2019) with a focus on the Global South in *Videogames in the Global South* edited by Phillip Penix-Tadsen. Aditya Deshbandhu's monograph *Gaming Culture (s) in India: Digital Play in Everyday Life* (Deshbandhu 2020) sets about an ambitious task and the extent to which it succeeds or fails will need to be assessed. Finally, two less-known but very significant research contributions will also need urgent attention. One is a doctoral dissertation on gaming parlours in Chandigarh by Gagunjoat S. Chhina (Chhina 2016) and the other is an MPhil thesis on fighting games and parlour in Delhi and Mussoorie by Prabhash Tripathy (Tripathy 2017), who has already been quoted earlier in this chapter.

Other than these, Xenia Zeiler has written a series of important articles focusing on a range of topics from game design to culture and Padmini Ray Murray has also contributed importantly to the field. Coming from a sociological and anthropological standpoint, Bharath Pallavalli's work on using serious gaming for policymaking and other case studies from India, also needs consideration. Both Zeiler's and Ray Murray's work have been mentioned earlier and will come up again in connection with the cultural contexts of gaming in India. Palavalli et al. (2021) make important contributions in attempting to solve transport congestion problems through game-based learning and uses the latter to address other social issues. To understand the *history* of gaming cultures in India, however, this chapter will focus on the research that addresses the topic directly.

As an early researcher pursuing games studies in India when I completed my MPhil thesis on videogames and storytelling from Jadavpur University, Kolkata, in 2005, I had been obviously taking an active interest in gaming cultures and the industry in India. After I completed my doctoral research, I was invited to contribute entries for an encyclopaedia and then later for the two anthologies mentioned above. In the first two contributions, I was attempting an overview of the field and trying to make sense of the cultures and the industry of what was a huge arena. As Tripathy has pointed out, there were areas that I had missed in my early research and there are likely to be others that I will not be able to cover even in this present book. It is important, however, to state this clearly as the very diversity of India and the multiplicity of languages and sources make any holistic coverage very difficult. In my chapter on Indian gaming in terms of gaming in the Global South, I have highlighted the fact that India cannot always fit into the easy categorisation of the Global South and have also started addressing the issue of the digital divide that I discuss in much more detail in the previous section:

> [H]ow the digital divide affects India and links to its positioning within the global south is a moot question. [...] one should neither forget claims of an internal north-south cultural divide in India, nor ignore the uneven distribution of access to digital knowledge within the

> vastly discrepant socio-economic tiers in the country. Also intriguing is whether the purported south-south collaboration that is supposed to occur within the countries of the global south is relevant to video games in India. (Mukherjee 2019)

Nevertheless, this analysis left many questions unaddressed and some issues just cursorily looked at that have been looked at in more detail in this book.

Judging from its title, Deshbandhu's monograph aims to address the gaming cultures in the everyday lives of Indian gamers but a large part of it is an introduction to how the author views Games Studies. The fourth chapter of his book is called 'Charting the Indian Gamescape' and while it aims towards a lofty goal it falls short in living up to its aim because of certain methodological lacunae. The 'Indian gamescape' is only addressed through interviews with 14 people, of whom three are women and the rest men, presumably of a similar age group and based on a 'snowball sampling method' wherein one participant provides referrals for the others and so on. The likelihood of diversity and variety in such a group is very limited and particularly since this group is very small (just 14 people to represent the gamescape of a country of over a billion), the conclusions are not reliable. The participants are probably from a higher social and economic stratum as they can afford high-end computers (mostly) and consoles; there is no indication that members from different linguistic groups, geographies, religions and castes have been included in the study. The research is based on gamer diaries and co-playing sessions. While it may not be possible to gather as much demographic data in such surveys, the group is way too small to enable any robust conclusions.

Nevertheless, the observations are important to note at least for academic purposes. A respondent called Chaithanya states:

> Earlier video game systems like the Sega Genesis and the ones from Nintendo were affordable but the Xbox and PlayStation have been priced on par with a computer. It is very difficult to convince one's parents that a video game console is worth the purchase. The computer is viewed as a device for the entire family with features for everyone whereas the video game console is only for the players. All my friends

> game on the computer, people who own consoles are rare. (Deshbandhu 2020)

A Sega Megadrive (also called Genesis in the USA) sold in India cost ₹14,000 in 1983 as mentioned in Chapter 2. As per an inflation calculation website, a hundred Indian rupees in 1983 would be worth 1585 Indian rupees today, an increase of fifteen times. As such, at today's rate, the price would be an impossibly high 2,217,6000 Indian rupees and certainly not 'affordable' by most Indian families. As already indicated, Nintendo sold very few units in India before it wrapped up its business. Even today, the ever-popular Nintendo Switch is priced comparably higher at around ₹ 35,000—the price of a reasonably capable mid-range laptop or desktop computer. Many of the players interviewed are from high-income groups and can actually afford a console in addition to their personal computers and mobiles. Deshbandhu's (2020) observations also need to be re-examined:

> The players were in a constant debate about the intended experience of the PC and the optimized one offered by the console while attempting to make decisions that suited their style of play, gaming preferences and their financial limitations in the constant search for what they called 'value for money.' […] By making larger marathon gaming sessions increasingly difficult, players have been forced to adapt and evolve their approaches to games.

Desbandhu does focus briefly on mobile games noting their portability and 'microsessions' of engagement but he does not emphasise the huge possibility and mass appeal of these games that have now come to the forefront in very recent times. Therefore, when Desbandhu refers to the 'value for money' or affordability, he is clearly speaking for a group of players who can afford to choose between PC and console games (which are overwhelmingly expensive in India and are rarely available as pirated copies). Recalling Prabhu's points regarding the poverty line or even Tripathy and Mudgal's points regarding the gaming shops where people from all social groups would mingle over arcade games, Deshbandhu's focus group seems quite limited and typically wealthy. Regarding mobile games, too, the perception has changed with the emergence of *PUBG mobile*, which regularly featured in eSports and marathon competitions, something that could not have been foreseen when his book was written. Deshbandhu, however, does also conduct his research in a gaming parlour but even here, both the gaming parlours he visits, Spawn and Diginet, are in Hyderabad and cater to an upwardly mobile clientele. As a player whom he interviews informs, 'the best thing about Spawn is the ability to play uninterrupted, the food is inexpensive and the drinks are not necessarily aerated you have options between lemonade, iced tea and at times butter milk and lassi in the summer', indicating a level of affluence. Reading between the lines of Deshbandhu's observations and survey data, a narrative of exclusivity emerges in how one reads the descriptions of gaming parlour culture. Deshbandhu, of course, does make an important note that will need more attention in the subsequent sections—he points out the lack of women gamers in these parlours.

For a much deeper engagement with the gaming parlour cultures, Gagunjoat S. Chhina's doctoral dissertation, *Video Gaming Parlours: The Emerging Field of Video Gaming in India* (2016) is of paramount interest. Chhina has worked extensively in Chandigarh and compared his findings to cybercafes and gaming parlours in Manchester, UK. This could also be usefully compared with Prabhash Tripathy's MPhil dissertation, which has already been referred to. Chhina describes his rationale as follows:

> As opportunities to engage in video gaming increased in India, a clear dichotomy developed between urban and rural areas. Opportunities to engage with the practice of video gaming differed greatly between cities and rural villages because of both cultural and infrastructural differences. I explore how the culture and infrastructure of Chandigarh allowed video gamers to have access to home-based video game hardware or public video game machines in a similar manner to the West, though 20 years or so later. (2016: 15)

Chhina has selected one of the wealthier cities of India and indeed its only 'planned city'. Chandigarh, which was designed by the Swiss-French architect Le Corbusier, and is the shared capital of the states of Punjab and Haryana. He too selects the elite gaming parlours in one of the wealthier cities (but not one of the major cities in India) and justifies his rationale as below:

> Indians define video game parlours as indoor venues where customers play video games on either consoles or computers. They are recent, appearing only about 2 to 3 years prior to my field research. Lavishly furnished, serving drinks and snacks, gaming parlours are comfortable and welcoming environments. I have focused on gaming parlours because they are social spaces in which video games play a pivotal role. An alternative would have been to also conduct my study by gaming booths located in smaller markets but these offer less shade and no shielding from the heat, and are exposed to road noise and pollution. Furthermore, they had a great deal going on in and around them because they were not dedicated video gaming spaces. (Chhina 2016: 57)

While the neglect of the gaming booths in smaller markets marks a considerable gap in research as the majority of India's population is exposed to the 'less shade and no shielding from the heat, and are exposed to road noise and pollution' (2016) and what other activities take place in tandem with gaming is also a matter of interest, nevertheless, Chhina provides a much more detailed context for the study of these parlours. The lavish furniture and the food and drink seem to be common to the Hyderabad gaming parlours that have already been described. Chhina, however, makes an important point regarding the location of these parlours: 'I had assumed gaming venues would be located in the shopping district—sector 17. Unfortunately, there were no gaming spaces in sector 17. It was in sector 35 where I discovered my two research sites: Indulgence and Oxide gaming parlours' (58). All the parlours are spacious, they are difficult to discover and are often sandwiched between other bigger establishments. Chhina goes on to observe that '[o]xide was significantly smaller than Indulgence and shared its first floor entrance with a high class Thai Massage parlour' (61). Whether this could mean that elite or otherwise, gaming parlours were located in fringe areas or less noticed areas is, of course, a moot question. Indeed, a personal interview with Tripathy (2021) and Mudgal's blog post (2020) both seem to indicate that gaming booths and parlours were located in the less prominent parts of the cities. At the time of writing this book, however, this author has checked that an Indulgence Gaming Lounge has opened up in one of the most prominent Chandigarh shopping malls. In Kolkata, for example, the major malls have a play area that contains arcade machines side-by-side with mini bowling alleys and rides.

Chhina's study is significant because it analyses the demographic and social factors and comments on their level of affluence: patrons consisted of four to twelve male high school students, groups of mid-to-late twenties male professionals such as bankers and children from six to twelve whose parents would use the space as a sort of creche while they went about their errands. Chhina notes that barring the very young children in the latter category all players in these gaming parlours were male. He also noted the hierarchy within the staff in the gaming parlours where the manager would not, for example, open the door for patrons. While the exclusively male patronage is also common to what Tripathy has observed, in Tripathy's study there is more of a mingling of classes:

> There were many 'chotus' who worked in the parlours, they were the 'house- gamer', the technician, the boss and managers. Almost all the gamers mention a 'chotus': most likely a teenager, who was good at all the games, would fix the machine if it malfunctioned. He was like the master of the 'dojo'. To Many gamers he was the one who offered the first challenge, they wanted to beat him in order to become champions (as they often call themselves). One gets a sense of intimacy and awe when gamers mention this master figure but then no one mentions him by his name. (2017: 66)

What is surprising is that Tripathy does not manage to obtain the name of even one of the so-called *Chotus*, unlike Chhina does with the Indulgence manager Harry who is often cited in the thesis. 'Chotu' is a North India endearment or slang (depending on the context) for someone who is considered little or small. The jack-of-all-trades technician-cum-manager is nevertheless relegated to a nameless belittling by the gamer elite. Ironically, he is also 'master of the "dojo"' (2017). Nevertheless, Tripathy does claim that videogame parlours proved to be more of an egalitarian space for school students: 'Rachit, another gamer from Delhi, states that he had access to both types of video game parlours as his friend's father ran a video game parlour, but he added that the expensive arcade was not a place he could visit every day. The local video game parlour was closer and affordable and the level of competition was higher' (2017: 111). He also mentions Tibetan refugee children in the hill-station Mussoorie flocking to the gaming parlours after school hours.

While this monograph still maintains that the gamer population is largely urban and affluent, it is important to look at the diverse communities of gamers who are less represented in the urban game space. All of the surveys identify the gaming parlours as being a predominantly male-dominated space. Chhina is the only researcher to have actually reviewed the scenario in rural India—of course, the rural parts of the state of Punjab may be vastly different from those of other states such as West Bengal. Chhina notes that '[w]hereas the urban experience mirrors to some extent the initial Western encounters with video game play in the 1980s, video game play experiences in rural India are very different [...] these encounters almost invariably involved a link to the diaspora and to the West' (Chhina 2016: 90). Chandigarh and the rural area around it are quite unique in this regard as many families here have relatives residing in the UK, USA and Canada. Despite being relatively affluent by Indian standards, there were other hindrances to owning computers and consoles:

> Electricity, particularly in the summer, could be unavailable for days. Therefore, where electricity was necessary, farmers would use diesel generators to supply it. The interviewees who had grown up in rural areas stated that their parents did not judge activities, such as watching television or playing video games, as warranting the use of the backup diesel generator. Furthermore, the variation in electricity currents was likely to blow out fragile computer circuitry. (Chhina 2016: 106)

The computer was also not perceived as essential to the family and as such even the most commonly cited reason in urban India—that it was needed for the children's education did not have much of an appeal. Most of the early encounters with videogames that Chhina mentions were in videogame shops where consoles were installed in makeshift wooden boxes. There is a hint of a variety homebrew culture here according to him and this may connect to the discussion on *jugaad* in Chapter 6.[1] An excerpt from an interview with the manager of the gaming cafe is quite a revelation:

> Harry: It was in my mama ji's village and there it was an army retired colonel and when he was retired in his free time he kept a console with Mario. Back then there were not very many games. We started Mario mostly or Contra. It was with a gamepad. It was in a wooden box [...] I was about 9 or 10 when I started playing, about 1998. (Chhina 2016: 108)

While earlier work on videogames in India, including my own, have mainly concentrated on interviewing urban gamers and game developers, much more still remains to be done and it is here that Tripathy and Chhina's research is of extreme significance in understanding videogame cultures in India. Speaking of in-depth surveys, while there is still a gap in the data obtained from rural India, the authors have carried out a number of surveys both online and offline from which further rich data can be obtained. Before analysing the survey results, however, it is necessary to view the available research regarding the other countries in the Subcontinent.

Gaming Cultures in the Indian Subcontinent: Looking Beyond India

There has been very little research on the other countries in the Subcontinent; consequently, it will be best to start with a discussion of gaming cultures in these places. Starting with the smallest country in the Subcontinent, Bhutan, which is probably the only country to get its television sets and the Internet at the same time—it got both in the 1990s—it is important to note how gaming culture has gained significance with an almost unparalleled rapidity in the region. The Bhutanese daily *Kuensel* sounds a note of interest and concern:

1 It must be noted, however, that the modified wooden cabinets and television sets that Chhina speaks of cannot be compared to a full-fledged homebrew culture as is described by Swalwell or Svelch as there is no group of people involved in making both hardware and software that is new and unique using their local skills; instead, the instances here are scattered and more a sort of making-do than the making of a local culture, per se.

> In the past decade and a half, video game parlours have mushroomed in Bhutan. In Thimphu alone, there are around 80 gaming parlours. It is usual to see these gaming centres packed with teenagers and even adults. [...] While we don't yet know if the gaming parlours are having an adverse impact, it would be wise to ensure that some guidelines are being followed by those who run these establishments. We would prefer our children and teenagers to spend their time in a gaming parlour rather than in a bar. (Kuensel Online 2016)

This longish excerpt from the newspaper article is instructive on many counts; it begins on a note of caution but is quick to indicate that gaming parlours have significant sociocultural potential. The relatively young IT culture in Bhutan is at pains to figure out the impact and potential of videogames in what seems to be one of the more mature reactions to the medium. In general, gaming seems to be a separate world to the majority of people in the country who happen to be non-gamers. Government responses such as draconian bans on games and the lack of serious engagement with games in terms of pedagogy or even gamer psychology have impeded bridging the knowledge gap regarding gaming. One could only speculate but most policymakers in the South Asian nations may not have any hands-on experience with gaming. Nevertheless, interest in the potential of videogames continues to grow—for example, a videogame developed in Bangladesh is teaching children in 350 schools how to address problems they face during puberty: '"We feel really alone and helpless when puberty starts and can't talk frankly about teenage issues" said a 15-year boy from Barisal during user-testing.' 'This type of game helps us learn about the right and wrongs of [growing up] by ourselves' (Sharif Hussain Shamim 2017). In Bhutan too, a game that is aimed at addressing youth unemployment issues has been designed by the UNDP (United Nations Development Programme). Even beyond such directly educational experiences, the cultural appeal of videogames is much bigger as will be discussed from survey data collected for this book. Judging from the gamers' groups on social media such as Facebook or Discord, however, one can get an idea of the impact of videogames on culture in the region. Gaming groups such as 'Gamers of Bangladesh', 'Pakistan PC Gamers' and 'Sri Lanka PC Gamers' often have large memberships ranging in the hundreds of thousands. Often these forums post gameplay videos or more interestingly, in terms of gamer experiences, details about their struggles in getting gaming equipment as has been mentioned earlier in this chapter.

There is also a rising culture of eSports in all of these countries. The growing popularity of eSports in Pakistan, which boasts stars such as Syed 'Sumail' Hassan and Arslan Ash, has already been mentioned in connection with its government's official recognition of eSports. Preceding Pakistan, the government of Sri Lanka recognised eSports as an official sport in 2019 and the country's team was 'set to make its inaugural appearance as a medal event at the 2019 Southeast Asian Games' (Ainsworth 2019). Nepal, Bhutan and Maldives all have active eSports societies. Indian eSports too is coming of age albeit very slowly. Ankit 'V3nom' Panth, India's celebrity eSports personality states:

> I would say its [sic] growing but we still need to see the consistency. I know there are tournaments with big prize pools happenings, big brands have started jumping in, it's better than before but still its not at its prime. According to me it still needs 2–3 more years to have more opportunities and become stable. Currently brands are just testing this. The viewer base is still not that much in the country and that's what is holding us back. We need to take this to the masses and let them know about it. (Rajesh 2019)

Panth concedes that the eSports scene in India is yet to become stable (especially given that only two to three organisations sponsor eSports and that the salaries are way below international standards) and given the aftermath of the Covid-19 pandemic, his prediction of two to three years may need longer to be fulfilled. As of the time of writing, in February 2021, the Indian Olympic Association has just officially accepted eSports as a medal event. Having said that, the publicity that eSports receives in the national media is minimal and the salaries that are paid to eSports gamers reflect the status of eSports in India. The appeal of eSports, however, goes far beyond celebrity status and cash awards for some. In Pakistan, a survey undertaken by researchers reveals that Muslim women 'use e-sports as a vehicle for an oppositional agency and personal freedom from the patriarchal system' (Hussain et al. 2021). Most of the women interviewed were from marginalised regions of Pakistan and played *PUBG*, *DOTA* and *Tekken 7*. One participant states, 'I cannot be negative in front of society (she laughed), but I can be who I am when I play *Tekken 7* (she laughed again), I can have any type of character I desired to select' (Husain et al. 2021). Many of the participants felt that the anonymity, privacy and the freedom of expression that the medium offered were their main reasons for engaging with it. They also state that they usually take up male identities in these games because male characters are stronger. Beyond the conventional understanding of videogames and eSports, many other aspects need to be looked at in the South Asian context, especially from the social and cultural perspectives that are quite unique to digital culture.

Gaming Cultures and the Indian Subcontinent: Some Observations from Survey Data

Umer Hussain et al.'s article (2021) is probably one of the first to feature research on gaming cultures in Pakistan in one of Game Studies major journals. At the time of writing, more academic research on Sri Lanka, Bangladesh and other countries of the Subcontinent is a key requirement. Information regarding the gaming cultures of these countries has been difficult to come by and for the purposes of this book, a survey was conducted among members of gaming groups in India, Pakistan, Bangladesh, Nepal and Sri Lanka. The author reached out to multiple gaming groups on social media in Bhutan and Maldives but was unable to elicit any responses. The first and second waves of the Covid-19 pandemic were raging in the Subcontinent during the time of conducting the survey; as such, physical surveys and field visits to gaming communities in these countries were not possible. The full survey results have been anonymised and shared with the participants' consent as Appendix Two in this book. In this section, for the sake of brevity, only the statistical summaries and some salient comments from respondents have been provided.

In India, most of the responses (52.5%) were obtained from the Whatsapp group Game Studies India. Other responses were obtained via other Whatsapp groups or referrals (15%), Facebook groups of gamers in all of these countries and personal referrals. Forty-one people responded to the survey of whom 78% were from India, 9.8% from Sri Lanka, 7.3% from Bangladesh, 4.3% from Pakistan and 2.4% from Nepal. The respondents were asked their gender and age. 80% of them were male and 20% were female while 85.4% were in the age group of 18 to 30 while 9.8% were between 30 and 40 and 4.9% above 40. The statistics bear out the relative novelty of the videogame medium and the fact that the gaming scene in all these countries is fairly male-dominated (although the two respondents from Pakistan were both women). 58.5% of the respondents said they were casual gamers while 31.7% claimed to be hardcore gamers. 4.9% were unsure and one respondent expressed doubts about the classification. No prior definition of casual and hardcore was provided in the survey and it was left to the participants to decide on the categorisation themselves without creating any preconceptions. Data regarding economic status was not requested and this will remain a lacuna in the survey; however, as the survey was conducted online, it may be assumed that all respondents had access to an Internet connection, possibly via a computer or a smartphone. To come to the main issue here, the participants were asked whether videogames have an impact on culture and 95.1% said that they do. Of the two people who disagreed, one said that videogames impacted storytelling and art and in so doing contradicted the earlier response. Of the cultural categories that they saw videogames as having an impact in, most respondents agreed on storytelling (85.4%) followed by the arts (75.6%) and then history, psychology, diversity and inclusiveness, philosophy, music, politics and social violence.

Almost half the respondents left a more detailed explanation of how videogames influenced culture in general. There was a wide range of responses, many focusing on the storytelling aspect because 'games are as influential as other art forms, if not more because of the way they let you embody a character and make choices in a way a book doesn't let you' and '[b]y using the art of storytelling and gaming together, it results in an introspective look into one's own perspective and what the player makes of the game in an individualistic way'. Others claim that videogames are 'points of common interest that become breeding grounds for further discussions about topics such as music, philosophy and storytelling, to name a few' and set up a 'feedback loop with culture'. One of the respondents states that '[i]t makes you violent but can help to talk to others as well'. Also, in synch with the discussion of gaming culture in the earlier sections, some respondents discussed gamification as a cultural phenomenon and others commented that 'eSports has become a rising cultural currency of certain nations'. One of them commented that videogames may have a cultural impact in Japan but not in his country—this leads to the next part of the survey that addresses the cultural impact of videogames in the region.

When the same question was asked regarding their own countries, the responses were somewhat different. One response sums it up well: 'I think they influence culture but they are not big enough yet to influence it at large. They influence it in niches. Until we come to games like *PUBG* which have influenced a whole generation, but I'm not sure in what ways.' Many others are of a similar tenor and perhaps, listing some of them will provide a better idea of what people think:

> In our country, the inclination to play and recognize video games as a part of culture increases steadily up the age pyramid up to a certain point when it breaks off sharply and videogames become nothing but 'distractions' and 'tools of teaching violence.'
>
> 'Not in my country, not yet.'
>
> 'Both in positive ways and negative ways. Teenagers who used to go out, socializing, and play cricket, climb trees have moved towards staying in room, and playing games, as well as some of the teenagers who used to do drugs and all.'
>
> 'As per my knowledge, videogames are yet to penetrate Indian subcultures on a substantial level.'
>
> 'Video games, especially online multiplayer ones, help people connect internationally. Not to mention, video gaming has become a growing market in the country. Indian themes in certain videogames, like Raji, also help in getting a glimpse into the variety of different cultures in the country via storytelling.'

These responses seem to indicate that for most people who have commented, videogames are not yet any important part of the culture of the Indian Subcontinent but many respondents agree that they make it possible for people in the Subcontinent to reach out to other cultures and thereby increase the level of cosmopolitanism in society. Also evident is the fact that the cultural impact of games is restricted to a certain age group and that people from this age-group struggle to make their concerns known to the policymakers.

The survey results have been published in full in the Appendix, of course, without disclosing the identities of the respondents. Google forms were used to collect the survey data, which was then assessed using Google Sheets and Form's inbuilt graph-generator. The survey was left open for one and a half months; at the time of writing, responses are still coming in and have been incorporated. To my knowledge, no prior survey has addressed the question directly and the responses received to provide a crucial overview of the gaming scene in the region.

Concluding Remarks

One of the respondents of the survey outlines the scenario of gaming culture in the Subcontinent really well: '[videogames] influence it in niches. Until we come to games like PubG [sic] which have influenced a whole generation, but I'm not sure in what ways'. On the one hand, there is a huge hue and cry about the games *PUBG* and *Freefire* either on account of the security of information or on account of making players violent (strangely, *Fortnite* and other similar games seem to escape the notice of the censors). On the other hand, there has been a relative marginalisation of videogame culture ever since the advent of these games in the Indian public spaces and later, the household and even on portable devices. As such, the fuller impact of casual games on the public has not been adequately gauged and just as a substantial degree of research is being done to assess the impact of social media on culture, further research is needed in connection to how videogames relate to discourses on pedagogy, violence and diversity among other things. It will also make the medium more transparent for those non-gamers such as parents or policymakers who are indirect but important stakeholders in-game cultures.

Whether one is concerned with the effects of *PUBG* or *Pokemon Go* on players, or whether one is recommending a videogame to be taught in the classroom, the ludic cultures of the region are paramount in defining the attitudes of players. The digital medium also, arguably, influences player behaviour and the fuller impact of videogames on the region is yet to be gauged. It might be said, however, that the digital medium and the interactivity have ensured some important cultural shifts that need to be studied further; this moment, however, is crucial as it marks a watershed wherein certain videogames such as *PUBG* are becoming a cultural byword and also a subject of controversy within a public that is still largely ignorant about the cultural potential of the medium.

Section Three

Representations

5

Representations of the Subcontinent in Videogames Global and Local

The controversy and confusion surrounding the videogame medium are intrinsically linked to how videogames and gaming cultures are represented both globally and to local communities, also those who are unfamiliar or less familiar with videogames. On a global level, there is the issue of a pervasive, if mostly unwitting, orientalism in the portrayal of the region and its culture. There is also a serious lack of familiarity with the gaming audiences of the Indian Subcontinent and their diversity among both global and local stakeholders. A likely result is that games get castigated as the medium that is corrupting the youth (although a wide range of age groups are involved in playing videogames) and as such become the object of vilification by the news media, the political powers and the public intellectuals. The other result is that globally produced triple-A and other game blockbusters routinely ignore the cultural developments in the Global South and this is reflected in their portrayals of the Subcontinent. This chapter will address both these aspects of representation of videogames in the Subcontinent.

Running over the Subcontinent: Two Stories of Cultural (Mis)Representation

Let us begin this section with two stories. The first story is about how an Indian restaurant in Osaka apparently contributed to videogame history in the early nineties. Apparently, two items on its menu, *dal* (lentils) and *seem* (hyacinth beans), were combined to name a character in *Streetfighter II*, the cult fighting videogame that was released in 1991. Dhalsim, the yoga master, is the Indian superhero in Capcom's *Streetfighter* franchise and also the epitome of Orientalism in videogames as is evident from his name itself. Wearing a garland of skulls and with the ability to spew a stream of flame, the character is certainly constructed following some stereotypes that have defined India and Indians in Western eyes for centuries. Clearly, the Capcom designers just needed to walk across the Indian restaurant across the street and look at the menu to form their impression of India, one that would be conveyed worldwide through their globally popular videogame.

The second story is the story of a moment of purported joy for *Grand Theft Auto 2* players. In a YouTube video of *GTA 2*, you can watch the blue car (the player) run over six tiny pixelated orange figures chanting a religious mantra and looking different in their orange dresses. The screen flashes the word, 'Gouranga!' According to author David Kushner, 'Baglow, DMA's writer and PR guy, had an idea of other people they could mow down in the game. The inspiration came from his own real-life travels. Whenever he passed through London airport, he always got hassled by Hare Krishnas, urging him to be happy. 'Gouranga!' they'd say, a Sanskrit expression of good fortune. Baglow hated it. Then a lightbulb went off over his head' (Kushner 2012). Also, apparently, this gave shape to the outlaw image of the *GTA* games that was to be their hallmark. Entertaining as they may be to some, both of these cases are characterized by an orientalist and a racist attitude.

Needless to say, there are some glaring errors in the conceptions of how Indians are named, of the tantric religious practices (which Dhalsim is often considered to follow) and also of the meaning of 'Gouranga'. Unpacking this further, Dhalsim's description has already been critically commented on earlier by myself, Rachael Hutchinson and Christopher Patterson. Patterson (2020) describes Dhalsim as follows:

> Dhalsim, an egregious stereotype of an Indian yogi who sports face paint, pupil-less eyes, an emaciated torso, and a necklace of skulls, can be recognized not as an 'odorless' Japanese aesthetic but as a queer exaggeration whose offensive traits signal not realism but a play style, with his ability to strike players from a distance using stretchable arms and legs, as well as his magical ability to incinerate enemies up close by shouting 'Yoga fire!' and spitting out a stream of flame.

Hutchinson (2020) also makes a similar comment when she describes Dhalsim fighting in a Hindu temple dedicated to Lord Ganesha:

> Statues of elephants line the walls, each with gold decorations on their trunks, some with brass or ceramic pots at their feet. Dhalsim himself sports golden shorts, gold bands at his wrists and ankles, and a necklace of skulls. This amalgam conflates Hinduism with death veneration and the worship of Khali [sic], collapsing the whole into an exotic picture of India.

Of course, countenancing Ganesha as a martial god may be quite difficult for most Indians; it is his brother Karthikeya (variously, Murugan or Skanda) who is the god of war in Hindu mythology. The elephants, gold and the necklace of skulls all present a stark orientalist picture as I have commented in my book. In the film *Streetfighter* (1994), Dhalsim is played by Roshan Seth who appears as a relatively frail and geeky Indian scientist, again reinforcing some common Western stereotypes about India.

Regarding *GTA*'s 'Gouranga' message, the less said the better as the whole episode of being exhilarated after running over a group of monks is sadistic and fairly brutal. The 'Hare Krishnas' whom Baglow claims to have been hassled by are a monastic order called International Society for Krishna Consciousness (ISKCON) that has its headquarters at Mayapur in the Nadia district of West Bengal, India. Founded by 'Swami Prabhupāda in New York City in 1966, ISKCON belongs to the *Gaudiya-Vaishnava sampradāya*, a monotheistic tradition within the Vedic or Hindu culture. Philosophically it is based on the Sanskrit texts *Bhagavad-gītā and the Bhagavat Purana,* or *Srimad Bhagavatam.* These are the historic texts of the devotional *bhakti yoga* tradition, which teaches that the ultimate goal for all living beings is to reawaken their love for God, or Lord Krishna, the "all-attractive one"' (ISKCON n.d.). ISKCON runs a series of rural communities, relief programmes, schools as well as temples and congregations. Gouranga, contrary to Kushner, does not mean 'Be Happy' but is the name of Chaitanya Mahaprabhu, a 15th-century Indian reformer who was instrumental in the Vaishavite Bhakti Movement. The mean of his name means 'the fair or golden complexioned'; ISKCON devotees distributed stickers saying 'Call out Gouranga and Be Happy', which may have been the reason for Kushner's mistake. Why running over monks who preach peace and happiness should be hilarious is, of course, difficult to explain.

Recent Portrayals of the Subcontinent in Videogames

From early portrayals to more recent times, the scenario has not changed much. Ubisoft's recent game, *Far Cry 4*, has as its locale the fictional country of Kyrat, located in the Himalayan foothills and very closely resembling Nepal. In fact, Ubisoft sent a team to Nepal to research the setting of the game. The team travelled to big cities like Kathmandu and Pokhara as well as to remote locations up in the Himalayan mountains and promised to bring to the game an authentic experience based on their research. Journalist Hannah Shaw-Williams (2014), however, had other impressions:

> While Thompson and Fournier may have been satisfied with what they learned on their trip, a petition with over 1,300 signatures from Nepalese people protests the fact that the trailer for *Far Cry 4* features native characters who speak Hindi, rather than Nepali. Despite Thompson's efforts not to create a 'Disney' version of Nepal, the petition's signatories fear that the game will create a false perception of their country.

There is more than just the use of Hindi in the game that could bother the Nepali people. As I have commented in some detail elsewhere (Mukherjee 2021), the game's treatment of religion is extremely problematic. The character of the *Tarun Matara*, the child goddess in the game, is modelled on the Kumari Devi in Nepal's Kathmandu. The game developers show the Kumari in a fairly negative light whereas the reality may not be as bleak. In his master's thesis on the topic, Bijay Tamang refers to the experience narrated by Rashmila Shakya who had been a Royal Kumari. Tamang states that 'Rashmila loves the tradition and tries to subvert the western feminist and child labour activist idea about Kumari and demands to continue the tradition for the sake of nationality and cultural unity. She further claims that Kumari is one of the identity markers of the nation and Nepal is famous all over the world as a place of "living goddess" [sic]' (Tamang 2017). In the game, the child Bhadra is the designated Tarun Matara and the player's decision to support one of the rebel leaders, Amita, results in the abolition of the practice while the decision to support Sabal, who is more of a conservative, results in Bhadra being made the Tarun Matara and those who oppose the institution being killed. The developers take the stand that the institution of the Kumari (who is chosen at a young age like the Dalai Lama but whose tenure ends after some time on obtaining adulthood) is an abuse of children's rights; this position may not sit well with the Nepali Hindu community who revere the Kumari as a living goddess. Judging from the testimony of another former Kumari, Chanira Bajracharya, a 19-year-old Nepalese student, she says she still looks up to the goddess: 'I feel I'm blessed and a lot of my success comes from those blessings' (Sarkar 2014) and also that the tradition encourages respect for women in a male-dominated society. Such misguided attempts on the part of the developers to portray the culture of Nepal are indeed many; those interested in a more detailed analysis may choose to read what I have written elsewhere (Mukherjee 2021) on the subject.

Another major element in the game, however, needs to be noted. The antagonist is quite strangely named Pagan Min. One might easily make a connection with the first name and its connotations of unchristian but there is another lesser-known but significant connection to South Asian history. Pagan Min was a Burmese king whose opposition to the British East India Company under Lord Dalhousie started the Second Anglo-Burmese War. Why the chief antagonist (or the game 'boss') should be named after an Asian ruler whose country was colonised by a European power is quite unclear. Unless one assumes an underlying colonial bias that lingers on in the developers' minds perhaps unconsciously. The orientalist portrayal of Nepal, of course, has been pointed out already in Gregory Grieve's comment on the treatment of Nepal as *Shangri La*. Typically, Shangri La also makes an appearance in *Far Cry 4* albeit in a state of hallucinogen-induced dreaming. Shangri La, of course, is a

Western myth dating back to James Hilton's novel, *The Lost Horizon* (1933). The Tibetan equivalent might be Shambala, the mythical land described in the Buddhist Kalchakra Tantra as a white valley where people lived in harmony and where war and strife are absent. As Grieve states it, the on-ground scenario is vastly different from such orientalist reconstructions and indeed, it has been so for centuries. When Lara Croft visits Nepal in *Tomb Raider: Legend* (Church 2006) to retrieve a Ghanaian artefact called Ghalali Key, she is only to be seen engaging in some impressive parkour in the Himalayas and on occasion engaging in firefights that involve blowing up helicopters. The Nepali people are largely absent as is any reference to their culture; the location merely serves as a backdrop for the colonial mindset of the Indiana Jones type exploration adventure of Lara Croft.

By now, it is clear that the portrayal of the Subcontinent in videogames is heavily reliant on stereotypes. In other examples, often protested about by the concerned nations, these countries are shown as failed states and terrorist hubs. In 2013, Pakistani businessmen managed to effect a ban on *Call of Duty: Black Ops II* (Treyarch 2012) and *Medal of Honor: Warfighter* (Danger Close Games 2012) both of which supposedly show the Pakistani Inter-Services Intelligence (ISI) as being connected to the Al Qaida terrorist group. According to a *Deutsche Welle* article:

> The All Pakistan Association of CD, DVD and Audio Cassettes Traders and Manufacturers recently released a statement announcing a countrywide ban on these games. The Association has always boycotted these types of films and games … The games ('Medal of Honor: Warfighter' and 'Call of Duty: Black Ops II') have been developed against Pakistan, and the association has completely banned their sale. (Shamil Shams 2013)

Quoting Emrys Shoemaker, communications analyst at London School of Economics, the *DW* article argues that 'These games reflect the ideology and the narrative of the people who write them. The information we have access to is largely controlled by Western media conglomerates. Those who do not have access or control over the media are at a disadvantage in terms of the ability to shape their own narratives' (2013). Other games such as *Splinter Cell: Double Agent* also feature Pakistan in connection with nuclear terrorism. According to Pieter Van den Heede, Kees Ribbens and Jeroens Janz, Pakistan is often counted in the countries of the Middle East in videogames and is usually a prominent location for the portrayal of violence and that as a consequence only a small section of such representation included other Asian countries such as China, India, the Philippines and Singapore. They go on to state 'that conflict-ridden countries like Sri Lanka, Myanmar, and Nepal were not depicted, while India and the Philippines, which have seen very destructive episodes of (armed) conflict and one-sided violence since 1989 as well, were hardly represented (each in only 2 of the 116 levels, or 1.7%).' (Van den Heede et al. 2018)

Sri Lanka is, incidentally, represented in *Tom Clancy's: Ghost Recon Predator.* As the newspaper, *Hindustan Times* reports, 'While the Liberation Tigers of Tamil Eelam (LTTE) were not named, the company, Ubisoft's promos leave little doubt about who the rebels were modeled on' (Patronobis 2010). The report also points out that such a portrayal 'could lead to protests from the remaining pro-LTTE diaspora groups is that the game's preview says the virtual rebels used civilians as human shields. The insurgents think, "...nothing of hiding among innocent civilians, of using people as a shield for their illegal and immoral campaign"' (2018). At the time of writing, the Tamil community in the Indian state of Tamil Nadu has protested the portrayal of Tamil people in the Indian OTT serial *Family Man 2* (*The Family Man* 2021) where the LTTE is shown as a terrorist organisation and has called it 'an attempt to discredit the struggle of the Eelam Tamils in Sri Lanka' (Madhav 2021). It is intriguing that majoritarian narratives in both the West and even within the Indian Subcontinent often make similar sweeping statements about a people. As van dan Heede et al. have noted though, the depiction of terrorism in Sri Lanka occurs in one game as opposed to the many games in which Pakistan is portrayed as a terrorist state. The other portrayal of Sri Lanka in videogames that comes to mind is *Indiana Jones and the Emperor's Tomb* (The Collective 2003), which is set in British-ruled colonial Ceylon. It is again not surprising as the film, *Indiana Jones and the Temple of Doom* (1984), which portrayed India in a rather negative light and was banned in the country for a while, was also shot in

Sri Lanka. Whether it be Nepal, Sri Lanka or India, orientalist portrayals of the cultures of the Subcontinent are commonplace in videogames.

Besides the two already mentioned, problematic representations of India abound in many other examples, some of which I have commented on elsewhere already. Siddhartha Chakraborti and Samya Brata Roy have both commented on how *Hitman* videogames perpetuate colonial stereotypes. Chakraborti (2015) critiques the representation of Sikhs in *Hitman 2: Silent Assassin*:

> [T]he player agent is again the much needed outsider who must impinge into the situation and save India from a danger which is indigenous in origin. The Golden Temple becomes the exotic location where the future of the Indian nation is to be determined through western intervention. India, far from being a sovereign nation, becomes a destination to which the western agent must travel in order to ensure the destiny of the Indian nation.

In my book, *Videogames and Postcolonialism,* I have also pointed out how in *Call of Duty: Modern Warfare 3* (Infinity Ward 2011) the American army battles the Russian in the Indian state of Himachal Pradesh but without any interference from the Indian armies. In this situation, where India is literally absent, again the Western overriding of India's sovereignty is fairly obvious. In his recent conference paper, 'Hitman 2 and its spectre of Mumbai: A city lost in translation' (Roy 2020), which deals with the newer iteration of *Hitman 2*, Roy brings up the overtly orientalist portrayal of Mumbai and the borderline silliness in the portrayal of the cityscape where shops have names such as 'Bakery Bread', 'Bhang Shop' and 'Clothes' and Bollywood films have names such as 'Snake and the Mongoose' in what he calls an 'essentialist reduction'. Continuing with the fauna, Roy shows how the Indian setting of the game contains distinctly oriental symbols such as peacocks. Continuing with the critique of orientalist misrepresentation, Chakraborti (2015) highlights the ludicrousness of the portrayal of Lara Croft fighting the god Shiva in *Tomb Raider 3* (Core Design 1998). Speaking of exoticizing Hindu gods, the *Uncharted* series also engages in a Lara-Croft or Indiana Jones-style portrayal of India as a location for treasure-hunting, quite in keeping with the colonial spirit of exploitation. In *Uncharted: The Lost Legacy*, the protagonists are looking for the 'tusk of Ganesh'. Ganesh is the famed elephant-god who brings prosperity; in the game, the tusk is a bejewelled mystical artefact. The events of the game revolve around the search for the artefact and although the protagonists agree to 'donate' the artefact to the Indian Ministry of Culture in the end, why they needed to explore and exploit what they consider exotic is a moot question. Likewise, in another *Uncharted* game, *A Thief's End,* the story is about finding the great Gunsway treasure fabled to be hidden by the pirate Henry Avery. While the story celebrates Avery's treasure, it completely ignores the Indian side of the story (the 'Gunsway' was the *Ganj i Sawai*, the Mughal emperor Aurungzeb's flagship, which was looted for days while its crew was raped and murdered). As I have commented elsewhere 'with an unmistakable Western bias, Avery the bloodthirsty pirate is to be glorified as a "prince of thieves" and a champion of liberty. One of the protagonists actually believes that he brings freedom to the oppressed and if it is at the cost of Eastern wealth, then that is because he had no choice' (Mukherjee 2020).

There are many such examples of representing Indian culture without heeding the sensitivities of the people of India. As I have commented, in *Age of Empires III: The Asian Dynasties*, the portrayal of Indian history is at best problematic: 'although the game features the Sepoy Mutiny of 1857 in one of its early missions and hints at the discontent against the East India Company, the colonial history of India is presented in a sanitized uniformity that views exploitation of resources in colonial India in the same light as perhaps one would see mining or farming in one's home country' (Mukherjee 2017b: 78). There are also dubious and historically incorrect assumptions about food habits in Mughal India. What is even more troubling is how Sid Meier's *Civilization* games portray Gandhi, often seen as India's foremost political figure both in the Subcontinent and globally. The 'nuclear Gandhi' in the *Civilization* series, which although not yet the topic of much discussion in India, could be construed as deeply offensive and even racist at many levels. What apparently started as a design glitch in the series was later built into the game on purpose. Game designer Jon Shafer seems to have found it a joke to make

Gandhi a perpetrator of nuclear war in *Civilization V*. Meier (2020) writes in his recently released memoirs:

> It is true that Gandhi would—eventually—use nukes when India was at war, just like any civilization in the game, and at the time this did strike a lot of players as odd. The real Abraham Lincoln probably wouldn't have nuked anyone either, but the idea was that every leader draws a line in the sand somewhere. It's also true that Gandhi would frequently threaten the player, because one of his primary traits was to avoid war, and deterrence through mutually assured destruction was an effective way to go about that.

Why representing a globally recognised figure of world peace from the Subcontinent as a nuclear war-monger can be considered funny is something that this author is unsure about. Despite seemingly going against the stereotype of Gandhi, the *Civilization* games, as I argue elsewhere, actually perpetuate an older colonial stereotype and fear as embodied in Winston Churchill's deep-seated resentment against Gandhian civil disobedience: 'Churchill's alarm seems to have been converted into the entirely non-Gandhian, very different, and yet very current fear of India as a nuclear-capable nation. In *Civilization's* version of history, not much has changed from the colonial times' (Mukherjee 2017: 79). Gandhi does get a somewhat different treatment in Joseph DeLappe's *Second Life* creation called 'March to Dandi'. According to journalist Warren Fry (2008), who reviewed the installation:

> DeLappe used a Nordic Trak Walkfit to traverse the 248-mile length of Gandhi's original march. His steps were converted into those of his avatar, MGandhi Chakrabati, via a handily wired connection to his laptop. MGandhi's progress through SL was projected on a wall facing DeLappe. While journeying in SL, DeLappe tried to find other users, give them a digital gift explaining the project, and invite them to walk with him.

DeLappe, who calls himself an activist and artist, may have had very noble intentions of portraying Gandhi's civil disobedience and his message of non-violence but the installation turned out to become something that completely missed the point of the Dandi March and the Salt Satyagraha. As Fry (2008) observes:

> The virtual representation of this famous act of civil disobedience and the bravura of durational performance were meant to somehow transmit Gandhi's message of peaceful protest. Instead, any attempt to engage the socio-historical complexities of Gandhi's actions or examine the potential pitfalls in overemphasizing his mythic status were overshadowed by DeLappe's go-it-alone performance art heroics and SL's modish glitz.

Not only does this installation miss the point of the Indian freedom struggle and Gandhian notions of Satyagraha but it is a travesty of the depth and gravity of a movement that thousands participated in. The notion of Civil Disobedience is entirely absent as is the oppression under a colonial power in the SL installation where an avatar resembling Gandhi, who was famous for his ascetism, is seen lounging on a sofa while the artist takes a break from walking. While this is not the place to argue about 'overemphasizing his mythic status', it is nevertheless imperative to point out how discourses from the global north underemphasize the achievements and the struggles of key figures from the Subcontinent even at the cost of disrespecting what they stand for.

The Subcontinent is constructed variously in videogames, particularly those originating in the global north. Although many of such representations are negative or insensitive to the local culture, there are, of course, some sympathetic portrayals of colonial India in games such as *Assassin's Creed: Syndicate* (Ubisoft Quebec 2015) where the exiled king of the Punjab, Duleep Sinhji, is featured in one of the side-quests and his dialogue with the protagonist is very revealing:

> Evie: 'Do you miss India?'
> Duleep: 'I remember... that my mother smelled of cinnamon. And when she cradled me in her arms in the summer heat, I would hold so still that she fell asleep. When I lost my kingdom, it hurt, but truly, when they took my mother away...' —Duleep explaining his attachment to his home country, 1868 in *Assassin's Creed Syndicate*'

Rarely represented in history books, Duleep Singhji or the 'Black Prince of Perthshire' finds a fairly important role in *Assassin's Creed: Syndicate.* In another section of the game, the exiled king tells the British prime minister, Gladstone, 'It is not a matter of money. I cannot stand idle and watch my homeland subjected to the yoke of an outsider's rule. My people are treated as slaves. I will die poor a 1000 times over if only to see them free' (Ubisoft Quebec 2015). Lately, there have been some attempts to represent the history of the Subcontinent, particularly that of the colonial period, from the perspective of the marginalized and the subaltern but such attempts are still comparatively few and far between.

Borrowed Concepts Unacknowledged: *Karma* and *Avatar*

From the representation of the Subcontinent's history and culture, it is necessary to move on to the representation of two philosophical concepts from Indic religions that are widely and very importantly featured in discussions on digital games. One of the most commonly used terms in gaming parlance is 'avatar' and as de Wildt et al. acknowledge this 'appropriation of avatar into tech and gaming contexts is a new use of Hindu religious terminology in an everyday context while it continues to evoke mystical and spiritual connotations' (de Wildt et al. 2020). There has been a parallel or perhaps derivative appropriation of the word in Hollywood films as evinced in James Cameron's blockbuster *Avatar* (2009) and *Avatar: The Last Airbender* (2005). Gautam Basu Thakur writes of Cameron's film that '[t]he anti-imperialist narrative of Avatar obscures a deeply Eurocentric mindset. In the guise of criticizing the West's violent appropriations of the Other, the film actually rehearses the old colonial narratives of European privilege, entitlement, and sovereign subjectivity. [...] Sully is the avatar of the West in the global present' (Thakur 2015: 87) In the *Avatar*, the protagonist, the disabled American soldier, Sully, is given a digital identity/prosthesis wherein he can inhabit the body of a Na'avi, an extra-terrestrial sapient species living on the lush jungle moon of the planet Pandora. Basu Thakur has already delved into the colonial context of the film but he does not spell out the implications of the use of the word 'avatar': the American soldier protagonist enters the Na'vi community in an 'avatar' or a digitally mediated identity and he also becomes a 'Toruk Makto' or the messianic tamer of a great leonopteryx or Toruk. Cameron's *Avatar* combines the messianic role of the avatar in Hindu philosophy and mythology and the sense in which the avatar has been perceived as an incarnation of a god, mostly of Vishnu, who is said to have ten avatars, all of whom descend to Earth at the time of a crisis and whose last avatar, Kalki, is yet to arrive but will signal the end of the *Kali Yuga* and bring destruction to the wicked. In fact, Cameron went on record stating that 'I didn't want to reference the Hindu religion so closely but the subconscious association was interesting and I hope I haven't offended any one in doing so' (Reuters 2010) and the similarity of the blue complexion of Cameron's protagonist to Krishna has also been commented on. In *Avatar: The Last Airbender*, too, the avatar is a character who can combine and control the four elements of air, water, Earth and fire; the character is again, a messianic character and a clear case of oriental exoticisation as Jane Iwamura notes in her critique of the portrayal of the oriental monk figure in Western cinema. A more detailed criticism has been made by a Tibetan student who points out the clear parallels with Tibetan Buddhism:

> The Air nomads are blatant stereotypes of Tibetan monks and lamas, and the 'Avatar' as a concept itself is inspired from Buddhist Bodhisattvas. This is made clear when the Dalai Lama selection process was mimicked for the 'Avatar' selection process. [...] The passing off of real history as an original idea for fiction, only further encourages the exotification of Asian cultures for Western entertainment, rather than the promotion of education, mutual respect, and understanding. (Wang 2021)

The Bodhisattvas are forms of the Buddha before he attained enlightenment and as such, are rebirths of Gautama Buddha. The orientalism and the exoticisation of the avatar figure have been clearly spelt out by her. It will be useful now to return to the use of the word in videogame culture.

In 1986, Chip Morningstar, designer of the videogame *Habitat*, tied the 'Sanskrit term "avatar" to [one's] real-time presence in an online world' (Britt 2008). Soon after, the novelist Neal Stephenson popularized this usage in *Snow Crash* (1992) and in little over a decade, the word has gained phenomenal currency in Game Studies, discussions of gameplay, virtual reality, social networking and even in a blockbuster film. This, arguably, is more popular than the original Sanskrit usage. Philip Rosedale, the creator of *Second Life*, defines avatar in the gaming sense as 'the representation of your chosen embodied appearance to other people in a virtual world' (Stokel-Walker 2013) The concept of the avatar is the key point of departure for analyses of in-game identity and involvement.

In the original Sanskrit usage, the avatar is an object of worship and is the manifestation of divinity that descends on Earth to destroy evil. The commonest English translation of the term is 'incarnation' (literally 'the being made flesh') and with this is also associated the idea of the cyclical appearance of divinity. Besides Vishnu, other gods such as Ganesha and Shiva also manifest themselves as avatars. 'Avatar' comes from the words 'ava' and 'tri' meaning 'below' and 'crossing' respectively— thus an avatar is the 'crossing-down' of a god to free humanity from evil. Geoffrey Parrinder (1997) identifies twelve characteristics of the Hindu doctrine of Avatar: avatars are real; if the human (the early avatars of Vishnu bear non-human or semi-human forms), they take worldly birth; they mingle the divine and human; they die; there is a historicity to some avatars; they are repeated; they are often exemplars of proper living; they have a mission and they guarantee divine grace. Further, the avatar is either a full manifestation of the deity or a partial one; it is also possible for the deity to manifest himself or herself as multiple avatars, simultaneously. As an example of the latter, the brothers Krishna and Balaram are both said to be avatars of Vishnu. In the epic *Ramayana*, Ram and Parashuram, both said to be avatars of Vishnu, meet each other. The time schema of the avatar concept is complex; unlike the one-time incarnation in Christian theology the avatars in Hindu philosophy are cyclic but they can also appear simultaneously and interact with each other. The other complexity is of course the relationship between the deity himself or herself and the avatar as the manifestation of the deity. As Freda Matchett (2001) points out that relationship between Krishna and Vishnu is 'something altogether more mysterious, the *¯a ´scarya* which reflects on earth the wonder that is Visnu.' Describing the relationship of Ram to Vishnu, Raimundo Panikkar comments that 'Rama in fact is totally human and totally divine, Rama is material and spiritual, temporal and eternal' (Panikkar: 38).

Morningstar's usage of the word is based on a very specific interpretation that 'seemed an appropriate mapping [...] in the sense that we humans are like deities, or at least external souls, with respect to a virtual world that exists only inside a computer simulation' (Kan 2010). Such usage ignores the complexity of the avatar in Hindu philosophy; it also misreads the original purported nature of the avatar. Elsewhere, I have tried to demonstrate how the dual processes of involvement and the multitelic nature of gameplay can both be captured in the notion of the avatar. Vishnu's *avatars* are, admittedly, not re-spawnings or repetitions as the reloaded instances of saved videogames; nevertheless, the term avatar does imply multiple 'descents' that somewhat resemble the videogame reloads and replays. The more common usage of the term or that of the mediated digital self does connect in some ways to the deity's earthly representation in a human or non-human form but it must be noted that the avatar in Hinduism is inseparable from the deity; this is not true of the videogame usage of avatar. It is, therefore, not surprising that little attention has been paid to the Indian origins of the term in gaming culture.

Another key concept in videogaming that derives from Indic philosophy is that of *Karma.* Generally, Karma is an in-game affordance that allows for moral decision-making and related outcomes. As a commentator states:

> Karma systems are a unique feature in many games, which takes into account the player's actions, inaction and their decisions, and shapes the world around them as well as their narrative as they progress. These systems can be overt and interactive, or very subtle instead. There are tons of games out there with karma systems—and some are done with more thought and nuance than others. (Dewan 2020)

In games such as Bioware's *Mass Effect* and Bethesda Softworks' *Fallout 3,* there is a clear-cut Karma-system and commentator Tobias Knoll observes. 'it is the only game that has a 'karma system' that actually uses the term 'karma' within the game' (Knoll 2018). *Far Cry 4*, however, also has an overtly named and elaborate karma system:

> Karma is a system used in Far Cry 4 that can reward or punish players based on their actions. [...] Karma is earned by performing good tasks for the Golden Path and citizens of Kyrat. You can do a number of things to increase your karma, including:
>
> The various Karma events that take place all around Kyrat, including saving a hostage from the Royal Army, helping the Golden Path during a skirmish, and protecting a group of civilians from wild animals. Spinning Mani Wheels, collecting Masks of Yalung, or collecting the four Thangkas will award generous amounts of Karma. Killing animals without guns or explosives, i.e. with throwing knives, bows, crossbows, or using your khukri to kill them will award small amounts of karma per each kill. There is a skill in the skill tree that allows you to multiply your Karma earnings many fold. Karma can also be taken away if you kill the Golden Path soldiers or civilians. However, once you reach the maximum Karma level, it will be impossible to lose it. (Karma 2021)

Set in a Nepal, where there is a large Buddhist population, *Far Cry 4* makes some token references to Buddhist notions of karma, in its insistence on saving hostages, not killing members of friendly groups, spinning mani wheels, collecting thangkas (Tibetan Buddhist paintings on cotton, silk or applique) or killing animals without explosives or guns—only it seems to ignore the very basic tenet of Buddhism or *ahimsa* (non-violence); indeed, it makes a travesty of the beliefs. Karma is indeed connected to Buddhist, Jain and Hindu beliefs although these religions have different approaches to it. Eminent anthropologist Gananath Obeyesekere (2006) states that while the word *karma* itself means 'action', the karmic theories are connected to rebirth eschatologies. Philosopher Jonardon Ganeri says that 'the idea of karma is that every human action has consequences, but it is not at all the claim that every human action is itself a consequence' (Gutting 2016, ch 9); Ganeri indicates that Karma in Indic philosophy works in complicated ways and is unlike what the musician John Lennon describes as 'Instant karma's gonna get you' (1970). Elsewhere, I have compared the rebirth eschatology of Indic religions to digital games and their save and reload mechanism. Even if, in some cases (such as in *Witcher 3*) the previous savegame may impact the players' statistics and the affordances with which they begin the game, the karma system in videogames does not map well to the karmic frameworks in Indic philosophy where the results of karma (*phala*) manifest themselves in multiple ways, across generations and even though a different person than the one who committed the act. Nevertheless, the cause–effect aspect of karma, especially when taking into account the reloaded lives of the protagonist, may still be useful element wherein Indic philosophy can be an influence on game design. In a similar vein, Knoll observes that 'the similarities of these elements, which indisputably occur in "karma systems" and are specifically named by players and game journalists, with earlier understandings of the karma concept are at least an indication that both are connected by the players; even if this happens largely unconsciously and by several detours' (Knoll 2018: 33).

Fallout 3 was supposedly the first game to use the term 'karma'; incidentally, the game never launched in India as Microsoft cited 'cultural sensitivities' as the impetus. Earnest Cavalli provides a possible reason: 'Then again, *Fallout 3* does feature mutant, two-headed cows that share a name with a caste of widely revered Hindu scholars and preachers. I can't imagine that mutating a people's sacred animal then naming the thing after their spiritual leaders would go over so well' (Cavalli 2008). Microsoft's decision to use that name and then not to release the game in India[1] is yet another stereotypical response that is insensitive to the cultural nuances of the region and ignores the subtler discussions that could benefit from being addressed by such a plural medium such as videogames.

Representations: Regional Games Studies and the Subcontinent

As thousands of players from the Subcontinent engage with the videogames that engage in sweeping orientalist stereotypes, there are

1 Incidentally, *Fallout 3* also features other Indian names but in roles that are not culturally offensive at all—Knight Captain Durga is named after the Hindu Goddess Durga; Durga is also a common name among Indian (mostly Hindu) women.

sometimes voices of protest such as those in Pakistan, Nepal and Sri Lanka, as outlined earlier in this chapter. The question that arises now is whether countries in the Indian Subcontinent are also looking at the videogame medium to promote an alternative ludic consciousness and also a representation of their diverse cultures from a local perspective. The geopolitics of the region is quite complex with India and Pakistan being political rivals and both nuclear-capable countries; nevertheless, there are many cultural overlaps and these countries have a shared colonial history and deep-rooted connections.[2] They also have their own unique cultural perspectives. As mentioned earlier, here Liboriussen and Martin's (Liboriussen and Martin 2016) conception of 'regional games studies' comes in useful as it helps researchers excavate the local game cultures that get overshadowed by the default Eurocentric and North America-centric norms of play and their videogame industries. Ideally, such representations serve to shape the videogaming cultures of these regions in a way that is inclusive of their extant ludic cultures and their sociocultural and economic requirements. They also facilitate the presentation of a stronger case for videogames to the state authorities, as in the case of Pakistan and India as discussed earlier.

Most of the commentary by international scholars on the gaming cultures in the Subcontinent centres on India. Whether they are upbeat about the scenario such as Ernest Adams (2009) or more cautious in their appraisal such as Adrienne Shaw (2013) and Casey O'Donnell (2014), there is a common motif that runs through their analysis and that is of the importance of the cultural distinctiveness of the region both in terms of its late entry into the IT culture and industry, its socio-economic status and its wealth of diverse local cultures. Friedman, of course, is an exception as he makes a case for the flat world of globalisation and ignores the local factors in game development. As far as local scholarship is concerned, there is an increasing degree of awareness about the Indian scenario. This is also being evidenced in the Subcontinent in general. Some of the key features that are common to one or more countries in the Subcontinent are the predominance of

2 These countries are also members of the South Asian Association of Regional Cooperation (SAARC).

mobile gaming (as opposed to PC and console gaming elsewhere in the world), the success stories of indie studios, the recent successes in eSports and finally, the use of mythological stories particularly from Hindu mythology[3] or from regional history. Of course, among many non-gamers and the authorities, videogames remain an enigma or are castigated as negative and violent such as in the recent *PUB-G* and *Freefire* bans in different countries in the region. Among the latter there are still many misconceptions prevalent about videogames as well as the lack of awareness about the medium: there are diverse instances like the 'Blue Whale Challenge' that was mistakenly described as a videogame in the Indian media and others like when a Pakistani minister mistook a plane landing in *Grand Theft Auto V* (Rockstar North 2013) for a real one and was trolled on social media after he praised the pilot (see Kaur 2019).

Local Cultures, Local Representations in and of Videogames

Riko Banerjee in his talk, 'What is it like to be a Gamer or pursue Game Studies in India?' (DiGRA 2020) raises some pertinent points regarding some major perceptual issues around gaming and game cultures. He raises the question of affordability stating that the minimum price for a gaming computer is probably one or two months' salary for a middle-class family in the Subcontinent and for the poorer sections of society, it is unthinkable to afford a PC or a console. Mobile phones, due to their having become more affordable and due to the recent wide reach of 4G networks across the Subcontinent, as discussed in Chapter Two, have become the medium of choice for a new group of gamers for whom *PUB-G* and *Freefire* are the staple gaming options. One needs to reiterate Prabhu's scathing comments on the affordability of games in a country such as India: 'how much of India is clumped around or just above those poverty lines? How many can even think of spending

3 As far as I am aware, other religious mythologies have not been represented in local videogames from the Subcontinent but the scenario, of course, is evolving.

on games? Is anyone even considering how much of India can afford games at all?' (Prabhu 2016).

It is in this context that the predominant position of mobile gaming needs to be considered. Earlier researchers (Shaw 2013, O'Donnell 2014 and Mukherjee 2015) were unable to predict the degree of the rapid 4G expansion and the surge in the number of smartphone users who would be taking to online gaming. Likewise, the mobile-based eSports culture was also not easy to predict even five years ago. Nevertheless, today, mobile gaming is being recognised in the region by governments seeking to legitimise eSports or at the other extreme, banning videogames and prosecuting those who play these games. Recently, there have also been situations where videogames have been associated with online gambling; Rishi Alwani states that 'India has a history of looking down on gambling, and gambling companies have been trying to relabel themselves as "real-money gaming", going as far as taking out full page ads on newspapers to curry-favour public opinion alerts the videogame community to the problems with such an association' (Alwani et al. 2021). Meanwhile, local eSports managers have been distancing themselves from gambling. As Akshat Rathee, the head of the Electronic Sports League (India) states: 'We believe esport [sic] does not deserve any gambling. We are not skill-based gaming, we are a sport. We are a sport because the physicality of responses of our participants leads to the result of a winner' (2021). There is another variation of this notion wherein the claim is that '[i] f you removed the money/prize-money out of Counter-Strike, League of Legends, Apex, Dota, whatever your poison may be, people will still be out there playing these same games tomorrow' (2021). Personally, this sounds quite an acceptable claim and one that separates online videogames from gambling games. The line, however, is thin and as a Pakistani news channel reports (*Lahore, Gambling Started under the Cover of Games* 2016), there are no laws defining the functioning of videogaming parlours and no taxes and the parlours soon switch to becoming gambling dens. As this chapter is being written, the High Court of Bombay is adjudicating whether the boardgame Ludo is a game of skill or chance (Chowdhury 2021). The premise here is to establish how far online ludo games (some have been referred to earlier) or games such as rummy and *teen patti* are to be judged as gambling apps.

There are also other far-reaching cultural impacts and trolling and hate-speech cultures have also evolved around these games. These and the stigma of violence often mark videogames as a negative influence in the minds of the majority in these countries who are non-gamers. On the other hand, the anti-gaming arrests that happened in India as well as the general neglect of a potential billion-dollar industry in the entire Subcontinent is the other problematic side of the coin. As indicated earlier, the lack of infrastructure and laws dedicated to videogames is also a problem. These problems are intrinsically connected with the local reception of videogames and they are not about to go away anytime soon. Perhaps, as Banerjee has indicated (*What is it like to be a Gamer or pursue Game Studies in India? - Riko Banerjee* 2020), more institutions teaching not only game development but also games studies as a discipline will help in changing the scenario. Developer Satyajit Chakraborty indicates, in a personal interview (2021), that the lack of a game design community is also a huge obstacle because there is no scope for sharing ideas.

Local content has become quite popular in the gaming scenarios of the Subcontinent. Some of the games have already been discussed in detail in the previous chapters and the investment of indie developers in local content is now a well-known fact. Adrienne Shaw's observations on the lack of history of videogames in India and how the English word 'gamer' does not have an Indian language equivalent have been commented on earlier. Drawing on her early and doubtless astute analysis, other commentators based in the Global North have made certain sweeping conclusions that may be defied by the recent development of local content. Ann-Marie Schleiner interprets Shaw's analysis to ask some important questions:

> What would an Indian digital gaming development scene equivalent to Bollywood be like and how would it happen? Which development trajectories should game industries at a national scale follow? Should an emerging national game industry aim to imitate the global North, such as Silicon Valley in California, or follow other models like the

> Southeast Asian 'Tiger' economic emphasis on technical education combined with export dependent economies? (Schleiner 2020: 42)

She also goes on to state that games do not need to be culturally specific because of the transnational portability of abstract game mechanics using the examples of games such as *Tetris*. Schleiner's comment raises many questions. What applies to abstract games such as *Tetris* may not be apt for games that draw on culture-specific narratives such as *Missing* but then there has been much prior research around these issues especially in connection with the ludology-narratology debates. The questions regarding whether the Indian game industry should necessarily emulate Bollywood is a moot question. Bollywood happens to have greater visibility than the other Indian creative industries but to assume that it should be the benchmark for the games industry is not altogether fair just as one cannot make an easy comparison of eSports with Cricket. Whether the local content in the videogames is part of a nationalistic endeavour needs more thought; most commentators speak about India but do not address the issues in the rest of the Subcontinent (where the Bollywood analogy does not work). That local content is being developed in all the countries in the Subcontinent has been shown in earlier chapters. Whether it is mythology-based (*Raji, Asura's Wrath, Threta* or *Unrest*, historical (*Heroes of '71* or *Nero*) or addressing a sociopolitical theme (*Missing*), the content of many of these indie games is deeply invested in local issues. Some games such as *Heroes of '71* and *Bhagat Singh* portray nationalist struggles for independence of Bangladesh and India, respectively. *Nero* (Arimac 2021) or *Niro* is based on a real-life sniper, Ranjith Madalena, who fought in the Sri Lankan Civil War. While these games promote specific narratives of nationalism, many of the other games address very different issues. Quite a few of the prominent local game developers in the region are invested in making local content that is not nationalistic but rather presents aspects of local culture that cover a variety of perspectives that may not yet be available to global audiences. Perhaps, the outcome here is not an imitation of either the Silicon Valley or the South East Asian 'tiger' economies focusing on technical education. So far, the recent games that have been successful in India have been mainly basing themselves on local culture. In fact, Steam organised an Indian Harvest Festival sale that featured the new games made in India and all of them had local cultural content. They were also all indie games. As the Sportskeeda.com website reports:

> For India, the biggest breakthrough in terms of Indie games happened with the release of 'Raji: An Ancient Epic.' The game was nominated for the 'Best debut Indie game' award at The Game Awards 2020. There is a separate fan-following for Indie games made in India. After the example set by Nodding Head Games, Frostwood Interactive is set to release another Indie title with the publishing support of Dino Digital. (Mukherjee 2021b)

The *Forgotten Fields* (Frostwood Interactive 2021) game is set in Goa and is about the memories of the developer's childhood; the local setting is an important part of the game's message. *Raji* has already been discussed at length earlier and the extent of localisation (including interfaces in Indian languages in addition to the Hindu mythology-inspired content) has been an important issue. It is no accident that there has been a rise in the number of indie studios in the region. The fact that they have chosen to project local content or content with regional influences needs more attention from a game cultures perspective.

In terms of game studies criticism, Liboriussen and Martin's article (2016), looks at the postcolonial trend in games studies research emerging from India; Zeiler and Mukherjee (2021) have also variously highlighted the local influences on videogame cultures in India as have Padmini Ray Murray and Chris Hand (2015) in their article on how *jugaad* informs the game design culture in India. Ray Murray and Hand explain how game design in India was deeply informed by the Indian context of the games and how instead of discarding new technologies quickly and allowing for a sedimented structure, the Indian game development ecosystem was about including a constellation of media rather than a stratified presence of older and newer media:

> [I]t was even more important that the 'Indianness' of the game should act as a corrective—leading us to consider how the game's Indian context informs its narrative and aesthetic design. *Meghdoot* was thus inspired by the allochronic nature of media forms in India—ancient

> modes of narrative dissemination such as oral storytelling still co-exist alongside cutting edge technologies, for example. This reality challenges [Jussi] Parikka's definition of media archaeology which sees media cultures as sedimented and layered. (2021)

The comparison to steampunk is obvious to anyone who is familiar with the concept of *jugaad* (loosely translated as a mix of DIY and hack); the flea markets of Indian cities are full of used and obsolete tech that are brought together in unique ways to make low-cost electronic devices. While *jugaad* is something that game developers speak of in terms of software development, there is also a different level of assemblage when one considers the content of the game and the 'allochronic' structure would, arguably, include multiple cultural elements that informed the gameplay. Ray Murray, together with a group of game designers from Bengaluru, also designed a game called *Darshan Diversion* (Kain *et al.* 2016) where they address the controversial prevention of women between the ages of 10 and 50 from entering the Sabarimala Temple. The game itself was made during the global game jam and was based on a popular news item featuring the controversy around the denial of entry to women. The Supreme Court of India passed a verdict that allowed women to enter the temple but the issue still remains controversial today. Indeed, instead of being structured as sedimented technologies, the game involves a plugging-in of multiple elements all at the same time. Further, the employment of a platformer mechanism to create an activist game is also a kind of *jugaad*, not least so emphasized by its situation in the Global Game Jam where it was finished under time and resource constraints.

While the development of games obviously is an important indicator of how gaming cultures are shaping up in the Subcontinent, player responses from across the region are also important testimonies that need to be considered. The author was compelled to rely on online surveys to gather such opinions as travel restrictions during the time of writing (due to the Covid-19 pandemic) did not permit much mobility. In the survey that was conducted for this book and in where 43 people participated, 20 answered the question, 'How do videogames influence your country's culture, if at all?' The survey is included as Appendix Two. Of these, one person was from Sri Lanka, two from Pakistan, one from Nepal, one from Bangladesh and 15 from India. Four of these participants were female and two of them were from Pakistan and two were from India. By and large, the responses are that gaming has a mixed effect on local culture but two respondents (one from India and the other from Nepal) have directly denied any influence of videogames on local culture. Others have agreed that these games increase social bonding, familiarity with other cultures, means of expressing themselves in public forums and even keeping the youth off drugs. Of course, issues of how policymakers view videogames is a matter of concern for many respondents as is the connection with videogames and violence. One of the respondents expresses fear because in India playing PUBG led to arrests while another expresses a nuanced viewpoint that the 'rise in popularity of multiplayer shooter games might echo the recent worrying rise of majoritarian mob violence and troubling political cultivation of discourses of victimization and misdirected socio-economic-political frustration'. The latter comment hints at the alt-right-like tendencies that may arise from such shooting game cultures. Recently, such tendencies, especially as evinced on public streaming channels, came under the scanner when the 'Arunachal Pradesh government [...] filed a case against a social media influencer from Punjab for his alleged racial remarks against a Congress MLA' (PTI 2021) who had been critical of the reintroduction of *PUBG* as *Battlegrounds-India*—while in this case, the parliamentarian was able to prosecute the offender, there are many cases where such behaviour goes unchecked. Connected to the discourse on violence and the negative effects of videogames, there is also the feeling that the impact of videogames is not understood properly by the older generations and a respondent from Bangladesh comments on how gaming in his country is mainly the preserve of those who are 10 to 30 years old. Among the respondents (who were admittedly all gamers) the general consensus was that videogames are important in forming communication skills. One participant also pointed to the rise of eSports as a cultural phenomenon, something that has been noted in an earlier chapter. The rise of the indie game companies that have pitched India as a prominently indie space of creativity (as opposed to just being centres for outsourced work or branches of global brands). One of the participants from India notes that 'nationalist sentiment and the still-independent nature of diverse game-making studios in India results in increasing numbers of Indian gamers, and speaks to Indian ethnic, religious and cultural tensions' and the observations made in this and earlier chapters reveal this as well. All of the survey responses are listed at the end of the chapter.

Videogames as Represented in Other Local Media

Long before films such as *Ready Player One* (2018)and somewhat in the tradition of other films based on playing videogames such as David Cronenberg's *Existenz* (Cronenberg 1999) or such films as the supernatural slasher *Stay Alive!* (2006), in 2011 the Hindi Bollywood blockbuster *Ra.One* (2011) starring Shah Rukh Khan was about a videogame character coming alive and trying to kill the game-designer's son. The film was a success and received national awards, including a Filmfare award although some reviewers were critical of Khan's attempt to reinvent himself in a superhero's role. The film's connection with Hindu mythology was commented on; Ra.One is a pun on Ravan, the demon-king of the epic *Ramayana* and G-One is a pun on the word *jivan* or life. Despite the comments on the technical prowess of the film, the reviews, in general, did not comment on the immersiveness of the videogame medium (although the game depicted a motion sensor-based system such as the current VR-enabled technologies) and issues such as reloads and multiple endings that could be there in videogames. The makers of the film did not consider such aspects of videogames in the storyline of *Ra.One* but initially there were plans to include more interactivity in the film: 'The challenge with *Ra.One* is to create a balance between the two distinctly different worlds of gaming and movies. The climax of the film will actually allow audiences to play the *Ra.One* game in theatres as they watch the film.' Barring the 3D version of the film no interactivity was added to the film although an eponymous videogame, which has been discussed in Chapter 3 was released simultaneously. Not much research has been done on the gaming aspects of *Ra.One* and the attempted meld of videogames with Bollywood needs more attention. Television also made a brief foray into the world of videogames through the live TV show *Games Bond*

(2005), aired in 2005. According to report on rediff.com, the series consisted of a live gaming session of *Counter Strike* (Valve Software 2000) and the aim was to bring gaming culture to prominence:

> Currently on air on Star One, *Games Bond* is based on a popular virtual game *Counter Strike* 1.6. and is hosted by model, actor Rahul Dev. 'The idea is to popularise the idea of gaming which is still nascent in India,' say Kanwaldeep Kalsi and Ankush Patel (CEO), co-founders of Kalkush & Company, that makes the show. (Krishnakumar 2005)

While the show had limited success. It was in a sense doing what recent streamers have been doing on platforms such as Twitch and YouTube. The involvement of actors such as Shah Rukh Khan (*Ra.One*), Akshay Kumar (*Fau-G*) and Rahul Dev (*Games Bond*) shows the overlaps between the media but the representation of videogames has never been consistent in the other aspects of Indian culture.

In fact, there are few literary references to videogames in the literature of the Subcontinent. Savithri Rajeevan, a leading Malayalam writer, has written a poem titled 'Video Game'. To quote a section of Rajeevan's (2003) poem:

> Revolver...no not the Uzi...
> Yes, the shotgun. One, two, three, four
> bound still by tape unarmed,
> innocently they approach me again. Deceased, yet so full of life.
> What to use now, to kill the dead? Or
> where is the remote button?
> Who will press it?

Rajeevan's poem is replete with images of violence and it is a difficult poem to understand and explain. She does, however, seem to point towards the reiterative nature of violence and the grim gameplay of dealing death to hordes of undead foes. The poem, however, presents a very cliched image of videogames and one wonders whether this is going to remain the persistent image of the medium in Indian culture. The poem has been translated into English by her son Yadu Rajiv, who has now gone on to become an award-winning Indian game designer. This example shows a rather unique connection between game design and literature, one which would be rare to find the world over. In a personal interview, Rajiv (2021) informed me that he and his mother were playing the early *Tomb Raider* games and the poem was inspired by Lara Croft's archaeological excavations and comparatively low-key violence thus giving the poem an added level of complexity.

Local Representations: A Summary of Academic Initiatives

The local reception of videogames in the Indian Subcontinent, today, marks an important departure in the ways in which culture and technology have been thought of in the region. The engagement with games after their rather late introduction to India has been documented albeit haphazardly. The rest of the Subcontinent is even less researched and it is only now that research articles are being published on Pakistan, Nepal, Bangladesh and Sri Lanka. Umer Hussain's article (Hussain et al. 2021) in *Games and Culture* on Pakistani women eSports participants was published as recently as March 2021; Gregory Grieve's short article published in *Gamevironments* in 2018 and my own article on *Far Cry 4* and Nepali history published in *Games and Culture* in 2021 are the few examples of publications on the countries other than India in the Subcontinent but at least this is an important beginning. Indian scholars have been active in writing about videogames in both academic and non-academic forums. There is now a chapter of the Digital Games Research Association (DiGRA) in India, which was launched at the time of writing this book.

Conclusion

One can only hope that such research initiatives shall spread all across the Subcontinent and South Asia at large. More work also needs to be done on the public gaming spaces such as gaming parlours or cybercafes and retail units that sell games in the Subcontinent as well as on the mobile gaming cultures. Similarly, the rather limited and often orientalised representation of the Subcontinent in videogames also needs to be rethought and resisted by developers. Instead of assuming a universal player (with European or American cultural backgrounds), videogames that represent the Subcontinent should invest in more research in local cultures and attempt to move away from colonial and orientalist preconceptions. Perhaps in response to the global representations and global interest in the region, local content has seen an upsurge and it will be interesting to see whether there is a continuity in this trend. It will also be important to examine how diverse and inclusive such new cultural developments are.

6

Absent Discourses in Game Cultures: The Case for Diversity

There are many gaps in what videogame cultures in the Subcontinent represent. The gender bias among gamers and developers is still huge as are other aspects that need a nuanced discussion of inclusiveness and diversity. A divide exists between a 'gamer' and 'non-gamer', where the latter are either excluded from discussions relating to videogames or choose to remain willfully ignorant regarding the appeal and the importance of videogames as a sociocultural phenomenon that is complex and cannot be judged by stereotypes. Similarly, economic disparity and the digital divide are problems that have been at the forefront of discussions recently. Caste-related and religion-related issues have been of extreme importance in the digital context although not much has been said in the context of videogames. Also, language is yet another major factor in defining how games are to be received in local communities. Last but not the least, the lack of access for gamers with disabilities remains a major cause for concern. The lack of representation and inclusivity in videogames in the Subcontinent is a veritable elephant in the room; scholars such as Padmini Ray Murray have been vocal about such disparities in the Indian context and recently Umer Hussain has written on the Pakistani gaming scenario but discussions on these topics are still few and far between. In this chapter, while the issues of disparity will be pointed at, it will be difficult to outline the scenario with any amount of accuracy as there is an acute lack of data and much more research needs to be put in by both the industry and academia before anything remotely resembling the situation can be described. It is, nevertheless, important to at least initiate the discussion and to connect it with the global discourses on inclusiveness and diversity in videogames.

The Digital 'Game' Divide: Economic and Linguistic Disparities and Videogames

As the second wave of the Covid-19 pandemic raged in India, the vaccination process came under scrutiny because many people were unable to access the digital application that was being used for registration. The Hon'ble Supreme Court of India instructed the government that:

> A vaccination policy exclusively relying on a digital portal for vaccinating a significant population of this country between the ages of 18–44 would be unable to meet its target of universal immunisation owing to such a digital divide. It is the marginalised sections of the society who would bear the brunt of this accessibility barrier. (The Hindu 2021)

The court order cited a 2018 National Statistics Office survey that mentions that 4% of rural households and 23% of urban Indian households possess a computer. While the figures may have improved, they cannot have improved so substantially to cover the entire population. The wireless teledensity in rural India is 59.3% as compared to 135% in urban areas according to the Telecom Regulatory Authority of India (2021). The court also noted that the app had accessibility issues and that visually challenged people could not use it. The digital divide has come to the forefront in education, Covid-19 vaccination and governance. Some of the key problems that have been raised have been those of access, whether it is of the devices and the media, the language, or physical abilities to access these sources of information. In the light of these discussions, perhaps it is necessary to also look at how inclusive videogames are in the Subcontinent.

An earlier chapter has already quoted Shailesh Prabhu's essay 'Breaking Down the Billion' (Prabhu 2016) where he points at the vast number of people below the poverty line in India and the consequent disparity in the population that can access videogame consoles, computers or even smartphones. Of course, as Prabhash Tripathy (2017) maintains, in the gaming parlours in Delhi, the situation was different and even those not economically well-off would participate in gaming bouts but this would still be an exception rather than the rule. Of course, such egalitarian gaming spaces are now gone as Gagun Chhina's (2016) dissertation makes us aware. Riko Banerjee's (*What is it like to be a Gamer or pursue Game Studies in India? - Riko Banerjee* 2020) talk, cited earlier, mentions a valid point: the price of a PlayStation 5 console or a medium-range gaming computer exceeds more than double the month's income of the majority of Indians. The same would apply to many countries in the Subcontinent and although there is a significant increase in the number of smartphones and access to high-speed Internet across the region; the disparity in access still remains a major issue. As far as physical accessibility is concerned, games created in the region have not taken into account the visually challenged and colour blind, such as the ones made abroad such as *Lost and Hound* (Daisy Ale Soundworks 2020) or *A Blind Legend* (Dowino 2015).

Language is yet another major reason for the disparity in access. Most videogames are not localised into Indian languages and English is assumed as the lingua franca in the region; however, people who do not read English may struggle to play many of the videogames. *PUBG* (PUBG Corporation 2017) and *Freefire* (Garena 2017), however, have a mass appeal despite their use of an English interface. Some Indian games such as *Missing* (Chakraborty 2016) have a local language version and attempt game localisation. *Missing* has a Bangla/Bengali version that was popular in India and in Bangladesh, which is predominantly Bangla-speaking. *Raji* recently received a Hindi voiceover in March 2021. According to designer Avichal Singh:

> 'Hindi voiceover has been a big ask since launch and leading upto launch,' he says. 'A lot of people have been asking why this isn't in Hindi. We had to explain that it takes months because there's a lot of audio in the game. For a team of our size, I think it took us eight to nine months to get the English audio to the quality it is. Now we are going to put Hindi voiceover.' (Alwani 2021)

This was presumably in response to the widespread criticism that the game was not accessible to Indians, as has already been mentioned already in Chapter 4.

The makers of the game have now addressed this issue and the localisation is set to happen. Localisation, however, is not an easy task and as Marcus Toftedahl states, linguistic, cultural context and technical issues are all at play. Of course, the first and second of these two combined in *Far Cry 4*'s use of Hindi instead of Nepali for a game that was to all purposes set in Nepal. A Change.org petition that said 'this petition is a fight against [sic] an identity of Nepalese people. Since this game shows us and our terrain, they must show actual fact about the place as well. Let's shake our hands and take some necessary action before it gets released in the global market. Once it is released we can't do anything. I believe this Game format should be in English or Nepali' (Thapa 2014) was signed by 3,260 supporters.

The Digital 'Game' Divide: Gender

While economic disparity and language have received some attention, there is little mention of gender as a major area of discrimination. Unlike in the Global North, the industry in India has not known a phenomenon such as Gamergate but whether there is no gender disparity is a moot question. In an interview, Moumita Paul, who was then employed as a game designer for Disney, was 'disappointed with the targeting of women in #Gamergate' and stated that she had 'seen many developers being insulted in popular gaming forums in Facebook, where they have faced "harmless" or "friendly" jokes targeted at women' (Mukherjee 2014). Others, such as Mohini Dutta, who is based in the USA and India, have had a similar response to #Gamergate. That the digital divide is deeply gendered is a commonly known fact. A report cited by the Deutsche Welle website (2020) states:

> 'As much as we may like to believe that India is sprinting alongside the world digitally, we cannot forget the huge mass of people who have yet to witness the dawn of computers. It is a reflection on rural India,' Mamta Kumari, a health activist from Bihar, told DW. Overall, the NFHS showed that only 42% of Indian women surveyed have ever used the internet, compared with 62% of men.

While the rural–urban digital divide is a serious one, when one considers the number of women accessing the Internet, the divide is more acute. Another report states that:

> More worryingly, the gap between men and women when it comes to mobile internet users is one of the highest amongst low and middle-income countries—50%. Most women (especially in rural settings) have shared phones or one phone in the family. [or] hand me down phones which are broken or malfunctioning. 31% women in India possess brick or basic phones which do not have internet access. (Jairath 2021)

When the general ratio of men and women with smartphones and mobile Internet is so skewed, it is evident that the same gap is also applicable to women playing videogames.

In fact, when one compares the number of women who play videogames on either their mobile phones or PCs and consoles, the numbers are likely to be far fewer. It must be mentioned here that surveys on videogames in the Subcontinent have not taken into account the digital divide based on gender. In the survey conducted across the Subcontinent for this book, only 19% of the respondents were women. More robust and extensive surveys are, however, needed. Umer Hussain et al. (2021) have completed a pathbreaking study in Pakistan on the eSports participation of Muslim women in Gilgit-Baltistan. In this article, the authors note that 'there is a dearth of scholarship to understand forces that shape marginalized Muslim women's experiences from Pakistan in e-sports [and] explore various sociological forces that shape Muslim women from Gilgit-Baltistan's (Pakistan) experiences while participating in e-sports' (2021). The study participants revealed that they faced systematic marginalisation and eSports had become a means for them to resist patriarchy. There are, of course, many important names in Indian eSports, such as Zerah Gonsalves, Shagufta Iqbal, Ibadoor K. Lynser and Saloni Pawar. Many of them are also live streamers and commentators. Bhutan's Pinda Rika Dorji has already been mentioned in this connection. The Bangladesh Esports Association (BESA) organised its first women's Dota 2 tournament in June 2019. Nevertheless, women gamers complain that there is a lack of support and career options for gamers in general but that 'women are stereotyped as non-gamers and when they do play games, people think it is for attention [and] women live-streamers often get harassed or bullied. Also, many women gamers still shy away from coming to the forefront' (Ahaskar 2019). Caroline D'Cruz (2019) writes about her experience of playing *PUBG*:

> Another experience I am subjected to while gaming (especially when playing PUBG) that when men find out I am a woman and then pester me to share my number or to talk to them. They find it extremely hilarious to call a woman a 'bitch' or 'whore' if I choose to ignore their advances. To put this in context, it's like receiving persistent texts from that one creepy dude in your 'others' inbox or on a dating app.

The verbal abuse and the gender-based harassment are something that designers such as Paul had commented on; the same issues are faced by players. Often there is a claim to create a level playing field and comparisons are made with countries such as South Korea where professional gaming attracts many more women. In fact, Samrat Dasgupta, writing in the computer magazine *Dataquest*, makes a similar note:

> We can take inspiration from South East Asia where women game developers are continuing to enhance existing games and create new formats with art styles and graphics that offer exclusive experiences to female gamers. Women gamers in South East Asia have become particularly drawn to MMORPGs (Massively Multiplayer Online Role-Playing Games), FPS (First Person Shooter) games and MOBA (Multiplayer Online Battle Arena) games, according to a recent study by Google and Niko Partners. (2021)

While the intention, here, seems laudable, Dasgupta is nevertheless perpetuating (albeit unconsciously) a gender bias where new formats are recommended exclusively for women gamers. When even well-intentioned commentaries often slide into a patronising tone or end up upholding the gender divide, the direness of the scenario is well evident.

So far, the opinions voiced by game developers and players have been considered. At this point, the content of games also needs to be discussed. The female protagonist of Raji has been praised by critics and as Rajvi Desai states, the videogame starring a teen girl 'defies industry stereotypes' (2019). According to her, the designers were able to effect such a change because of a more inclusive audience:

> The designers didn't set out to create Raji as a girl—it's not a mere gesture to appease any equality rhetoric, said Avichal Singh, one of Raji's game designers. People relate to the struggles of the protagonist, which was the focus of the storyline, he said. One of the reasons they could do that, according to Singh, is because the audience for video games has matured and diversified in recent times. (2019)

As Desai claims, in games such as *Raji*, a conscious effort has been made to challenge patriarchy and the toxicity around gender bias. Desai (2019) reports:

> It's not a mere gesture to appease any equality rhetoric, said Avichal Singh, one of *Raji*'s game designers. People relate to the struggles of the protagonist, which was the focus of the storyline, he said. One of the reasons they could do that, according to Singh, is because the audience for video games has matured and diversified in recent times, which has normalized creating games that represent non-traditional protagonists and environments.

While Desai and the makers of *Raji* are perhaps right to be hopeful, the story is not the same for many games that are developed in India. Dibyadyuti Roy and Aditya Deshbandhu's (Roy and Deshbandhu 2021) study of the games marketed by Zapak, which was referred to in Chapter 3, addresses how the gender divide is enforced by games that are made on the assumptions that women employees are lazy or that they are more concerned with dressing-up. Similarly, objectification of women, whether as a result of postcolonial masculinist anxieties (as Roy and Deshbandhu contend) or in other contexts, is also something that is evinced in the games that they describe. Of course, there are also games such as *Missing-Game for a Cause* and *(Un)Trafficked* that directly address child trafficking and prostitution, thus highlighting key problems that women face in parts of the Subcontinent.

In the earlier quotation, Dasgupta lauds women game developers in South East Asia and uses them exemplars; however, as far as design is concerned, there are some key names in the Subcontinent as well, both in game design and research. Two names that come to mind are Poornima Seetharaman, the only Indian to make it to the Women in Games Hall of Fame, and Sadia Bashir from Pakistan who has been recognised by the US Embassy at the Women Entrepreneurs Summit in 2016 for her accomplishments. Seetharaman is a lead designer at Zynga, India, and Bashir is the founder of the Pixel Arts Academy. While there are emerging success stories, Seetharaman cautions regarding gender bias in the industry. She points out that often working conditions are skewed in favour of men and often women are denied the due credit that they deserve. She says that:

> Of course, we have faced gender inequalities. For the women attendees in the audiences who are new in the industry or are even gamers, if they do not hear about our experiences, they may wonder if they are the ones doing something wrong; I don't want that. (Bhavani 2021)

She also talks about how most of the female voices are white and how important it is for BIPOC women voices to be heard in the industry. As already mentioned, games research has also seen important interventions, both local and global, from researchers such as Padmini Ray Murray from India and Amani Naseem for the Maldives, both of whose research has been discussed in the earlier chapters. Although not based in India, Meghna or 'Meg' Jayanth, who is one of the world's foremost game writers, having worked on games such as *80 Days* and *Sunless Seas* also has her roots in India just as Mitu Khandakar, the co-founder of Glow-Light Games and a professor at New York University's game centre, originally hails from Bangladesh.

The Digital 'Game' Divide: Race, Caste and Subalternity in the Ludic Cyberspace

Of course, the question of racial discrimination is extremely relevant for all genders. In India (and to an extent in Nepal and Bangladesh), one also needs to address discrimination on the basis of caste. In videogames, whether in terms of play culture or development, casteism is not yet being addressed in discussions. In the software industry and, in general, on social media, questions of caste-based discrimination find increasing relevance. A recent report in *The Washington Post* states:

> The legacy of discrimination from the Indian caste system is rarely discussed as a factor in Silicon Valley's persistent diversity problems. […] Dalit engineers and advocates say that tech companies don't understand caste bias and have not explicitly prohibited caste-based discrimination. A subaltern cyberspace with interesting and important consequences not only for the Dalits—the 'untouchable' castes of India—but for political culture in the age of digital media. (2020)

The term 'Dalit' means 'oppressed', 'broken' or 'crushed' (Dalits 2015) and has now come to symbolise a movement for change and for the eradication of the centuries-old oppression under the caste system. As Pramod Nayar writes, 'emergence of a subaltern cyberspace with interesting and important consequences not only for the Dalits—the "untouchable" castes of India—but for political culture in the age of digital media' (2014). Nayar speaks of the lack of access due to which 'the digital divide as far as Dalits are concerned, we can assume, remains unbridged' (2014). There are Dalit websites, such as Round Table India, Dalit and Adivasi Students' Portal, Ambedkar.org, and Savari as well as the YouTube channel Dalit Camera, that construct the public sphere for the Dalit communities and, of course, numerous Facebook groups, Twitter handles and other social media. Nayar views these efforts as means of presenting an alternative history of India where Dalit communities from all over the world might be able to meet. Nayar states the global nature of the digital presence of Dalits via 'these communities of interest, or "webs of affinity", as Lisa Nakamura terms them—initially dealing with India, Nepal and Bangladesh, now incorporate into their vision fields and fields of action, issues normally ignored by Dalits in India' (2014). It is intriguing that Nayar invokes Nakamura (Nakamura 2013) whose 'cybertypes' theory is a key entry point into discussions of racism in videogames. So far, however, there has been no study of Dalit communities playing videogames and being part of the industry in the Subcontinent. As far as traditional sports are concerned, casteism is rife even today as is in evidence from the *New Indian Express's* report that states 'two upper caste men in Haridwar stood outside [hockey] star striker Vandana Katariya's home at Roshnabad village and started hurling casteist abuses' (The New Indian Express 2021), and blaming India's hockey defeat in the Tokyo Olympic semi-finals on the Dalit players in the team. Incidentally, Katariya became the only Indian woman to score a hat-trick in the Olympics. What implications caste can have for videogame cultures is as yet unknown and is a key area of potential research, especially when compared to scholarly work that has been done on racism and other challenges to diversity and inclusiveness in videogames globally by scholars such Nakamura, David Leonard, Kishonna L. Gray (Gray and Leonard 2018) and Adrienne Shaw (2013). In response to similar questions, the role of the subaltern in cyberculture has been addressed in Radhika Gajjala's seminal work *Cyberculture and the Subaltern* (2012), where she addresses 'how voice and silence shape online space in relation to offline actualities [and] how offline actualities and online cultures are in turn shaped by online hierarchies as well as different kinds of local access to global contexts', thereby pointing out how the online space results in the erasure and the silencing of certain communities and the subsequent rendering of them as 'subaltern'. Padmini Ray Murray's *Darshan Diversion* has already been mentioned in connection to the intervention that it makes to assert gender rights, but Ray Murray also addresses issues of caste-based discrimination through her research. Whether videogames too can become a space for such inclusive thinking is something to consider. Just as the graphic novel medium, such as in *Bhimayana* (Natarajan 2011a) and *A Gardener in the Wasteland* (Natarajan 2011b), has been chosen to represent the Dalit perspective, videogames could perhaps emerge as a medium to represent the concerns of Dalit communities and other minority groups.

Concluding Remarks

While the Subcontinent has neither seen an overtly vast gender divide and discrimination as was seen in the Gamergate controversy in the United States, nor such movements corresponding to the Black Lives Matter in gaming culture (for example, when in response to the widespread BLM movement, the indie game website itch.io released a BLM bundle), it is still to witness issues of digital divide based on gender, class, caste, economic prosperity and religion. This chapter merely grazes the surface of the issues involved and that too more in terms of the Indian context, as the availability of data from the rest of the Subcontinent regarding these issues is scant. In fact, there is not much to go on regarding the situation in India either—mainly due to the lack of adequate research. Nevertheless, judging from the Indian context, it serves as a necessary prelude and reminder that much more detailed research on the disparity in videogame cultures and the industry is needed. Before concluding this overview of the Subcontinent's ludic investment in digital games, it is important to highlight the need for a diverse and inclusive gaming culture and industry.

7

What Wakens the Sleeping Giant?

The Subcontinent itself, as has been noted in various chapters earlier, is very culturally diverse and this diversity is reflected in its gaming cultures as well. At the same time, videogames are relatively new as an entertainment medium and are now poised to come of age, speaking from multiple perspectives. The novelty of the medium leaves much that is yet to be understood and communicated by the different stakeholders, whether local or global. In an article published before the *PUBG* ban in India, a commentator wrote:

> There's no denying that PUBG Mobile took India by storm, thriving like no other in the Indian Subcontinent. [...] The game now has more than 600 million downloads in 2020, with that number continually on the rise due to the "stay at home culture" that has recently become a somewhat perplexing part of our daily lives. Anyone can play, all you need is a touch screen phone. (Bhostekar 2020)

While the game has been banned in many parts of the Subcontinent, it has also returned in new versions and also brought more multiplayer gaming in its wake. With online games stores such as Steam's local pricing and the increased access to high-speed broadband that brings PC game downloads within reach, there is a shift from piracy to legitimate game downloads. All of this means that the Subcontinent can potentially become a more viable source of revenue for the global videogame industry, a fact that governments too are aware of when they suddenly speak of promoting the local toy and games industry. Among local policymakers, videogames are still an enigma. There are concerns regarding how videogames promote violence but without any proven systematic academic research to back these concerns up—often draconian laws and bans are put in place. The jury is literally out on these games even as the judiciary of Pakistan, Nepal, India and

Bangladesh have all been called upon to adjudicate whether to ban some of these games or even to judge the nature of a game (whether it is a game of skill or one that promotes gambling). At the time of writing this, *PUBG*, which was banned in India on the grounds of cybersecurity issues, has been brought back by a different company as *Battlegrounds India*. At the same time, there has also been a comparative growth in the number of local games made in the Subcontinent and many of these fall back on local mythology and history. With the fast growth of mobile Internet and the increase in the number of smartphones, mobile gaming continues to show more potential whereas the newer consoles and dedicated VR devices (such as the Oculus Rift and the HTC Vibe) are still comparatively prohibitively priced for the gamers in the regions. For many casual and most hardcore gamers, PC gaming is the popular way to go. As far as global games are concerned, the Subcontinent has featured in many blockbuster triple-A videogames and such portrayals have also given rise to scholarship that has brought them under critical scrutiny. Academic scholarship on game cultures in the Subcontinent per se is still wanting but there is increased research activity with many younger scholars writing doctoral theses on the subject in their own countries or while studying abroad.

One reason for this summary is to point out how vibrant the videogame cultures of the region are becoming and to also note the disjunct between such vibrancy and the traditional modes of entertainment and sport as well as the digital divide between those who play videogames and those who do not. The other reason is to show the huge potential, both cultural and economic, in global as well as local terms, of bridging such a divide. Thirdly, the aim is to establish points of dialogue between the global industry and gaming cultures with those in the Subcontinent in ways that will be inclusive and diverse. Not to pontificate but to suggest a few timely interventions, this book attempts to provide an overview, albeit limited, of the region rather than a single country, which could benefit both local and global stakeholders. So far, most of the publications on the subject gravitate towards India and ignore its neighbours despite the large gaming populations and diverse gaming cultures. Some countries, in particular, get ignored altogether. In fact, a recent list of a hundred South Asians important in the world of gaming mentions personalities from India, Pakistan, Bangladesh and Sri Lanka but misses out Nepal, Bhutan and the Maldives entirely (SAHM 2021).

The larger overview enables a comparative look at the common and also the differences elements in gaming cultures that the region shares. While exploring points of convergence in gaming cultures, it would be very helpful to create regional bodies that could assist both game developers and researchers. Together with such endeavours, another major area in which those working in the industry and research should consider focusing their attention to is establishing a dialogue between governments and experts on gaming, whereby key questions regarding security-related issues and behavioural issues like violence in videogames are addressed and clarified; moreover, such forums could also advise governments regarding the support that can be provided for the games industry. Similarly, such discussions should also cover the setting up of educational institutions that can train future game developers as well as courses on games research in existing higher education institutions. Such examples abound in the countries of the Global North and could be used as models in the region. There is also a rich repository of local content such as historical narrative and mythology as has often been tapped into by both mainstream and indie developers. The indie scene in the region is picking up and support, both financial and logistical, for such entrepreneurship will be more than welcome. As explained in the introduction and subsequently, the gaming culture in the region is a product of transculturation and glocalisation, where often Western cultural elements are quite predominant. The game industry is different from other entertainment industries in this regard as it had a comparative later start and its initial content was mainly borrowed from the West; however, the games industry and gaming cultures in the different countries of the region need to speak to the film industry and other entertainment media. Such attempts have been made in Bollywood but have not been very successful but more and better-coordinated efforts are needed.

As triple-A games in development such as *Threta* show the potential of achieving huge popularity, as the recent success of *Raji* has proven, the Subcontinent needs its own blockbuster titles. Perhaps, while mods such as *Grand Theft Auto: Punjab* and video spin-offs such as Taha Ismail's *Grand Theft Auto: Dhaka City Stories* (2016) are important to the subcultures around gaming, what the region needs are triple-A franchises of its own, based on glocalised models and with transmedial texts, such as with the Pokemon videogames and cartoon films, which have contributed to the popularity of Japanese videogame franchise across the world. As eSports are getting recognised by governments officially and as nations have started taking more interest in improving local games technologies, the Subcontinent has a chance of making a mark in the global gaming scenario. Very importantly, the potential of the region as a market—the drop in *PUBG* market value was 14 billion USD and its share prices fell by 2% after it was banned in India (India. com Business Desk 2020)—is becoming more obvious. Game designer Ernest Adams had once identified India as a 'sleeping giant' considering its potential in the gaming industry and culture; how far this is true is a moot question at the moment but it is a comment that may apply not just to India but to the entire Subcontinent in time as it gives new meanings to gaming culture(s) and game development.

Bibliography

1Up Gaming. *Gamer Girls of India*. N.p., 2019. Film.

———. *Indian Heroes of PUBG*. N.p., 2019. Film.

24 News HD. *Lahore, Gambling Started under the Cover of Games*. N.p., 2016. Film.

Adams, Ernest. 'The Promise of India: Ancient Culture, Modern Game Design.' *The Designer's Notebook*, 2009. https://www.designersnotebook.com/Lectures/India/india.htm/.

Agarwal, Priyangi. '"Is It Ok to Play Videogames While We're Observing Roza?"' *The Times of India*, 21 June 2013. https://timesofindia.indiatimes.com/city/lucknow/is-it-ok-to-play-videogames-while-were-observing-roza/articleshow/21203213.cms/.

Ahaskar, Abhijit. 'Outsourcing of Game Development Work to India Gains Traction.' *mint*, 5 August 2020. https://www.livemint.com/technology/tech-news/outsourcing-of-game-development-work-to-india-gains-traction-11596591463870.html/.

———. 'Women Advance through the Ranks in India's Gaming Arena.' *mint*, 16 May 2019. https://www.livemint.com/technology/tech-news/women-advance-through-the-ranks-in-india-s-gaming-arena-1558022093740.html/.

Ahmed, Ather. '13 Video Games That Will Definitely Keep You from Whining About Your Roza.' *MangoBaaz*, 10 June 2017. https://www.mangobaaz.com/video-games-for-ramazan/.

Ainsworth, Jeremy. 'Sri Lanka Recognises Esports as an Official Sport.' *Esports Insider*, 8 October 2019. https://esportsinsider.com/2019/10/sri-lanka-recognises-esports/.

Ali, Ishaq. 'Retro Love: A Trip Down Memory Lane with Cadillacs And Dinosaurs.' *iXie Gaming*, 17 February 2020. https://www.ixiegaming.com/blog/retro-love-a-trip-down-memory-lane-with-cadillacs-and-dinosaurs/.

Alwani, Rishi. 'Indian Gambling Companies Want to Be Categorised as Esports and Gaming.' *IGN India*, 9 February 2021. https://in.ign.com/india/154842/news/indian-gambling-companies-want-to-be-categorised-as-esports-and-gaming/.

———. 'Meet Ogre Head, the Indian Studio behind Asura, One of the Cooler Indie Games Coming out This Year.' *Tech in Asia*, 24 September 2014.

https://www.techinasia.com/meet-ogrehead-the-indian-studio-behind-asura-one-of-the-cooler-indie-games-coming-out-this-year/.

——. 'Nintendo Switch Sales Dominate Internationally, Get Dominated in India—The Mako Reactor.' *The Mako Reactor*, 6 August 2020. https://themakoreactor.com/features/nintendo-switch-sales-india-figures-2020/15695/.

——. 'Raji: An Ancient Epic Hindi Voiceovers Announced, GOG Version Released.' *IGN India*, 25 March 2021. https://in.ign.com/raji-an-ancient-epic/156653/news/raji-an-ancient-epic-hindi-release-date-gog-pc/.

———. 'The Death of Trine: A Cautionary Tale about Game Development in India.' *Tech in Asia*, 29 July 2014. https://www.techinasia.com/the-death-of-trine-a-cautionary-tale-about-game-development-in-india/.

——. 'Yoddha: How Kargil and Bollywood Inspired India's First PC Game.' *NDTV Gadgets 360*, 5 August 2016. https://gadgets.ndtv.com/games/features/yoddha-the-warrior-how-kargil-and-bollywood-inspired-indias-first-pc-game-868980/.

American Psychological Association. 'APA Reaffirms Position on Violent Video Games and Violent Behavior.' 3 March 2020. Accessed 2 September 2021, https://www.apa.org/news/press/releases/2020/03/violent-video-games-behavior/.

Andrado, Mahesh. 'Beyond Gaming: The History of GamerLK.' *ReadMe*, 21 February 2018. https://www.readme.lk/gamerlk-story/.

'Antariksha Sanchar: Transmissions in Space.' n.d. Accessed 30 August 2021, https://sketchfab.com/models/a01cd8c5f85b4b73bd0ebcb2143202fa/embed/.

Arimac. 'Kanchayudha — A Case Study.' 15 July 2017. Accessed 31 August 2021, https://medium.com/teamarimac/kanchayudha-a-case-study-5957fcd18448/.

Arora, Akhil. 'Raji: An Ancient Epic Review: A Feminist Fable and a Commendable Debut.' *NDTV Gadgets 360*. 28 August 2020. https://gadgets.ndtv.com/games/reviews/raji-an-ancient-epic-review-nintendo-switch-2286347/.

Baidar, Aishwarya. 'Meet Muni Bahadur Shakya, a Pioneering Nepali Computer Scientist: The Record.' *The Record*. 24 August 2021. https://www.recordnepal.com/meet-muni-bahadur-shakya-a-pioneering-nepali-computer-scientist.

Bandyopadhyay, Kausik. *Mahatma on the Pitch: Gandhi and Cricket in India*. New Delhi: Rupa Publications India, 2017.

Bandyopadhyay, Kausik and Boria Majumdar. *A Social History of Indian Football: Striving to Score*. London and New York: Routledge, 2018.

Bandyopadhyay, Sibaji. 'Sibaji Bandyopadhyay of Gambling: A Few Lessons from the Mahābhārata.' *Mahabharata Now*. Edited by Arindam Chakrabarti and Sibaji Bandyopadhyay. Routledge India, 2014.

Banerjee, Utpal K. *Computer Education in India: Past, Present and Future*. New Delhi: Concept Publishing Co, 1996.

Bastin, Rohan. 'Ritual Games for the Goddess Pattini.' *Social Analysis: The International Journal of Social and Cultural Practice* 45, 2 (2001): 120–142.

Bell, William Brent. *Stay Alive*. Hollywood Pictures, Spyglass Entertainment, Endgame Entertainment, 2006. Film.

Bhavani, Divya Kala. 'We Need More Female Leaders in Gaming, Says Indian Game Designer Poornima Seetharaman.' *The Hindu* 8 March 2021. https://www.thehindu.com/life-and-style/poornima-seetharaman-interview-video-games-gender-equality-india/article34017986.ece.

Bhostekar, Sushant. 'PUBG Mobile: More Than Just a Game in India.' *Medium* 21 July 2020. https://esposocial.medium.com/pubg-mobile-more-than-just-a-game-in-india-ba75ed5642dc.

Bolter, Jay David and Richard Grusin. *Remediation: Understanding New Media*. Reprint edition. Cambridge, Mass.: MIT Press, 2000.

Bose, Mihir. *The Magic of Indian Cricket: Cricket and Society in India*. London and New York: Routledge, 2006.

Britt, Aaron. 'Avatar.' *The New York Times* 8 August 2008. *NYTimes.com*. Web. 5 Sept. 2021. https://www.nytimes.com/2008/08/10/magazine/10wwln-guest-t.html.

Cameron, James. *Avatar*. Twentieth Century Fox, Dune Entertainment, Lightstorm Entertainment, 2009. Film.

Cavalli, Earnest. '"Cultural Sensitivities" Bar Fallout 3 from India.' *Wired*. 22 October 2008. https://www.wired.com/2008/10/cultural-sensit/.

Chakrabarti, Arindam. *Deho Geho Bondhutwo: Chhoti Sharirok Tarko*. Kalakātā: Anustup, 2008.

Chakraborti, Siddhartha. 'From Destination to Nation and Back: The Hyperreal Journey of Incredible India.' *Journal of Gaming & Virtual Worlds* 7, 2 (2015): 183–202.

Chen, Chi-Ying. 'Is the Video Game a Cultural Vehicle?' *Games and Culture* 8, 6 (2013): 408–427. *SAGE Journals*. Web.

Chhina, G.S. 'Video Gaming Parlours: The Emerging Field of Video Gaming in India.' PhD Thesis, University of Manchester, 2016. https://www.research.manchester.ac.uk/portal/files/54584781/FULL_TEXT.PDF.

Chowdhury, Srimoyee. 'Ludo, a Game of Chance or Skill, Bombay HC to Decide. Memes Flood Twitter.' *Hindustan Times*, 6 September 2021.

https://www.hindustantimes.com/trending/ludo-a-game-of-chance-or-skill-bombay-hc-to-decide-memes-flood-twitter-101623053715986.html.

'Colombo Ride Mobile Game Goes 3D.' *The Sunday Times*, 27 August 2021. https://www.sundaytimes.lk/100509/Magazine/sundaytimesmirror_05.html.

Consalvo, Mia. *Atari to Zelda: Japan's Videogames in Global Contexts*. Illustrated edition. Cambridge, MA: The MIT Press, 2016.

———. 'There Is No Magic Circle.' *Games and Culture* 4, 4 (2009): 408–417. *SAGE Journals*. Web.

———. 'Visiting the Floating World: Tracing a Cultural History of Games Through Japan and America.' *DiGRA '07 - Proceedings of the 2007 DiGRA International Conference: Situated Play*. Tokyo: N.p., 2007.

Cronenberg, David. *EXistenZ*. Dimension Films, Alliance Atlantis Communications, Canadian Television Fund, 1999. Film.

'Dalits.' *Minority Rights Group*. 8 September 2021. https://minorityrights.org/minorities/dalits/.

Dasgupta, Samrat. 'Women Become the Key Drivers of Online Gaming in India.' *Dataquest*, 8 September 2021. https://www.dqindia.com/women-become-the-key-drivers-of-online-gaming-in-india/.

Dawes, Liam. 'Forgotten Fields Is a New Narrative Adventure from the Dev of Rainswept.' *GamingOnLinux*, 30 August 2021. https://www.gamingonlinux.com/2020/06/forgotten-fields-is-a-new-narrative-adventure-from-the-dev-of-rainswept.

D'Cruz, Caroline. "'m A Female Gamer in India & Deal with Worse Men Than Those on Dating Sites." *iDiva*, 26 November 2019. https://www.idiva.com/news-opinion/womens-issues/female-gamers-in-india-deal-with-sexism-while-playing-pubg-and-cod/18004684.

de Wildt, Lars et al. '(Re-)Orienting the Video Game Avatar.' *Games and Culture* 15, 8 (2020): 962–981. *SAGE Journals*. Web.

Desai, Govindbhai H. 'The Coming Census of India.' *Indian Review* October (1910).

Desai, Rajvi. 'Video Game Starring A Teen Girl in Ancient India Defies Industry Stereotypes.' *The Swaddle*, 5 June 2019. https://theswaddle.com/video-game-starring-a-teen-girl-in-ancient-india-defies-industry-stereotypes.

Deshbandhu, Aditya. *Gaming Culture(s) in India: Digital Play in Everyday Life*. 1st edition. London; New York: Routledge India, 2020.

Deutsche Welle. 'India's Digital Divide Grows among Rural Women.' *Deutsche Welle*, 15 December 2020. https://www.dw.com/en/indias-digital-divide-grows-among-rural-women/a-55949074.

Dewan, Kevin. 'Karma Systems in Games - Inviting Choice Rather than Intention. *SQUAD*, 11 March 2020. https://squadstate.com/feature-2/karma-systems-in-games-inviting-choice-rather-than-intention.

DiGRA India. *First Person Encounters #7: Abhi, Creator of Venba*. N.p., 2021. Film.

———. *Games Studies Adda Podcast: Adda on Ludonomics*. N.p., 2021. Film.

———. *What Is It like to Be a Gamer or Pursue Game Studies in India? - Riko Banerjee*. N.p., 2020. Film.

Dikshit, Neeraj. 'Tech Flashback: India's First 3D Game Let Users Become Bhagat Singh and Shoot at Nasty Imperialists.' *Scroll.in*, 24 August 2017. https://scroll.in/magazine/847321/tech-flashback-indias-first-3d-game-let-users-become-bhagat-singh-and-shoot-at-nasty-imperialist.

DiMartino, Michael Dante and Bryan Konietzko. *Avatar: The Last Airbender*. Nickelodeon Animation Studios, 2005. Film.

D.K. Krishna and Raj Nidimoru. 'Family Man 2: Season 2.' *The Family Man*. N.p., 4 June 2021. Television.

Donlan, Christian. 'Raji: An Ancient Epic Review - a Gorgeous Adventure through Architecture and Myth.' *Eurogamer*, 18 August 2020. https://www.eurogamer.net/articles/2020-09-02-raji-an-ancient-epic-review-a-gorgeous-adventure-through-architecture-and-myth.

Dorji, Tshering. 'Online Game Platform for Youth Launched.' *The Bhutanese*, 25 October 2014. https://thebhutanese.bt/online-game-platform-for-youth-launched.

Drishti. 'Poverty Estimation in India.' *Drishti*, 10 October 2019. https://www.drishtiias.com/to-the-points/paper3/poverty-estimation-in-india.

Education Desk. '"Ye PUBG Wala Hey Kya," PM Modi Replies to Online Game Distress Parent | Education News, The Indian Express.' *The Indian Express*, 30 January 2019. https://indianexpress.com/article/education/pariksha-pe-charcha-2-0-iye-pubg-wala-hey-kia-pm-modi-replies-to-online-game-distress-parent-5559786.

Elise Favis. 'Visa Restrictions Prevented Two Pakistani Women from Attending GDC. So They Made a Game about It.' *Washington Post*, 13 February 2020. https://www.washingtonpost.com/video-games/2020/02/13/visa-restrictions-prevented-two-pakistani-women-attending-gdc-so-they-made-game-about-it/.

ET bureau. 'Why Did the Simputer Flop? - The Economic Times.' *The Economic Times*, 23 July 2015. https://economictimes.indiatimes.com/news/science/why-did-the-simputer-flop/articleshow/48180974.cms.

ET Online. 'Games without Frontiers: Indians, Pakistanis Team up for ESports - An Unheard Alliance.' *The Economic Times*, 17 December 2020. https://

economictimes.indiatimes.com/news/politics-and-nation/games-without-frontiers-indians-pakistanis-team-up-for-esports/an-unheard-alliance/slideshow/79773559.cms.

Fickle, Tara. *The Race Card: From Gaming Technologies to Model Minorities: 22.* New York: New York University Press, 2019.

Forbes. 'Sadia Bashir.' *Forbes Lists*, 2018. https://www.forbes.com/profile/sadia-bashir/.

Friedman, Thomas L. *The World Is Flat: A Brief History of the Globalized World in the Twenty-First Century*. London: Allen Lane, 2005.

'From the Vault: The Lost.' *Irrational Games*, 15 November 2011. http://irrationalgames.ghoststorygames.com/insider/from-the-vault-the-lost/.

Gajjala, Radhika, ed. *Cyberculture and the Subaltern: Weavings of the Virtual and Real*. 1st edition. Lanham, Md: Lexington Books, 2012.

'Games for Change.' *Games for Change*. https://www.gamesforchange.org/who-we-are/about-us/.

Ghoshal, Abhimanyu. 'Why Has Nintendo Ignored India for 30 Years?' *Qrius*, 5 January 2018 https://qrius.com/nintendo-ignored-india-30-years/.

Good, Owen. 'India's First Game Gets India's First Game Controversy.' *Kotaku*, 18 April 2009. https://kotaku.com/indias-first-game-gets-indias-first-game-controversy-5217826.

Gowariker, Ashutosh. *Lagaan: Once Upon a Time in India*. N.p., 2002. Film.

Grieve, Gregory Price. 'An Ethnoludography of the Game Design Industry in Kathmandu, Nepal.' *Gamevironments* 8 (2018): 49.

GSM Association. *Country Overview: Pakistan*. GSM Association, 2016.

Guha, Ramachandra. *A Corner of a Foreign Field: The Indian History of a British Sport*. Illustrated edition. London: Picador, 2003.

Gupta, Sahil Mohan. 'What Steve Jobs Did in India 35 Years Ago.' *NDTV Gadgets 360*, 6 June 2012. https://gadgets.ndtv.com/others/news/what-steve-jobs-did-in-india-35-years-ago-225246.

Gutting, Gary. *Talking God: Philosophers on Belief*. 1 edition. New York: W. W. Norton & Company, 2016.

Hanson, Ben. 'How Steve Wozniak's Breakout Defined Apple's Future.' *Game Informer*, 2015. https://www.gameinformer.com/b/features/archive/2015/10/09/how-steve-wozniak-s-breakout-defined-apple-s-future.aspx.

Hashmi, Mobina. 'At the Limits of Discourse: Political Talk in Drag on Late Night Show with Begum Nawazish Ali.' *South Asian History and Culture* 3, 4 (2012): 511–531.

Hern, Alex. 'Playing Video Games Doesn't Lead to Violent Behaviour, Study Shows.' *The Guardian*, 21 July 2020. http://www.theguardian.

com/games/2020/jul/22/playing-video-games-doesnt-lead-to-violent-behaviour-study-shows.

Hilton, James. *Lost Horizon*. Reissue edition. New York London Toronto: Harper Perennial, 2012.

'History.' *Pakistan International Airlines*. https://www.piac.com.pk/corporate/about-us/history.

historyofhowweplay. 'Super Sales Six.' *The History of How We Play*, 4 November 2017. https://thehistoryofhowweplay.wordpress.com/2017/11/04/super-sales-six/.

Howson, Andre. 'A Roundup of Top Game Studios in Sri Lanka.' *roarmedia*. 11 October 2016. https://roar.media/english/tech/insights/a-roundup-of-top-game-studios-in-sri-lanka.

Huizinga, Johan. 'De vidûsaka in het indisch tooneel.' University of Groningen, 1897.

———. *Homo Ludens: A Study of the Play-Element in Culture*. London: Routledge and Kegan Paul, 1949.

HundredProofSam. 'Why the Zeebo Will Fail in India.' *IndianVideoGamer.com*, 31 March 2009. https://www.indianvideogamer.com/forums/index.php?/topic/8711-why-the-zeebo-will-fail-in-india/.

Hussain, Mazin. 'Inside Sri Lanka's Gaming Culture.' *SuperJump*, 13 April 2021. https://superjumpmagazine.com/inside-sri-lankas-gaming-culture-1d15a87bd30d.

Husain, Osman. 'Gaming Startups in Pakistan Grow despite the Lack of a Local Market.' *Tech in Asia*, 16 April 2015. https://www.techinasia.com/gaming-startups-pakistan-grow-lack-local-market.

Hussain, Umer et al. '"I Can Be Who I Am When I Play Tekken 7": E-Sports Women Participants from the Islamic Republic of Pakistan.' *Games and Culture* (2021).

Hutchinson, Pamela. 'The Birth of India's Film Industry: How the Movies Came to Mumbai.' *The Guardian*. 25 July 2013. http://www.theguardian.com/film/2013/jul/25/birth-indias-film-industry-movies-mumbai.

Hutchinson, Rachael. *Japanese Culture Through Videogames*. London: New York: Routledge, 2019. Print.

———. *Japanese Culture Through Videogames*. 1st edition. S.l.: Routledge, 2020.

Hyde, Thomas. *De Ludibus Orientalibus*. Oxford: Sheldonian Theatre, 1694.

IAMAI - nielsen. *Digital in India - 2019 Round 2 Report*. IAMAI - nielsen, 2019.

Ikigai Law. *Unpacking a Billion Dollar Industry: Digital Games and Sports in India*. IAMAI, 2021.https://cms.iamai.in/Content/ResearchPapers/fd643e10-7c1a-469a-a14b-e80d7f06e351.pdf.

India.com Business Desk. 'PUBG Ban Impact: Tencent Loses $14 Billion in Market Value, Its Shares Fall Over 2% After India Bans PUBG | India.Com.' *India.com*, 3 September 2020. https://www.india.com/business/pubg-ban-impact-tencent-loses-14-billion-in-market-value-its-shares-fall-over-2-after-india-bans-pubg-4130206/.

'India's Prime Minister Appeals for Games Based on "Indian Culture and Folk Tales."' *GamesIndustry.biz.* https://www.gamesindustry.biz/articles/2020-08-26-indias-prime-minister-appeals-for-games-based-on-indian-culture-and-folk-tales.

Induruwa, Abhaya. 'Information Technology Development in Sri Lanka - A Review.' *Journal of the National Science Foundation of Sri Lanka* 27 (1999): 209–254. *ResearchGate*. Web.

International Telecommunication Union. *Information and Communication Technology in the Atolls: Maldives Case Study*. 2004. https://www.itu.int/ITU-D/ict/cs/maldives/material/CS_MDV.pdf.

'Is Cricket Killing Other Sports in India?' *Sportstar*, 12 June 2004. https://sportstar.thehindu.com/magazine/is-cricket-killing-other-sports-in-india/article29642925.ece.

———. *Sportstar* 12 May 2021. https://sportstar.thehindu.com/magazine/is-cricket-killing-other-sports-in-india/article29642925.ece.

ISKCON. 'About Us.' *ISKCON EASY*. https://iskconeasy.com/about-us/.

Islam, Mahmudul. 'The Unexplored Potential of Game Development in Bangladesh.' *The Business Standardi*, 6 December 2020. http://www.tbsnews.net/feature/panorama/unexplored-potential-game-development-bangladesh-167773.

Ismail, Taha. *GTA: Dhaka City Stories*. N.p., 2016. Digital.

IT & Telecommunications Division. *IT Policy and Action Plan*. Islamabad: IT & Telecommunications Division Ministry of Science & Technology Government of Pakistan Islamabad, 2000. http://lgkp.gov.pk/wp-content/uploads/2014/03/National-IT-Policy.pdf.

'Itihaasa- Research and Digital.' *Itihaasa - Research and Digital*. 2020. https://itihaasa.com/listing/timeline.

Iwabuchi, Koichi. *Recentering Globalization: Popular Culture and Japanese Transnationalism*. Durham, NC: Duke University Press, 2002.

Jafri, Wajhi. 'State of Play: Is Videogame Development on the Rise in Pakistan?' *Dawn*, 30 April 2019. https://www.dawn.com/news/1475376.

Jairath, Anushree. 'Why the Digital Divide Has Overwhelmingly Worsened Women's Health.' *The News Minute*, 19 May 2021. https://www.thenewsminute.com/article/why-digital-divide-has-overwhelmingly-worsened-women-s-health-149133.

Jayan, T.V. 'Games They Played.' *The Telegraph Online*, 14 February 2011. https://www.telegraphindia.com/science-tech/games-they-played/cid/432148.

Joho, Jess. 'Rituals Presents the Surreal Fragmentation of Narrative in a Post-Colonial India.' *Kill Screen*, 11 September 2014. https://killscreen.com/previously/articles/ritual-presents-surreal-fragmentation-narrative-post-colonial-india.

Jones, William and Hiram Cox. *The Indian Game of Chess*. Edinburgh: Priv. printed for the Aungervyle society, 1883. *HathiTrust*. https://catalog.hathitrust.org/Record/011743119.

Jordan, Jon. '"We're Not India": Dawn Patrol Reveals How Sri Lankan Developers Are Fighting Preconceptions.' *pocketgamer.biz*, 2013. https://www.pocketgamer.biz/asia/interview/55134/were-not-india-dawn-patrol-reveals-how-sri-lankan-developers-are-fighting-preconceptions/.

Joshi, Priyanka. 'HCL Infosystems Enters the Gaming Zone.' *Business Standard India*, 20 August 2010. https://www.business-standard.com/article/technology/hcl-infosystems-enters-the-gaming-zone-110082000031_1.html.

Jugantor. 'দেশে নিষিদ্ধ হচ্ছে ফ্রি ফায়ার ও পাবজি গেম.' *Jugantor*, 21 May 2021. https://www.jugantor.com/national/425643/%E0%A6%A6%E0%A7%87%E0%A6%B6%E0%A7%87-%E0%A6%A8%E0%A6%BF%E0%A6%B7%E0%A6%BF%E0%A6%A6%E0%A7%8D%E0%A6%A7-%E0%A6%B9%E0%A6%9A%E0%A7%8D%E0%A6%9B%E0%A7%87-%E0%A6%AB%E0%A7%8D%E0%A6%B0%E0%A6%BF-%E0%A6%AB%E0%A6%BE%E0%A7%9F%E0%A6%BE%E0%A6%B0-%E0%A6%93-%E0%A6%AA%E0%A6%BE%E0%A6%AC%E0%A6%9C%E0%A6%BF-%E0%A6%97%E0%A7%87%E0%A6%AE.

Kaur, Amanpreet. 'Fact Check: Pakistan Politician Shares Animation Video as a Real-Life Incident - Fact Check News.' *India Today*, 7 July 2019. https://www.indiatoday.in/fact-check/story/fact-check-pakistan-politician-shares-video-reallife-incident-1563940-2019-07-07/.

Kalasi, Kanwaladeep, and Ankush Patel. 'Games Bond.' Star One, 2005. Television.

Kan, Michael. 'What Is an Avatar? Creators Chip Morningstar and Randy Farmer Trace the Ancient Roots of the Latest Buzzword.' *Business Trends Around the Globe*, n.d. http://heritage-key.com/blogs/michael-kan/what-avatar-creators-chip-morningstar-and-randy-farmer-trace-ancient-roots-latest-/.

'Karma.' *Far Cry Wiki*, n.d. https://farcry.fandom.com/wiki/Karma.

'Karma Systems in Games - Inviting Choice Rather than Intention.' *SQUAD*, 11 March 2020 https://squadstate.com/feature-2/karma-systems-in-games-inviting-choice-rather-than-intention/.

Kemp, Simon. *Digital 2021: The Maldives*. Datareportal, 2021.

Khan, Aaquib. 'A Video Game Glorifies Bangladeshis Liberation War: But Is That All It Does?' *Firstpost*, 15 June 2018, https://www.firstpost.com/long-reads/a-popular-video-game-series-glorifies-bangladeshs-liberation-war-but-is-that-all-it-does-4510847.html/.

Khan, Shaharyar M. *Cricket Cauldron: The Turbulent Politics of Sport in Pakistan*. London: New York: I.B. Tauris, 2013.

Kidambi, Prashant. *Cricket Country: The Untold History of the First All India Team*. Penguin Viking, 2019.

Knoll, Tobias. '"Instant Karma"—Moral Decision Making Systems in Digital Games.' *Religions* 9, 4 (2018): 131.

Kocurek, Carly A. *Coin-Operated Americans: Rebooting Boyhood at the Video Game Arcade*. 1st edition. Minneapolis: University of Minnesota Press, 2015.

Kokab, Tabonda. 'Pakistan Female Game Designer on a Mission for Change.' *BBC News*, 5 July 2018. https://www.bbc.com/news/world-asia-43966675.

Kris Graft. '3G-Powered Zeebo Game Console Reconfigures for Education In India.' *Game Developer*, 12 January 2011. https://www.gamedeveloper.com/pc/3g-powered-zeebo-game-console-reconfigures-for-education-in-india.

Krishnakumar, Aparna. 'The Name's Bond. Games Bond! - Rediff.Com Business.' *The name's Bond. Games Bond!*, 10 August 2005.https://www.rediff.com/money/2005/aug/10game.htm.

Kuensel Online. 'Using the Video Game Culture.' *Kuensel Online*, 6 July 2016. https://kuenselonline.com/using-the-video-game-culture/.

Kundi, Ghulam Muhammad, Bahadar Shah and Allah Nawaz. 'Digital Pakistan: Opportunities & Challenges.' *JISTEM - Journal of Information Systems and Technology Management* 5 (2008): 365–390.

Kuorikoski, Juho. *Finnish Video Games: A History and Catalog*. Jefferson, North Carolina: McFarland & Co Inc, 2015.

Kushal. 'History of Computer in Nepal & History of Computer Education in Nepal.' *Kushal The Knowledge for All*, 29 March 2018. http://kushal.net.np/?p=136.

Kushner, David. *Jacked: The Unauthorized behind-the-Scenes Story of Grand Theft Auto*. London: Collins, 2012.

Lakhsya. 'CEO's Update: The Year That Was | Lakshya Digital.' *Lakshya Digital*, 2021. https://lakshyadigital.com/ceos-update-covid19/.

'Laws of Bhutan- Bhutan Information and Media Act 2006.' *Asian LII*, 2006. http://www.asianlii.org/bt/legis/laws/bicama2006402/.

'Laws of Nepal - Information Technology Policy 2057.' *Asian LII*, 2000. http://www.asianlii.org/np/legis/laws/itp2057311/.

Lee, Mary-Ann. 'Bangladesh Gets Its First Bangla Language Mobile Game.' *Tech in Asia*, 30 December 2014. https://www.techinasia.com/bangladesh-bangla-language-mobile-game.

Lennon, John. *Instant Karma! (We All Shine On)*. Abbey Road, London: N.p., 1970. Audio Recording.

———. *INSTANT KARMA! (WE ALL SHINE ON). (Ultimate Mix, 2020) - Lennon/Ono with The Plastic Ono Band*. N.p. Film.

Liboriussen, Bjarke and Paul Martin. 'Regional Game Studies.' *Game Studies* 16, 1 (2016). Web. 2 July 2021. http://gamestudies.org/1601/articles/liboriussen.

'Ludii Portal.' N.p., n.d. Web. 1 September 2021. https://ludii.games/details.php?keyword=Baghchal.

Madhav, Pramod. 'The Family Man 2 Smear Campaign against Sri Lankan Tamils, Says State IT Minister Mano Thangaraj - Binge Watch News.' *India Today*, 25 May 2021. https://www.indiatoday.in/binge-watch/story/the-family-man-2-smear-campaign-against-srilankan-tamils-says-state-it-minister-mano-thangaraj-1806598-2021-05-25.

Madhurja, Ahmmed and Soumik Siddique. 'Our Negligence of the Ever-Growing Gaming Industry.' *The Daily Star*, 4 March 2020. https://www.thedailystar.net/opinion/news/our-negligence-the-ever-growing-gaming-industry-1875901.

Mag the Weekly. 'Pakistan's Gaming and Animation Industry.' *Mag the Weekly*, 3 August 2018. http://magtheweekly.com/detail/3596-pakistans-gaming-and-animation-industry.

Mahmud, Zeeshan. *Essays on Bangladesh Cricket*. Createspace Independent Pub, 2016.

Majumdar, Boria. *Eleven Gods and a Billion Indians: The On and Off the Field Story of Cricket in India and Beyond*. Noida: S&S India, 2018.

———. 'Mohun Bagan's "battles" against the Raj | Kolkata News.' *The Times of India*, 15 August 2013. https://timesofindia.indiatimes.com/city/kolkata/mohun-bagans-battles-against-the-raj/articleshow/21836516.cms.

Majumdar, Boria and Nalin Mehta. 'When Dhyan Chand and India's Olympians Refused to Salute Hitler.' *The Wire*, 2021. https://thewire.in/books/dhyan-chand-india-olympics-hitler.

Mansur, Risabh. 'Facing the Biggest Japanese Video Game Makers, Mumbai-Based Mitashi Revolutionised Gaming in India. Here's How.' *YourStory.com*, 11 January 2019. https://yourstory.com/smbstory/facing-the-biggest-japanese-video-game-makers-mumbai-based-mitashi-revolutionised-gaming-in-india-heres-how/amp.

Matchett, Freda. *Krishna, Lord or Avatara?: The Relationship between Krishna Nd Vishnu*. Routledge, 2001.

Mathias Fuchs, Sonia Fizek. *Rethinking Gamification*. N.p., 2014. Web. 5 September 2017. http://archive.org/details/RethinkingGamification.

Meier, Sid. *Sid Meier's Memoir! – A Life in Computer Games*. Illustrated edition. New York: W. W. Norton & Company, 2020.

Mellawa, Ranjan. *Winds Behind the Willows: A Sri Lankan's Life in Love with Cricket 2017*. Sri Lanka: Damian Ranjan Mellawa, 2017.

Menon, Nikhil. '"Fancy Calculating Machine": Computers and Planning in Independent India.' *Modern Asian Studies* 52.2 (2018): 421–457.

———. 'India's First Computers and the Cold War.' *The Caravan*, 1 April 2018. https://caravanmagazine.in/lede/india-first-computers-cold-war.

Mignolo, Walter D. 'The Global South and World Dis/Order.' *Journal of Anthropological Research* 67, 2 (2011): 165–188.

Ministry of External Affairs India. *India-Maldives Relations*. Ministry of External Affairs India, 2014.

Ministry of Information and Communications and Royal Government of Bhutan, Thimphu. *Information and Communications Technology (ICT) Policy for Bhutan: A White Paper*. Thimphu: Ministry of Information and Communications Royal Government of Bhutan, Thimphu, 2003.

Mitra, Soumen. 'Babu at Play: Sporting Nationalism in Bengal: A Study of Football in Bengal, 1880–1911.' *Bengal: Yesterday and Today*. Ed. Nisith Roy and Ranjit Roy. Calcutta: Papyrus, 1991.

Mitter, Sohini. 'Indian Internet Is More Rural, Local, and Mobile-First than Ever.' *YourStory.com*, 12 May 2020. https://yourstory.com/2020/05/half-billion-active-users-indian-internet-rural-local-mobile-first/amp.

Moray, Deepali. '20 Years of Internet in India.' *News18*, 15 August 2015. https://www.news18.com/news/tech/20-years-of-internet-in-india-on-august-15-1995-public-internet-access-was-launched-in-india-1039859.html.

Mudgal, Sparsh. 'A Heartfelt Tribute to The Neighbourhood Gaming Parlour, The OG 90s Kid Adda.' *Scoop Whoop*, 18 January 2020. https://www.scoopwhoop.com/gaming/tribute-to-the-neighbourhood-gaming-parlour/.

Mujahid, Yousaf Haroon. 'Digital Opportunity Initiative for Pakistan.' *The Electronic Journal of Information Systems in Developing Countries* 8, 1 (2002): 1–14.

Mukherjee, Souvik. 'Blue Whale: It's Not a Videogame.' *Kolkata News - Times of India*, 26 August 2017. https://timesofindia.indiatimes.com/city/kolkata/blue-whale-its-not-a-videogame/articleshow/60229757.cms.

———. 'Crab-Rangoons in Kyrat: (Re)Writing South-Asian History in Far Cry 4.' *Games and Culture* (2021): 15554120211005240. *SAGE Journals*. Web.

———. 'India.' *Encyclopedia of Video Games: The Culture, Technology, and Art of Gaming*. Ed. Mark J. P. Wolf. ABC-CLIO, 2012.

———. 'India.' *Video Games Around the World*. Ed. Mark J. P. Wolf. Boston, Massachussetts: MIT Press, 2015.

———. 'Replaying the Digital Divide: Videogames in India.' *Video Games and the Global South*. Ed. Phillip Penix-Tadsen. ETC Press, 2019.

———. 'Same Old Battle in New Cultural Space.' *The Times of India*, 15 December 2014.

———. *Videogames and Postcolonialism: Empire Plays Back*. London: Springer, 2017.

Mukherjee, Subhradeep 'Bucketbaba.' 'Forgotten Fields: An Aspiring Story of an Author Finding His Roots.' *Sportskeeda*, 5 April 2021. https://www.sportskeeda.com/esports/forgotten-fields-an-aspiring-story-author-finding-roots.

Mukhopadhyay, Debobroto. *Mashrafe*. Bangladesh Cricket Supporters' Association, 2016.

Munasinghe, Mohan. *A National Computer Policy for Sri Lanka (COMPOL Report)*. N.p., 1983.

Naha, Souvik. 'Cricket, Entertainment, Glamour Industry and Promotional Culture in India, 1913–2013.' *Sport in History* 35, 3 (2015): 464–489.

Nandy, Ashis. *The Tao of Cricket: On Games of Destiny and the Destiny of Games*. Oxford: OUP India, 2000.

Narayanan, Chandresh. 'How the Cult of Sanath Jayasuriya Pulled India-Sri Lanka Cricketing Ties from Drifting Apart.' *ThePrint*, 30 March 2019. https://theprint.in/pageturner/excerpt/how-the-cult-of-sanath-jayasuriya-pulled-india-sri-lanka-cricketing-ties-from-drifting-apart/214470/.

Naseem, Amani et al. 'Playmakers in the Maldives.' *Playful Disruption of Digital Media*. Ed. Daniel Cermak-Sassenrath. Singapore: Springer, 2018. 113–139.

NASSCOM. *India's Game Studio Directory*. New Delhi: NASSCOM, 2012.

Natarajan, Srividya. *A Gardener in the Wasteland: Jotiba Phule's Fight for Liberty*. New Delhi: Navayana, 2011.

———. *Bhimayana: Experiences of Untouchability*. 1st edition. New Delhi: Navayana, 2011.

Nayak, Chetan. 'FAU-G Review: Good Graphics Let down by Boring Gameplay.' *The Indian Express*, 28 January 2021. https://indianexpress.com/article/technology/gaming/fau-g-review-good-graphics-let-down-by-boring-gameplay-7163955/.

Nayar, Pramod. 'The Digital Dalit: Subalternity and Cyberspace.' *Sri Lanka Journal of Humanities* 37 (2014).

News18. 'Pakistani PUBG Players Are Tweeting to PM Imran Khan to Unban the Popular Game.' *News18*, 27 July 2020. https://www.news18.com/news/buzz/pakistani-pubg-players-are-tweeting-to-pm-imran-khan-to-unban-popular-game-2737503.html.

Newspaper, Bhutan's Daily. 'Using the Video Game Culture.' *Kuensel Online*, 6 July 2016. https://kuenselonline.com/using-the-video-game-culture/.

No Boss Gaming. 'Cholun Ghure Ashi Mostafar Jogot Theke.' N.p., Television. No Boss Gaming.

NOC Team. 'Computer Age in Pakistan.' *Code Week*, 11 August 2009. codeweek.pk.

Norman, Jeremy. '"Brain", the First PC Virus Epidemic, Created in Lahore, Pakistan: History of Information.' *Jeremy Norman's History of Information*, n.d. https://www.historyofinformation.com/detail.php?id=1676.

Obeyesekere, Gananath. *Karma and Rebirth: A Cross Cultural Study*. Motilal Banarsidass Publishe, 2006.

O'Donnell, Casey. *Developer's Dilemma: The Secret World of Videogame Creators*. Cambridge, Massachusetts: The MIT Press, 2014.

———. 'The Work/Play of the Interactive New Economy: Video Game Development in the United States and India.' Rensselaer Polytechnic Institute, 2008.

Ortiz, Fernando. *Cuban Counterpoint: Tobacco and Sugar*. Trans. Harriet de Onís. Illustrated edition. Durham: Duke University Press, 1995.

Orwell,George.'TheSportingSpirit|TheOrwellFoundation.'*TheOrwellFoundation*, 1945. https://www.orwellfoundation.com/the-orwell-foundation/orwell/essays-and-other-works/the-sporting-spirit/.

———. 'The Sporting Spirit | The Orwell Foundation.' *The Orwell Foundation*, 8 May 2021. https://www.orwellfoundation.com/the-orwell-foundation/orwell/essays-and-other-works/the-sporting-spirit/.

Pakgamers.com. *Game Developers Survey (GDS '19) - Pakistan*, 2019. https://docs.google.com/forms/d/e/1FAIpQLSd_ALN5fDSbgMR6lB4tPU72D6P-P1FI4imau8isGkmfAdI883Q/viewform.

Palavalli, Bharath M., Sruthi Krishnan and Yashwin Iddya. 'Enabling Public Participation in Shaping the Inclusive Energy Transition Through Serious Gaming—Case Studies in India.' *Shaping an Inclusive Energy Transition*. Ed. Margot P. C. Weijnen, Zofia Lukszo and Samira Farahani. Cham: Springer International Publishing, 2021. 231–244.

Palmer, Dan. 'National Olympic Committee of Sri Lanka Announces Esports Partnership.' *Inside the Games*, 2 March 2020. https://www.insidethegames.biz/articles/1091353/sri-lanka-esports-partnership-signed.

Pandey, Rohan. 'Ghajini The Game: Review.' *Game Guru*, 6 February 2009. https://www.gameguru.in/action/2009/06/ghajini-the-game-review/.

Pandey, Shailesh B. and Nischal Regmi. 'If You Build It, Will They Come? Exploring Narratives That Shape the Internet in Nepal.' *Science, Technology and Society* 25, 3 (2020): 444–464.

Parrinder, E. G. *Avatar and Incarnation: The Divine in Human Form in the World's Religions*. Oxford, England; Rockford, MA: Oneworld Publications, 1997.

Patronobis, Sutirtho. 'Fighting LTTE on Playstation.' *Hindustan Times*, 19 August 2010. https://www.hindustantimes.com/world/fighting-ltte-on-playstation/story-aWkRFUZzMNR1er6FDSgw2H.html.

Patterson, Christopher B. *Open World Empire: Race, Erotics, and the Global Rise of Video Games: 26*. New York: New York University Press, 2020.

PC Mag. 'Definition of Simputer - PC Mag Encyclopedia.' *PCMAG*, n.d. https://www.pcmag.com/encyclopedia/term/simputer.

Penix-Tadsen, Phillip. *Cultural Code – Video Games and Latin America*. 1st edition. Cambridge, MA: MIT Press, 2016.

——. *Video Games and the Global South*. ETC Press, 2019.

Perera, Ajith Chrysantha Stephen. *The Golden Era of Sri Lankan Cricket*. Talangama; Great Britain: Acumen Books, 1999.

Phalke, Bhalachandra D. *Raja Harishchandra*. Phalke Films, 1913. Film.

Pham, Brandon. 'Raji: An Ancient Epic & Crossing the Finish Line.' *Game Developer*, 17 December 2020. https://www.gamedeveloper.com/disciplines/raji-an-ancient-epic-crossing-the-finish-line.

PIB Delhi. 'Government Blocks 118 Mobile Apps Which Are Prejudicial to Sovereignty and Integrity of India, Defence of India, Security of State and Public Order.' *Press Information Bureau Government of India*, 2 September 2020. https://pib.gov.in/pib.gov.in/Pressreleaseshare.aspx?PRID=1650669.

'Playing Video Games Doesn't Lead to Violent Behaviour, Study Shows.' *The Guardian*, 21 July 2020. http://www.theguardian.com/games/2020/jul/22/playing-video-games-doesnt-lead-to-violent-behaviour-study-shows.

'Playmakers in Maldives.' *The Maldives Exodus Caravan Show*, 2013. http://the-maldives-exodus-caravan-show.com/operation-noose/.

Prabhu, Shailesh. 'Breaking down the Billion.' *GamesIndustry.biz*, 2 November 2016. https://www.gamesindustry.biz/articles/2016-11-02-breaking-down-the-billion.

Pradhan, Gopi. *Study of the Development of ICT in the Kingdom of Bhutan*. IDRC, 2001.

Prashar, A.S. 'Bhagat Singh in Animation Game.' *Chandigarh Tribune*, 6 August 2002. https://www.tribuneindia.com/2002/20020806/cth2.htm.

Premchand, Munshi. 'Shatranj Ki Khiladi [The Chess Players].' *Madhuri* (1928).

PricewaterhouseCoopers. *Global Entertainment & Media Outlook 2018–2022*. 2021. https://www.pwc.in/industries/entertainment-and-media/global-entertainment-and-media-outlook-2018-2022.html.

Priyadershini S. 'Tradtional Board Games: From Kochi to Iraq.' *The Hindu*, 1 October 2015. https://www.thehindu.com/features/metroplus/society/tradtional-board-games-from-kochi-to-iraq/article7711918.ece.

PTI. 'PM Modi Calls for Innovation in India's Toy Sector, Asks People to Be "Vocal for Local Toys."' 24 June 2021. https://theprint.in/india/pm-modi-calls-for-innovation-in-indias-toy-sector-asks-people-to-be-vocal-for-local-toys/683936/.

———. 'YouTuber Paras Singh Booked in Arunachal for Racist Remarks against Congress MLA Ninong Ering.' *The New Indian Express*, 25 May 2021. https://www.newindianexpress.com/nation/2021/may/25/youtuber-paras-singh-booked-in-arunachal-for-racist-remarks-against-congress-mla-ninong-ering-2307055.html.

Punathambekar, Aswin and Sriram Mohan. *Global Digital Cultures: Perspectives from South Asia*. Illustrated edition. Ann Arbor: The University of Michigan Press, 2019.

Raessens, Joost. 'The Ludification of Culture.' *Rethinking Gamification*. Ed. Mathias Fuchs, Sonia Fizek, and Paolo Ruffino. Lüneburg: meson press eG, 2014.

Rahool, Munir. 'Review: This Army Public School Attack Game Fails on Every Front.' *Dawn*, 18 January 2016. http://www.dawn.com/news/1232492.

Raihan, Siam. 'Bangladesh's First Open World Game Agontuk Releases Gameplay Trailer.' *Dhaka Tribune*, 16 November 2019. https://www.dhakatribune.com/showtime/2019/11/16/bangladesh-s-first-open-world-game-agontuk-releases-gameplay-trailer.

Rajan, Nalini, ed. *Digital Culture Unplugged: Probing the Native Cyborg's Multiple Locations*. 1st edition. Taylor & Francis, 2007.

Rajeevan, Savithri. 'Video Game.' Trans. Yadu Rajiv. *Indian Literature* 47, 3 (2003): 76–78.

Rajesh, Manish. 'Gamer in Focus - Ankit 'V3nom' Panth - Team Brutality.' *digit.in*, 10 October 2019. https://www.digit.in/features/gaming/gamer-in-focus-ankit-v3nom-panth-50588.html.

Ramasubramanian, Sowmya. 'India Tops Worldwide Game Downloads List in 2020.' *The Hindu*, 16 November 2020. https://www.thehindu.com/sci-tech/technology/india-tops-worldwide-game-downloads-list-in-2020/article33106400.ece>.

Rana, Prajesh S.B. 'Starting Small, Aiming Big: Game Development in Nepal.' *The Kathmandu Post*, 6 October 2020. https://kathmandupost.com/science-technology/2020/10/06/starting-small-aiming-big-game-development-in-nepal.

Ray Murray, Padmini and Chris Hand. 'Making Culture: Locating the Digital Humanities in India.' *Visible Language* 49, 3 (2015): 141–155.

Ray Murray, Padmini and Souvik Mukherjee. 'From the Outside Looking In: Creating a Serious 'art Game in India - a Case Study.' *2013 5th International Conference on Games and Virtual Worlds for Serious Applications (VS-GAMES)*. N.p. 2013. 1–3. Web.

Ray, Nirbed and Projit Bihari Mukharji. 'Sedentary Games and the Nationalist Project: A Silent History.' *The International Journal of the History of Sport* 22, 4 (2005): 699–707.

Ray, Satyajit. *The Chess Players*. N.p., 1977. Film.

Readme. 'Kanchayudha: What to Expect from a Sri Lankan Encounter.' *ReadMe*, 10 December 2016. https://www.readme.lk/kanchayudha-expectations/.

Reuters. 'Avatar May Be Subconsciously Linked to India: Cameron | Entertainment News, The Indian Express.' *Indian Express*, 15 March 2010. https://indianexpress.com/article/entertainment/entertainment-others/avatar-may-be-subconsciously-linked-to-india-cameron/.

———. 'Fawad Chaudhry Promises Pakistani Gamers New Opportunities.' *The Express Tribune*, 13 January 2021. http://tribune.com.pk/story/2279799/fawad-chaudhry-promises-pakistani-gamers-new-opportunities.

Reynolds, Author Alison. 'Pakistan Gets Wired: The Development of a Computing Center at the University of Islamabad.' *Blogging Hoosier History*, 8 May 2013. https://blogs.libraries.indiana.edu/iubarchives/2013/05/08/islamabad/.

Roy, Dibyadyuti and Aditya Deshbandhu. 'Anxious Postcolonial Masculinity in Online Video Games: Race, Gender and Colonialism in Indian Digital Spaces.' *Gender, Place & Culture* (2021): 1–20.

Roy, Samya Brata. 'Hitman 2 and Its Spectre of Mumbai: Samya Brata Roy.' New Delhi: N.p., 2020. *YouTube*. https://www.youtube.com/watch?v=Kox_vg3OhrM.

Roychowdhury, Adrija. 'No Bull, This Could Be Why Tamil Nadu Is Obsessed with Jallikattu.' *The Indian Express* 19 January 2017. https://indianexpress.com/article/research/no-bull-this-could-be-why-tamil-nadu-is-obsessed-with-jallikattu-4482132/.

Ruffino, Paolo, ed. *Independent Videogames: Cultures, Networks, Techniques and Politics*. 1st edition. Routledge, 2020.

'SAHM.' *POC IN PLAY*. N.p., 2021. https://www.pocplay.org/sahm.

Sarkar, Monica. 'Feminism for Goddesses: Does Goddess Worship Empower Girls?' *The Guardian*, 5 March 2014. http://www.theguardian.com/global-development-professionals-network/2014/mar/05/india-hinduism-goddesses-feminism-global-development.

Ṣāstrī, Tiruvēṇgaḍāchārya. *Essays on Chess, Adapted to the European Mode of Play: Consisting Principally of Positions or Critical Situations Calculated to Improve the Learner and Exercise the Memory*. Bombay: Printed for the author, by M.D. Cruz, 1814.

Schiller, Herbert I. *Mass Communications and American Empire*. Boston: Beacon Press, 1971.

Schleiner, Anne-Marie. *Transnational Play: Piracy, Urban Art, and Mobile Games*. Amsterdam: Amsterdam University Press, 2020.

Schreier, Jason. *Press Reset: Ruin and Recovery in the Video Game Industry*. New York: Grand Central Publishing, 2021.

Schulz, Mark. *Xenozoic Tales*. Princeton, Wisconsin: Kitchen Sink Press, 1987.

Sen, Biswarup. *Digital Politics and Culture in Contemporary India: The Making of an Info-Nation*. New York: Routledge, 2016.

Shamil Shams. 'Video Games Show Pakistan in 'bad Light' | DW | 24.01.2013.' *Deutsche Welle*, 21 January 2013. https://www.dw.com/en/video-games-show-pakistan-in-bad-light/a-16547732.

Sharif Hussain Shamim. 'Gaming for Good: Answering Those Awkward Questions about Puberty in Bangladesh.' *BBC Media Action*, 9 January 2017.https://www.bbc.co.uk/blogs/bbcmediaaction/entries/a337c3d3-7874-4615-9f0e-396f7a8d8ddc.

Sharma, Abhishek. 'DNA Exclusive: How Much Money Are Indians Spending on Gaming? IGDC Convenor Rajesh Rao Tells.' *DNA India*, 19 November 2020. https://www.dnaindia.com/technology/interview-dna-exclusive-how-much-money-are-indians-spending-on-gaming-igdc-convenor-rajesh-rao-tells-2857393.

Sharma, Chiranjib and Gohin Sonowal. *Sports History of Assam (Vol. I): Traditional Games and Sports*. Olympia Prakashan, 2017.

Sharma, Dinesh. 'George Fernandes and the Infamous IBM Exit.' *The Wire*, n.d. https://thewire.in/government/full-story-george-fernandes-and-the-infamous-ibm-exit.

Sharma, Dinesh C. *The Outsourcer – The Story of India's IT Revolution*. 1st edition. Cambridge, Massachusetts: MIT Press, 2015.

Shaw, Adrienne. 'How Do You Say Gamer in Hindi? Exploratory Research on the Indian Digital Game Industry and Culture.' *Gaming Globally: Production, Play and Place*. Ed. N. Huntemann and B. Aslinger. New York: Palgrave Macmillian, 2013. 226–250.

Shaw-Williams, Hannah. '"Far Cry 4" Documentary Explores Nepal, But Nepalese People Protest Game.' *Game Rant*, 11 August 2014. https://gamerant.com/far-cry-4-videos-nepal-controversy/.

Sheth, Hemani. 'Ludo King Surpasses 500 Million Downloads Worldwide, Adds New Features.' *@businessline*, 9 January 2021. https://www.thehindubusinessline.com/info-tech/ludo-king-surpasses-500-million-downloads-worldwide-adds-new-features/article33535620.ece.

Shimkhada, Deepak. 'A Preliminary Study of the Game of Karma in India, Nepal, and Tibet.' *Artibus Asiae* 44, 4 (1983): 308–322.

Shyamasundar, R. K. and M. A. Pai. *Homi Bhabha and the Computer Revolution*. New Delhi: Oxford University Press, 2011.

Simons, Iain and James Newman. *A History of Videogames: In 14 Consoles, 5 Computers, 2 Arcade Cabinets... and an Ocarina of Time*. London: Welbeck Publishing Group, 2018.

Singh, Gurmit. 'War Gaming.' Indian Institute of Technology, Kanpur, 1979.

Singh, Jagmeet. 'How Ludo King Became a COVID Quarantine Sensation in India.' *NDTV Gadgets 360*, 21 May 2020. https://gadgets.ndtv.com/games/features/ludo-king-creator-vikash-jaiswal-total-users-downloads-india-success-2232634.

Singh, S. Ronendra and Thomas K. Thomas. 'HCL Infosystems to Exit PC Manufacturing Business.' *The Hindu BusinessLine*, 12 March 2018. https://www.thehindubusinessline.com/info-tech/hcl-infosystems-to-exit-pc-manufacturing-business/article20689854.ece1.

Sinha, Anubhav. *Ra.One*. Red Chillies Entertainment, Eros Worldwide, Prana Studios, 2011. Film.

Sinha, Bhabani Prasad. Interview with Professor Bhabani Prasad Sinha. 5 July 2020.

Sippy, Ramesh. *Sholay*. NH Studioz, Sippy Films, 1975. Film.

'Skoar.' *Digit.in*, n.d. https://www.digit.in/gaming/.

Sohel, Mostafizur Rahaman. *ICT Journey of Bangladesh*. BASIS, 2016. https://www.itu.int/net4/wsis/forum/2016/Content/AgendaFiles/document/0ffca517-b27d-4f61-a21f-1da8541021f5/Bangladesh_BASIS_MRahman_WSIS2016.pdf.

Someshwara. *Manasollasa of King Someshwara*. Ed. Gajanan K. Shrigondekar. Baroda: The Oriental Institute, 1939.

'South Asian Digital Diasporas and Cyberfeminist Webs: Negotiating Globalization, Nation, Gender and Information Technology Design.' N.p., n.d. https://scholar.google.com/citations?view_op=view_citation&hl=en&user=3jkDhC0AAAAJ&citation_for_view=3jkDhC0AAAAJ:qjMakFHDy7sC.

Souza, Steven E. de. *Street Fighter*. Capcom Entertainment, Edward R. Pressman Productions, 1994. Film.

Spielberg, Steven. *Indiana Jones and the Temple of Doom*. Paramount Pictures, Lucasfilm, 1984. Film.

———. *Ready Player One*. Warner Bros., Amblin Entertainment, Village Roadshow Pictures, 2018. Film.

'Sri Lanka: Internet Penetration Rate 2019.' *Statista*, 2019. https://www.statista.com/statistics/765516/internet-penetration-rate-sri-lanka/.

'Sri Lankan Gaming Industry Trends.' *Colombo Telegraph*, 11 April 2019. https://www.colombotelegraph.com/index.php/sri-lankan-gaming-industry-trends/.

Star Digital Report. 'High Court Directs Govt to Ban PUBG, Free Fire for 3 Months.' *The Daily Star*, 16 August 2021. https://www.thedailystar.net/news/bangladesh/crime-justice/news/high-court-directs-govt-ban-tiktok-pubg-free-fire-2153431.

'Star Wars Rogue One in Maldives. The Shooting Location for Planet Scarif in the Beautiful Laamu Atoll.' *Dreaming of Maldives - The Blog. Your Unique Travel Guide to the Maldives*, 24 October 2016. https://www.dreamingofmaldives.com/maldives-blog/star-wars-rogue-one-in-maldives-the-shooting-location-for-planet-scarif-in-the-beautiful-laamu-atoll/.

Statista. 'Most Spoken Languages in the World.' *Statista*, 2021. https://www.statista.com/statistics/266808/the-most-spoken-languages-worldwide/.

———. 'Number of Smartphone Users in India 2015-2022.' *Statista*, July 2021. https://www.statista.com/statistics/467163/forecast-of-smartphone-users-in-india/.

Statista Research Department. 'India - Number of Mobile Gamers 2016-2022.' *Statista*, 19 March 2021. https://www.statista.com/statistics/739508/number-of-mobile-gamers-india/.

'Steam Community: Raji: An Ancient Epic.' N.p., n.d. Web. 2 September 2021. https://steamcommunity.com/app/730390/reviews/?browsefilter=toprated&snr=1_5_100010.

Stephenson, Neal. *Snow Crash*. New York: Bantam Books, 1992.

Stokel-Walker, Chris. 'Second Life's Strange Second Life.' *The Verge*, 24 September 2013. https://www.theverge.com/2013/9/24/4698382/second-lifes-strange-second-life.

Stuart, Keith. 'PlayStation 2 at 20: The Console That Revealed the Future of Gaming.' *The Guardian*, 4 March 2020. http://www.theguardian.com/games/2020/mar/04/sony-playstation-2-at-20-console-future-of-gaming.

Suarez, Ricardo. 'La Tienda de Juan.' *Deus ex Machina*, 17 June 2015. http://deusexmachina.es/la-tienda-juan/.

Sukumar, Arun Mohan. *Midnight's Machines: A Political History of Technology in India*. Gurgaon: Penguin Viking, 2019.

Sulapani. *Sulapani's Chaturanga- Dipika*. Ed. Manomohan Ghosh. Calcutta: Metropolitan Printing and Publishing House, 1936.

Sundaram, Ravi. *Pirate Modernity: Delhi's Media Urbanism*. 1st edition. London: Routledge, 2011.

Svelch, Jaroslav. *Gaming the Iron Curtain: How Teenagers and Amateurs in Communist Czechoslovakia Claimed the Medium of Computer Games*. Cambridge, Massachusetts: The MIT Press, 2018.

Tamang, Bijay. 'Redefining of Kumari Myth in Rashmila Shakya's From Goddess to Mortal.' Thesis. Faculty of Art in English, 2017. *107.170.122.150:8080*. Web. 4 September 2021. http://107.170.122.150:8080/xmlui/handle/123456789/2012.

Taylor, T.L. *Play Between Worlds – Exploring Online Game Culture*. Cambridge, Mass.: MIT Press, 2009.

Team YS. 'The 'MADE IN INDIA' Software Industry.' *Your Story*, 2010. https://yourstory.com/2010/12/the-made-in-india-software-industry/amp.

Tech 2 News Staff. 'PlayStation 5 Goes out of Stock Just Minutes after Its Official Launch in India- Technology News, Firstpost.' *Tech2*, 3 February 2021. https://www.firstpost.com/tech/news-analysis/playstation-5-goes-out-of-stock-just-minutes-after-its-official-launch-in-india-9266421.html.

Telecom Regulatory Authority of India. *Press Release No.16/2021*. Telecom Regulatory Authority of India, 2021. https://trai.gov.in/sites/default/files/PR_No.16of2021.pdf.

Tewari, Saumya. 'Ludo King's Parent Company Clocks $20 Million in Revenue in 2020.' *Mint*, 8 January 2021. https://www.livemint.com/companies/start-ups/ludo-king-s-parent-company-clocks-20-million-in-revenue-in-2020-11610112124290.html.

Thadani, Karmanye. 'The Delhi I Grew Up In.' *Khurpi*, 14 May 2016. http://khurpi.info/the-delhi-i-grew-up-in/.

Thakur, Gautam Basu. *Postcolonial Theory and Avatar*. 1st edition. London; New York: Bloomsbury Academic USA, 2015.

Thapa, Nissan. 'Correct the Language Used in Far Cry 4. Aware the Game Developers of Far Cry 4 That Nepalese People Speak Own Language Called Nepali Not Indian (Hindi).' Change.org. N.p., 2014.

Thapliyal, Adesh. 'How 'Raji: An Ancient Epic' Falls into the Indian Far-Right's Trap.' *Vice*, 27 October 2020. https://www.vice.com/en/article/m7ajbv/raji-ancient-indian-epic-far-right-hindu-nationalism.

The Daily Star. 'Bangladesh behind Nepal, Pakistan in Smartphone Use.' *The Daily Star*, 31 March 2021. https://www.thedailystar.net/backpage/news/bangladesh-behind-nepal-pakistan-smartphone-use-2069457.

The Family Man (TV Series 2019) - IMDb. N.p. Film.

The Hindu. 'On CoWIN, Supreme Court Flags Digital Divide.' *The Hindu*, 2 June 2021. https://www.thehindu.com/news/national/on-cowin-supreme-court-flags-digital-divide/article34711169.ece.

'The Mako Reactor • Japan Video Games News, Reviews & More.' *The Mako Reactor*. N.p., n.d. https://themakoreactor.com/.

The New Indian Express. '"India Lost Because It Has Too Many Dalit Players": Casteist Slurs Thrown at Hockey Star Vandana-The New Indian Express.' *The New Indian Express*, 8 May 2021. https://www.newindianexpress.com/sport/olympics/2021/aug/05/india-lost-because-it-has-too-many-dalit-players-casteist-slurs-thrown-at-hockey-star-vandana-2340559.html.

Thomas, Pradip N. *Digital India: Understanding Information, Communication and Social Change*. 1st edition. Los Angeles: SAGE India, 2012.

Toftedahl, Marcus, Per Backlund and Henrik Engström. 'Localization from an Indie Game Production Perspective: Why, When and How?' Digital Games Research Association (DiGRA), 2018. http://urn.kb.se/resolve?urn=urn:nbn:se:his:diva-16133.

———. 'Missing: Understanding the Reception of a Serious Game by Analyzing App Store Data.' *International Journal of Serious Games* 5 (2018): 3–22.

Trendsdesk. 'PUBG Is Shutting down in India and People Are Bidding Farewell on Social Media with Memes.' *The Indian Express*, 31 October 2020. https://indianexpress.com/article/trending/trending-globally/pubg-farewell-memes-pubg-ban-reaction-6909784/.

Tripathy, Prabhash Ranjan. 'Playing Cyborg: A Study of Video Game Parlours in Delhi and Mussoorie.' MPhil. Jawaharlal Nehru University, 2017.

Tshedup, Younten. 'E-Sport: A Booming Culture.' *Kuensel Online*, 4 July 2016. https://kuenselonline.com/e-sport-a-booming-culture/.

US Department of State. 'Background Notes: Maldives 06/96.' *US Department of State Archive*, 1996. https://1997-2001.state.gov/background_notes/maldives_0696_bgn.html.

Van den Heede, Pieter, Kees Ribbens and Jeroen Jansz. 'Replaying Today's Wars? A Study of the Conceptualization of Post-1989 Conflict in Digital 'War' Games.' *International Journal of Politics, Culture, and Society* 31, 3 (2018): 229–250.

Vivekananda, Swami. *Lectures from Colombo to Almora*. Third, 42nd reprint edition. Calcutta: Advaita Ashrama, 2010.

Wang, Hui. 'Lineage of Line Age: Transculturation of Global Play-Scape Video Games in East Asia.' *Recreation and Society in Africa, Asia and Latin America* 7 (2019). https://journal.lib.uoguelph.ca/index.php/rasaala/article/view/5832.

Wang, Veronica. 'Tibetan Representation in Avatar: The Last Airbender.' *Kollaboration San Francisco*. N.p., n.d. https://www.kollabsf.org/

kollabblogposts/2020/10/15/tibetan-representation-in-avatar-the-last-airbender.

Washington Post. 'India's Engineers Have Thrived in Silicon Valley. So Has Its Caste System.' *Washington Post,* 27 October 2020. https://www.washingtonpost.com/technology/2020/10/27/indian-caste-bias-silicon-valley/.

Watts, Rachel. 'Venba Is an Upcoming Cooking Game about an Indian Mother Restoring Her Lost Recipes.' *PC Gamer*, 26 January 2021. https://www.pcgamer.com/venba-is-an-upcoming-cooking-game-about-an-indian-mother-restoring-her-lost-recipes/.

Wazir, Burhan. 'Pakistan's Sticky Wicket.' *The World Today,* September 2014.

Wolf, Mark J. P., ed. *Video Games Around the World*. Massachussetts: The MIT Press, 2015.

World Video Game Hall of Fame. *A History of Video Games in 64 Objects*. Illustrated edition. New York: Dey Street Books, 2018.

Yee, Nick. 'What Men and Women Consider Hardcore Gaming Are Not the Same.' *ironSource LevelUp*, 12 September 2019. https://medium.com/ironsource-levelup/what-men-and-women-consider-hardcore-gaming-are-not-the-same-e39b06093456.

Zachariah, Rebecca. 'Game for Success.' *The Times of India*, 17 August 2011. https://timesofindia.indiatimes.com/business/india-business/game-for-success/articleshow/9628599.cms.

Zeiler, Xenia. 'Digital Humanities Practices and Cultural Heritage: Indian Video Games.' *Exploring Digital Humanities in India: Pedagogies, Practices, and Institutional Possibilities* (2020): Web. 23 August 2021. https://researchportal.helsinki.fi/en/publications/digital-humanities-practices-and-cultural-heritage-indian-video-g.

———. 'Gamified Embodiment Experiences in Indian Video Games.' *Digital Religion 2:0* (2021) *researchportal.helsinki.fi*. Web. 23 August 2021. https://researchportal.helsinki.fi/en/publications/gamified-embodiment-experiences-in-indian-video-games.

———. 'The Durga Puja Mystery: An Educational Video Game about Indian Culture.' (2020) *researchportal.helsinki.fi*. Web. 23 August 2021. https://researchportal.helsinki.fi/en/publications/the-durga-puja-mystery-an-educational-video-game-about-indian-cul.

———. 'The Global Mediatization of Hinduism through Digital Games: Representation versus Simulation in Hanuman: Boy Warrior.' *Playing with Religion in Digital Games* (2014): 66–87.

———. 'The Indian Indie Game Development Scene: History and Cultural Heritage as Game Themes.' *Gamevironments* 5 (2016): 257–263.

Zeiler, Xenia and Souvik Mukherjee. 'Video Game Development in India: A Cultural and Creative Industry Embracing Regional Cultural Heritage(s).' *Games and Culture* (2021) *researchportal.helsinki.fi*. https://researchportal.helsinki.fi/en/publications/video-game-development-in-india-a-cultural-and-creative-industry--2.

Zeiler, Xenia and Suzie Thomas. 'Special Issue: Video Games and Cultural Heritage.' (2021): *researchportal.helsinki.fi*. Web. 23 August 2021. https://researchportal.helsinki.fi/en/publications/special-issue-video-games-and-cultural-heritage.

Zimmerman, Eric, and Heather Chaplin. 'Manifesto: The 21st Century Will Be Defined By Games.' *Kotaku*, 9 September 2013. https://kotaku.com/manifesto-the-21st-century-will-be-defined-by-games-1275355204.

Appendix One: Timeline

Timeline of Videogame-related Events in India

Year (date)	Event	Type	Notes
1931	Hollerith machines brought to India	Hardware	The colonial government of India brought Hollerith machines to perform the complex calculations at the Defence Accounts Department (DAD) in 1931
1945	WIPRO founded	Company	The company was not involved in IT during its early years. It began as a manufacturer of vegetable and refined oils in Amalner, Maharashtra
1955	First Computer in India Installed	Hardware development	HEC-2M designed by A.D. Booth was installed at the Indian Statistical Institute (ISI), Calcutta
1955	Design of a pilot machine began at TIFR	Hardware development	It became operational in 1956
1959	TIFRAC (TIFR Automatic Calculator) completed	Hardware development	Full-scale version of TIFR's pilot machine, formally commissioned in February 1960, was named in 1962
1966	ISIJU-1 built in Calcutta	Hardware development	In Calcutta, the Indian Statistical Institute in collaboration with Jadavpur University continued the work of developing indigenous computers, and the ISIJU-1 was built

Year (date)	Event	Type	Notes
1967	Establishment of Tata Consultancy Services (TCS)	Company	The company was established in Mumbai
1973	TCS partners with Burroughs to begin India's export of IT Services	IT Development	TSC partnered with Burroughs Corporation, USA, to distribute and support its products in India as well as build software that would be exported to various Burroughs units and clients across the world and converted a hospital accounting system written in Burroughs Medium Systems COBOL to Burroughs Small Systems COBOL. At this point, TCS did not yet have a Burroughs computer on which to carry out the conversion. The team improvised by writing a 'filter' in assembly language on the ICL 1903 to parse the source code and convert it to the Small Systems version. This was the very first recorded instance of an offshore software delivery done out of India, 45 years ago, accomplished using automation (source: https://www.tcs.com/tcs-50)
1973	Satish Bhutani joins Atari	Personal achievement	Of Indian descent and fresh out of college from Texas University, he joined Atari in 1973 to be their export administrator to both Europe and the soon-to-be important market of Japan

Year (date)	Event	Type	Notes
1976	HCL Technologies founded	Company	It is an Indian multinational information technology (IT) services and consulting company, headquartered in Noida, Uttar Pradesh, India. It is a subsidiary of HCL Enterprise. Originally a research and development division of HCL, it emerged as an independent company in 1991 when HCL entered into the software services business
1979	Captain Gurmeet Singh writes a tank warfare simulation game for his MTech	Publication	Captain Gurmit Singh wrote his MTech thesis on a simulation game of tank warfare in 1981 where he programmed an entire war game for a DEC 1090 system
1970s–1980s	WIPRO shifts focus towards IT and computing industry	IT Development	
1981	Infosys founded	Company	Registered as Infosys Consultants Private Limited on 2 July 1981. It is one of the major IT companies in India
1980s	Backyard Innovation of the 1980s	Market/ Production Shift	In order to face a closed economy, Lajpat Rai Market in the 1980s was part of backyard innovation. While importers brought video games into the market, the quantities and prices were not suitable to meet the demand of video games in the local markets as well as that of outside Delhi. Many of the traders in the market made clones of NES (Nintendo Entertainment System) games.

Year (date)	Event	Type	Notes
			The Samurai gaming consoles was one such clone. The traders carefully assembled the chips of 9 IC (Integrated Circuit) boards in their shops. They imported the chips and the cartridges from China. The assembling and packaging was done in the local market. In this way, the traders at Lajpat Rai Market increased the quantity of gaming products
Mid-1980s	Nintendo licenses its consoles to Samurai, a local vendor, for Indian markets	Market/ Production Shift	Samurai failed to sell 'even 200 to 300 machines across the country in a month,' thus eventually ending this development
1988	NASSCOM established	Developer/ Company	A not-for-profit industry association, it is the apex body for the IT BPM industry in India. It is focused on building the architecture integral to the development of the IT BPM sector through policy advocacy, and help in setting up the strategic direction for the sector
1991	Mitashi starts business as a videogame console maker	Developer/ Company	From humble beginnings in the central Mumbai suburb of Ghatkopar as a video console gaming company in 1991, Mitashi (initially called Maze Marketing) morphed into a 480 crore consumer electronics player with a presence in TVs, ACs and washing machines. It also made a Cricket game that was very popular

Year (date)	Event	Type	Notes
1995	VSNL introduces Internet in India	IT Development	Internet got introduced in India in 1986 but it took a decade to make it available for the public. VSNL was first launched the internet in India on 15 August 1995
1995	Introduction of Sega Consoles into Indian market	Market/ Production Shift	Emerged as a rival to Nintendo products, but did not do very well because of high prices
1996	First Cyber Cafe in India opened	IT Development	Simply named CyberCafe, this cyber cafe opened at Mumbai's Leela hotel in 1996. It is soon followed by Delhi's Cyber Club at the ITC Maurya hotel. Both of them no longer exist
1997	Dhruva Interactive founded	Developer/ Company	India's first game developer, it was founded by Rajesh Rao
1997	Introduction of Snake game in Nokia feature phones	Game Development	Nokia entered the Indian market in 1994
1999	UTV Indiagames founded	Developer/ Company	Founded by Vishal Gondal as a five-member team, currently a video game publisher across various platforms for the South Asian market
2000	*Yoddha: The Warrior*	Videogame launch	India's first 3D game, and the first FPS from India and possibly also the first commercially sold PC game in the country
2001	PlayStation 2 launched in India	Market/ Production Shift	The console only grew in sales in the later years of the decade
2001	ESPN Super Selector	Videogame launch	Fantasy cricket game run by ESPN Star Sports, it was created by Joy Bhattacharjya

Year (date)	Event	Type	Notes
2002	*Bhagat Singh: The Game*	Videogame launch	Developed by Mitashi and published by Lumen Phon Multimedia, this shooter game borrows on the nationalist history of India and the life of Bhagat Singh for its premise
2003	*SKOAR!* Magazine	Publication	Started in 2003 as a bi-monthly publication by Jasubhai Digital Media Pvt. Ltd. as a sister publication to Digit (an Indian technology magazine). Eventually, it expanded into a magazine, website and community dedicated to video games in India
2003	Ironcode Gaming established	Developer/ Company	An independent game developer that publishes innovative games, it was founded by Pallav and Gaurav Nawani
2004	Lakshya Digital established	Developer/ Company	It is a premier provider of art, animation and Vfx services for the video games industry
2005	Ingenuity Gaming established	Developer/ Company	Ingenuity works with land-based, mobile and online companies worldwide to deliver games to all major platforms. This multi-channel game developer and studio has developed 500 games since 2005
2005	First MPhil thesis submitted on videogames and storytelling	Publication	An MPhil thesis was submitted on videogames and storytelling to Department of English at Jadavpur University, Kolkata
2006	Gameshastra founded	Developer/ Company	It was headquartered in Hyderabad

Year (date)	Event	Type	Notes
2006	NASSCOM Gaming Forum established	Organisation	The Forum has active support and participation from Digital Chocolate, Electronic Arts, ChaYoWo games, Playdom, iBibo, Jump Games, 99 Games, Mpowered.in, Hashtag Studios, Hungama Digital and many more. It has five active city chapters—Mumbai, Delhi, Hyderabad, Pune and Bangalore—each of which regularly hosts developer meet-ups
2007	Flipkart founded by Sachin and Binny Bansal	Organization	Flipkart is one of India's leading e-commerce marketplaces today
2008	Ubisoft Entertainment India Pvt Ltd	Developer Game Studio/ Company	Ubisoft Pune was legally incorporated as Ubisoft Entertainment India Pvt. Ltd. on 9 May 2008. It is a video game production studio based in Pune, India. The company is owned and operated by Ubisoft Entertainment, headquartered in Paris, France, and is primarily committed to developing gaming consoles and mobile games
2008	First NASSCOM Game Developers' Conference/ Convention, GDC	Conference/ Convention	India's primary platform for showcasing, inspiring, learning and dialogue, organised annually under the NASSCOM Gaming Forum
2008	*Ghajini*	Videogame Launch	Ghajini, developed by FXlabs and Geetha Arts, is a third-person action game based on the 2008 Bollywood film of the same name that starred Aamir Khan and was hailed to be India's first true 3D PC game

Year (date)	Event	Type	Notes
2009	*Hanuman: Boy Warrior*	Videogame launch	Developed by Aurona Technologies Hyderabad for Sony Computer Entertainment Europe, 2009, video game for PlayStation 2. Billed as the first console game developed entirely in India
2009	*Desi Adda: Games of India*	Videogame launch	A collection of cultural games from India, based on traditional Indian sports. First game developed entirely in India to be released on the PlayStation Network, and included three languages
2010	*The Legend of Vraz*	Videogame launch/ Award	This is the first arcade game based on Miniature Indian Paintings and was launched in 2010. It won the Best PC game Award at FICCI BAF Awards 2010 in Mumbai. It was developed by Zatun and was also their debut PC game
2012	Souvik Mukherjee writes an entry on India in the Encyclopedia of Videogames	Publication	Souvik Mukherjee wrote an entry on India in the *Encyclopedia of Videogames Encyclopedia of Video Games: The Culture, Technology, and Art of Gaming* ed. Mark J.P. Wolf
2012	Shailesh Prabhu makes his award-winning puzzle game, *Huebrix*	Videogame launch	Shailesh Prabhu of Yellow Monkeys Studio makes *Huebrix*
2013	Amazon India starts business	Organization	In early June 2013, Amazon.com launched their Amazon India marketplace without any marketing campaigns

Year (date)	Event	Type	Notes
2013	Adrienne Shaw publishes essay on gaming culture in India	Publication	Adrienne Shaw published her chapter 'How Do You Say Gamer in Hindi? Exploratory Research on the Indian Digital Game Industry and Culture' in Gaming Globally eds. N. Huntemann and B. Aslinger
2014	Studio Oleomingus	Developer/ Company	Independent game and arts studio, based in Chala, India, is founded by Dhruv Jani who runs it in collaboration with Sushant Chakraborty and Vivek Savsaiya
2014	*TeenPatti* Games	Videogame launch	TeenPatti Gold has been developed by Bengaluru-based studio, Moonfrog Labs, and is among the highest grossing games in India
2014	Casey O'Donnell publishes *Developer's Dilemma: The Secret World of Videogame Creators*	Publication	Written by Casey O'Donnell, this book is a critical inspection of the collaborative process of game development, drawing on extensive fieldwork in game studios in the United States and India
2014	*Unrest*	Videogame launch	This videogame thematically draws on Ancient India and was developed by Jaipur-based developers, Pyrodactyl. The game won two awards—namely Softpedia: Indie Game of the Year 2014 and NASSCOM Indie Game of the Year 2014
2014	*Guardian of the Skies*	Videogame launch	First video game produced by the Indian Air Force

Year (date)	Event	Type	Notes
2014	Video Games Fest	Conference/ Convention	It was held at Bengaluru as a showcase for game designers and developers; it was also held in the following years at Bengaluru and Pune
2014	*Lovely Planet*	Videogame launch	This is an innovative and colourful FPS game developed by New Delhi-based QuickTequila and was published by tinyBuild. Moroever it was the first game developed by an Indian to make it to Wii U and X box One
2015	Steam pricing in Indian Rupees	Videogame event	
2015	Launch of *Stay, Mum*	Videogame launch	A videogame that takes the form of a narrative puzzle that explores the relationship between a mother and son. It was developed by the New Delhi-based experimental game studio, Lucid Labs
2015	Launch of *Socioball*	Videogame launch	Socioball is an isometric puzzle game developed by Yellow Monkey Studios and was released in 2015
2015	Indian Gaming Expo (IGX)	Conference/ Convention	It was held in Mumbai on 14–15 November
2015	Souvik Mukherjee writes a chapter on India in *Videogames across the World*	Publication	Souvik Mukherjee wrrote a chapter on India in *Videogames across the World* ed. By Mark J.P.Wolf

Year (date)	Event	Type	Notes
2016	*Darshan Diversion*	Videogame Launch	Created by Padmini Ray Murray, Joel Johnson and K.V. Ketan for the Global Game Jam, an annual game-creation event, in 2016. The game was inspired by recent incidents of priests at Indian temples, particularly Sabarimala, preventing women from entering the temple premises, especially while menstruating
2016	Rockstar Interactive India LLP	Developer/ Company	A studio of Rockstar Games, formed by absorbing Dhruva Interactive, located in Bangalore
2016	Establishment of All India Gaming Federation (AIGF)	Organisation	Apex body of skill-based online gaming industry in India
2016	Steam allows all financial wallets and even cash-on-delivery	Organisation	Novaplay, Steam's financial partner made all digital financial transactions and even cash-on-delivery possible, thus revolutionising the marketing of games online by Steam
2017	*Asura: Vengeance Edition*	Videogame launch	The game developed by Ogre Head Studio was released in April 2017. It won the NASSCOM Game of the Year Award in 2017. It draws on on Indian cultural and mythological tropes

Year (date)	Event	Type	Notes
2017	Blue Whale Ban	Videogame Ban	Blue Whale Challenge is a suicide game in which the player is given certain tasks to complete for a period of 50 days and the final task is to kill oneself. The player is also asked to share photos after finishing the challenge. On 11 August 2017, the Government of India directed Internet providers to immediately remove the links of the dangerous online game
2017	Indian Federation of Sports Gaming (IFSG) formed	Organisation	A self-regulatory industry body that protects consumer interest and creates standardised best practices in the sports gaming industry
2017	*Scribbled Arena*	Videogame Launch	This multiplayer shooter game was developed by Mumbai-based developers Apar Games and won several awards such as Best PC Game India at FICCI BAF Awards 2017. It thematically draws on arcade tank battles but refashions them in a doodle avatar
2018	Launch of *The Last Train*	Videogame Launch	The Last Train is a Survival Adventure Game developed by Mumbai based Smash Game Studios and reimagines some of the most poignant epsiodes of WWII by re-creating a scenario where Japan has the opportunity of retailiating post the Hiroshima-Nagasaki bombings by America.

Year (date)	Event	Type	Notes
			The player takes the role of one of the last surviving train pilot in a post world War 2 America and helps locate the more humane dimensions of the aftermath of war by helping survivors reach their families across the country. The game was an Indie Game of the Year Finalist
2018	Launch of *Alter Army*	Videogame launch	Alter Army is a fast-paced action game developed by Vague Pixels. This is the debut game of this Japiur based video game development studio which was founded by two 16-year-olds—Mridul Bansal and Mridul Pancholi
2019	*Missing: Game for a Cause*	Videogame launch	An RPG produced by Leena Kejriwal and Satyajit Chakraborty to create awareness on the thousands of girls trafficked into prostitution in India
2019	*Scarfall: The Royale Combat*	Videogame launch	An Indian online and offline multiplayer battle royale game developed by Surat based gaming and IT service provider company XSQUADS Tech LLP
2019	*Mx. Democracy*	Videogame launch	The game was by the Election Commission in India in collaboration with National Institute of Design, Bengaluru (NID-B). The game touches on the voter registration process—types of voters and forms, enforcing model code of conduct, voter slip distribution, preparing the ballot, poll day preparations and polling process

Year (date)	**Event**	**Type**	**Notes**
2019	*Indian Air Force: A Cut Above*	Videogame launch	launched by Air Chief Marshal B.S. Dhanoa, this is a 3D mobile game.
2019	GamesLit Conference/ Convention: Games at the Margin	Conference/ Convention	GamesLit was the first international conference on Game Studies to choose an Indian venue. The three-day conference was hosted by Presidency University, Kolkata
2019	Souvik Mukherjee writes a chapter on India in *Videogames and the Global South*	Publication	Souvik Mukherjee's chapter 'Replaying the Digital Divide: Videogames in India' is published in *Videogames and the Global South* ed. by Phillip Penix-Tadsen
2020	Aditya Deshbandhu publishes *Gaming Culture(s) in India*	Publication	Aditya Deshbandhu, a professor in Indian Institute of Management, Indore, published *Gaming Culture(s) in India: Digital Play in Everyday Life*
2020	*Raji: An Ancient Epic*	Videogame launch	Nodding Heads Studio gained international acclaim for their indie game, *Raji: An Ancient Epic*
2021	*FAU-G (Fearless and United Guards)*	Videogame launch	*FAU-G* is an action game developed by nCore Games and is a tribute to the Indian Armed Forces
2021	*Battlegrounds Mobile India*	Videogame launch	*PUBG* relaunches as a new title called *Battlegrounds Mobile India* under the management of Krafton

Timeline of Videogame-related Events in Pakistan

Year (date)	Event	Type	Notes
1964–1967	Pakistan International Airlines computerised its operations via an IBM 1401 machine	IT Development	Coming around a decade later than the early Indian computers, these computers offered a semi-digital system
1968	Computer Centre set up in University of Islamabad	IT Development	Accomplished through collaboration with University of Indiana
1977	Establishment of Systems Ltd.	IT Development	Pakistan's first Software House
1979	Digitalization of government departments such as the Water and Sanitation Agency (WASA)	IT Development	Systems was the first informational technology company in the country that provided the Oracle-based software
1980s	The Pakistani Army inducted computers	IT Development	Its departments were computerised by the 1990s
1990	The Telephone and Telegraph Department was converted into the Pakistan Telecommunications Company (PTCL)	IT Development	PTCL started local dial-up connections in 1995
1992-93	First dial-up email service set up by Digicom Pakistan Pvt. Ltd.	IT Development	
1994	Private dial-up set up by Digicom Pakistan	IT Development	

Year (date)	Event	Type	Notes
2000	National IT Policy	Legislation	As part of this policy, the Pakistani government developed the IT Action Plan wherein 5 billion Pakistani Rupees were committed to the development of the IT infrastructure in 2000–2001 alone
2000s	Beginning of videogame development in Pakistan	Game Developer	
2000s	Early game development companies such as Trango Interactive, Wireframe Technologies and Fork Particle set up their studios in Islamabad and Lahore	Games Market	These studios also carried out outsourcing contracts from international players such as Zynga, Sega, Disney and THQ
2008	Pakistani VfX designer Mir Zafar Ali won an Oscar for Best Visual Effects	Personal achievement	This is as per the Pakistani magazine, *Weekly*. Ali, who designed the visual effects for Golden Compass, would go on to do so for *The Life of Pi*
2009	Mindstorm Studios signed a contract the British company Codemasters to collaborate on the Cricket Revolution game that was apparently supported by the Pakistani Cricket star, Shoaib Malik.	Game Development	

Year (date)	**Event**	**Type**	**Notes**
2019	Digital Pakistan Policy	Legislation	Launched by prime minister Imran Khan
2020	Pakistan bans *PUBG* and then revokes the ban	Legislation	Pakistan too banned PUBG Mobile earlier this year. The country's telecommunication authority (PTA) had temporarily suspended the battle royale title because of complaints received from various sections of the society. The suspension, however, was later lifted after a meeting between Pakistan Telecommunication Authorities and Proxima Beta Ltd (PB) representatives
2021	Arslan Ash becomes *Tekken 7* world champion	Personal achievement	Pakistan's Arslan Ash Siddique won the International WePlay Ultimate Fighting League (WUFL) Tekken 7 tournament
2021	Umer Hussain publishes article on Pakistani women eSports players	Publication	Umer Hussain at al. published their article '"I Can be Who I Am When I Play Tekken 7": E-sports Women Participants from the Islamic Republic of Pakistan' in the Game Studies journal, *Games and Culture*

Timeline of Videogame-related Events in Sri Lanka

Year	Event	Type	Notes
Early 1970s	IBM 1130 computers introduced in the country	IT Development	The universities in Moratuwa and Peradeniya used them to teach FORTRAN programming and later the computer was used by the engineering undergraduate students in preparing course work on power system load flow studies in Electrical Engineering, structural design in Civil Engineering, machine component design in Mechanical Engineering, etc. The computing system at Moratuwa was also used for administrative purposes when in the late seventies, the university payroll and the University Provident Fund statements for the UGC were computed on this
1983	Framing of COMPOL—National Computer Policy by Sri Lankan Government.	Legal policy	Due to the combined efforts of NARESA (Natural Resources Energy and Science Authority of Sri Lanka) and universities in Moratuwa and Peradeniya, COMPOL was framed by the Sri Lankan government. Some of the key objectives of COMPOL involved ensuring an efficient regulation of computer technology in all spheres of Sri Lankan life and benefit the lifestyle of its citizens. This framework was built under the leadership of President J. R. Jayewardene and also led to the formation of a committee who was in charge of drawing up a National Computer Policy Report which was accepted and led to the formation of CINTEC

Year	Event	Type	Notes
1984	Establishment of CINTEC—Computer and Information Technology Council of Sri Lanka	Legal body	This council was developed after the National Computer Policy Report developed by the COMPOL mandated committee was accepted. The council's name was changed in 1994 to Council of Information and Technology by the Science and Technology Department but it retained its acronym CINTEC
1992	Internet introduced among the academic and research community	IT Development	
1995	First Commercial ISP launched	IT Development	
2002	Launch of e-Sri Lanka Project	Government Initiative	Launched in November 2002, this project was entrusted with the task of developing an ICT roadmap for Sri Lanka by helping disseminate IT services and associated knowledge in fairly inaccessible areas (such as rural Sri Lanka, etc.)
2003	Implementation of the Information and Technology Act (2003) and establishment of ICTA	legal body	The e-Sri Lanka project ensued the implementation of the Information and Technology Act (2003) and led to the establishment of ICTA—Information and Technology Agency that has been operational since 1 July 2003. The ICT Agency was established as a government owned private company and was responsible for facilitating the e-Sri Lanka Policy

Year	Event	Type	Notes
2007	Establishment of Game Technology Solutions	Game Developer	Establishment of this Sri Lankan game development studio located in Dehiwala, Sri Lanka. They are the pioneers of mobile gaming in Sri Lanka. They also develop educational games since 2014
2007	Establishment of Gamer. lk (GAMER (GAMER LK)—Sri Lanka's only and most popular gaming forum	Gaming Forum establishment	This is the largest gaming platform of Sri Lanka. It was founded by Raveen Wijayatilake, who completed his postgraduate degree from University of Southampton
2008	Release of *The Colombo Ride* developed by Game Technology solutions	Game Release	This is Sri Lanka's first Sinhala mobile game and was developed by one of Sri Lanka's major gaming companies, Game Technology Solutions. Its second instalment won the title of 'Best in South Asia' at the mbillionth Award 2010 edition held in New Delhi, India and was released in 2009. Its third instalment 'Colombo Ride 3D' was nominated as a top five finalist at Mashable Awards 2010
2011	Establishment of Arimac	Digital product Developer	Arimac is one of Sri Lanka's premier digital product development company. It works in the fields of Mobile and Enterprise Solutions, Artificial Intelligence and Machine Learning, Immersive Technologies, and Game Design and Development
2017	Launch of Kanchayudha by Arimac	Game Release	It is an episodic historical game developed by Arimac using Unreal Engine and is based on Sri Lankan mythology and local culture

Timeline of Videogame-related Events in Bangladesh

Year	Event	Type	Notes
1968	First Computer brought into the country—an IBM 1620	IT development	This was during Bangladesh's existence as East Pakistan
1980s	Formal introduction of computers into the country	IT development	
1987	Bangladesh Computer Samity established	Organisation	Popularly known as BCS, the national association of information and communication technologies companies in Bangladesh. Mostafa Jabbar was its president for four consecutive terms
1988	Bijoy—Bengali digital keyboard	IT development	This Bengali digital keyboard was created by Mostafa Jabbar
1990s	Introduction of arcade games like *Mustapha* and *Street Fighter II*	Games Market	Mustapha was the local name for Capcom's Cadillacs and Dinosaurs (one of the characters it featured is called Mustapha)
1997	Bangladesh Association of Software and Information Services (BASIS) established	Organisation	The national association of software and information and communication technologies companies in Bangladesh

Year	Event	Type	Notes
2002-03	*Dhaka Racing*	Game Release	The game was developed by eSophers Ltd and was the first 3D game to have been developed in Bangladesh. Its demo version was released in 2002 for Microsoft Windows and the product was available for the commercial market in 2003. It thematically draws on the streets of Dhaka. The game also features traditional Bangladeshi vehicles such as rickshaws, autos , etc—players can choose these vehicles for their races
2004	*Arunodoyer Agnishikha*	Game Release	Developed by Trimatrik Interactive Studio and published by SHOM Computers, this is a first-person shooter game based on the Bangladeshi Liberation War
2014	*Ludo Friends*	Game Release	Developed by TapStar Interactive, *Ludo Friends* draws on the popular household board game Ludo and is Bangladesh's first Bengali (Bangla) digital board game
2016	Release of *Heroes of '71*	Game Release	This shooter game has been developed by Mindfisher Games (formerly known as Portbliss games) and was released on the birth anniversary of Bangladesh in 2016. It was a video game funded by Bangladesh Computer Council and Information and Computer Technology and deals with Bangladesh's war of independence against Pakistan

Timeline of Videogame-related Events in Nepal

Year	Event	Type	Notes
1971	First computer introduced	IT Development	For the purpose of conducting the national census
1979	First microcomputer in Nepal developed	IT Development	Created by Muni Shakya
1983	Nepalese font developed	IT Development	Developed by Muni Shakya
1990s	Universities in Nepal started an ICT programme	Academia	
1995	First e-mail service started	IT Development	started by the private firm, Mercantile Communications
1997	Telecommunications Act passed by the government	Legal Policy	
2000	IT Policy drafted	Legal Policy	Named the Information Technology Policy, 2057
2016	Yarsa Games founded	Game Developer	The Pokhara-based game studio was founded by NJ Subedi
2016	Sroth Code Games founded	Game Developer	The now defunct game studio was founded by Uttam Adhikari in Tinkune, Kathmandu
2019	Red Tail Fox Pvt. Ltd. (Red Tail Fox Studio) founded	Game Developer	Red Tail Studio is a creative design and tech development company focused on tech development, game development, digital product shipment/ distribution and internet marketing. Founded by Uttam Adhikari in Kathmandu

Timeline of Videogame-related Events in Bhutan

Bhutan			
Year	**Event**	**Type**	**Notes**
1963	Bhutan received its first telecommunication links	IT Development	
1998	Bhutan received its national telecommunication network	IT Development	Established with Japanese aid whereby Thimphu, the capital city, got direct access to the world outside
1999	Bhutan Telecommunication Act	Legal Policy	Television and Internet were introduced together at this time
2006 (July)	Bhutan Information Communication and Media Act passed	Legal Policy	Purpose is to provide for a technology and service sector neutral regulatory mechanism which implements convergence of information, computing, media, communications technologies and facilitates for the provision of a whole range of new services
2003	ICT Whitepaper drafted	Legal Policy	It provides a framework for developing computer technology in the country and states that Bhutan will harness the benefits of ICT to realize the Millennium Development Goals and enhance Gross National Happiness (GNH)
2016	Dota 2 Bhutan Summer League 2016	eSports Tournament	*Dota 2* is among the most popular games in Bhutan

Timeline of Videogame-related Events in the Maldives

1955	The first telephone exchange built	Telecom	
1968	Telephones open to public for the first time	Telecom	Maldives became independent in 1966, shortly after telephony was opened to the public
1996	Internet comes to Maldives	Telecom/ Internet	Dhivehi Raajjeygé Gulhun or Dhiraagu is the oldest and major telephone and Internet provider
2004	Dial-up Internet connectivity	Telecom/ Internet	
2013	Playmakers in Maldives event	Game event	Researcher Amani Naseem organised the 'Playmakers in the Maldives' event, where ten game designers from different countries created new games with and for people in the capital Malé
2017	*Star Wars: Rogue One Scarif*		
2020	*Thakuru Wars* online game released	Game development	
2021	High-speed broadband connections are commonly available	Internet	

Appendix Two: Survey

Title: Videogames and Culture

Medium: Online survey conducted using Google Forms. The survey was anonymous although participants were provided the option to mention their emails if they wanted a copy of the results. The results have been anonymised entirely.

Descriptive text: This is a research survey being conducted independently to gauge how far videogames influence culture, and are seen as cultural artefacts in the Subcontinent. The results of the survey will be communicated to you if you wish and will also be published in my forthcoming book. I am a videogame researcher from India with over twenty years of experience in Games Studies. If you wish to contact me, please feel free to email me at prosperoscell@gmail.com

The questions and responses are listed below and the textual responses are presented verbatim.

Do you consider yourself a casual gamer or a hardcore game?
43 responses

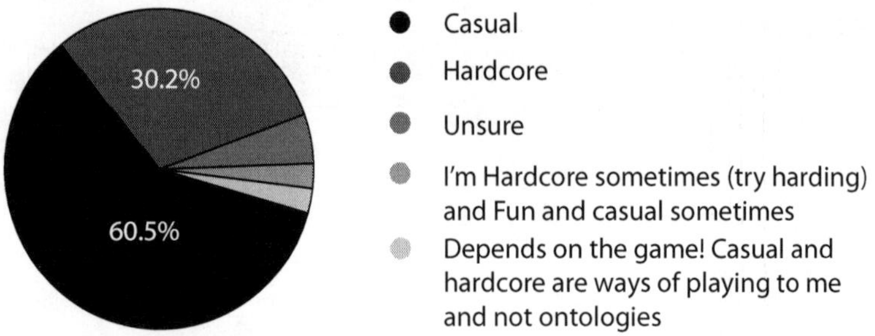

What is you gender?
42 responses

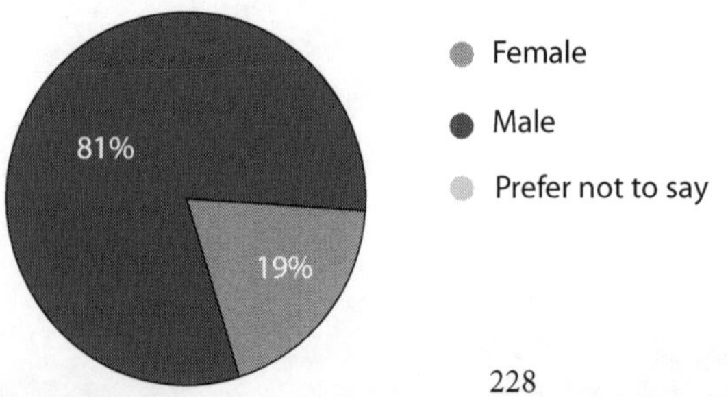

What age group do you fall in?
43 responses

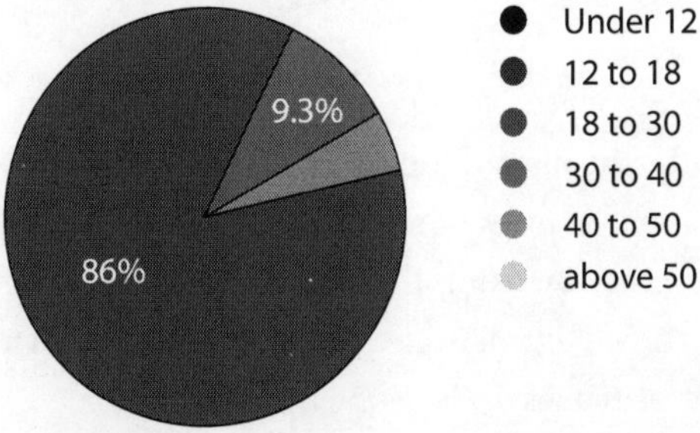

Do you think videogames have an impact on culture?
43 responses

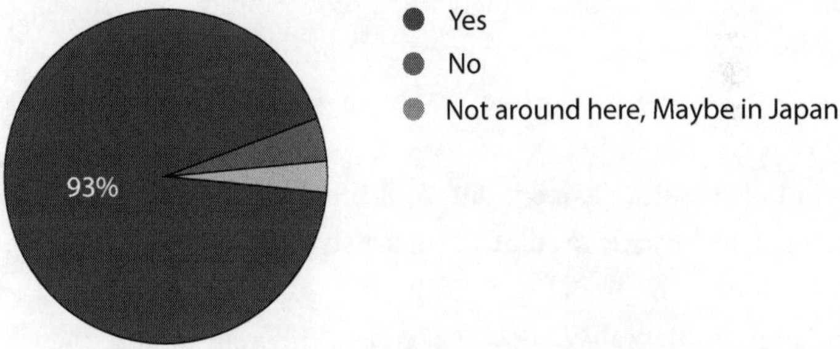

In which of these categories do you think games influence culture?
43 responses

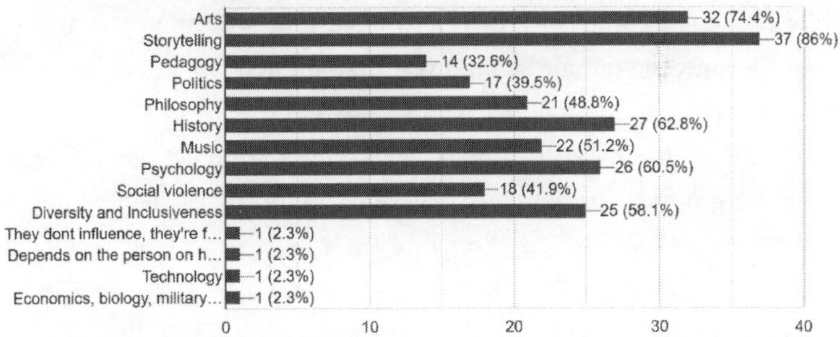

Would you care to elaborate on how videogames influence culture? 22 responses

Good For Mental Health

I feel games are as influential as other art forms, if not more because of the way they let you embody a character and make choices in a way a book doesn't let you.

They don't influence, they're for entertainment and fun with friends.

Videogames have often drawn inspiration from and shown social violence, the darker themes that convey other sides of society during certain circumstances, and more. By using the art of storytelling and gaming together, it results in an introspective look into one's own perspective and what the player makes of the game in an individualistic way.

Video games influence pop culture greatly from YouTube content to memes and more interestingly their contribution to language. Certain terms have undergone semantic augmentation such as 'noob' 'op(veropowered)' 'gg(good game)' 'tank/tanky'.

Everyone has his or her preferences. Each and every one of us has some kind of reason to game it out. And the things and actions done in games maybe be toxic to someone or satisfying to someone..not that I'm telling him or her a sadist when he feels excited blowing out the alien brain onto the wall. But everyone has a different mindset which he/she works on. Thus games effects [sic] each one of us differently.

Videogames are a new form of storytelling. Many have a storyline to follow. I see games as any other medium of art, along the lines of books, songs, movies and all. So yes, they influence the way we think and perceive 'real life' and hence, influence culture.

First and foremost as points of common interest that become breeding grounds for further discussions about topics such as music, philosophy and storytelling, to name a few. Further videogames often carry over elements of the above endemic to the places they were made and allow players to be exposed to ideas from places other than the one they live in.

Video games affect our brain activity. So this directly influences our thinking pattern. This allows us to be more open-minded in things, think deeper and think quickly, rather than just following the common social acceptance.

Since they are a new, emerging form of entertainment with their own mode of storytelling (and therefore product differentiation in the market), they attract, influence and cultivate their own breed of consumers. Therefore, depending on the game, consumers become more sensitive to choice and consequence, become accustomed to social violence, associate cause/effect relations in succeeding or failing to exit a labyrinth, etc.

Videogames as cultural artifacts emerge from within the culture, their influence hence, comes from within. Videogames change the prevalent notions of the ludic in culture via challenging them, appropriating them or propagating an alternative notion.

Videogames break away from the simple reader-writer context and dichotomy. They break the space between the reader and the text and allow a secondhand experience of a particular subculture, through the Player Character or Avatar.

It makes you violent but can help to talk to others as well.

eSports has become a rising cultural currency of certain nations. For example, in Denmark, after a dominating run in three consecutive CSGO majors (the biggest and most prestigious CSGO tournament) by a Danish team named Astralis, the Danish government decided to make the team a public-sector undertaking. The team and the sport became hugely popular and recognised in the whole state, and several scholarships and stipends were introduced for the benefit of eSports. This was surprisingly promoted by politicians and political parties who actually advocated the benefits of eSports and video games in general. Other than that, video games have often led to cultural re-conceptions of certain countries, states and cultural populations, just like anime and manga. Game soundtracks have gone on to become chartbusters, introducing people to genres they never would have heard or heard of before were it not for those games (read: Mick Gordon and the Doom soundtrack—metal through and through). Discovery feature in recent Assassins Creed games is a unique way to promote pedagogy through games.

Just like books, they leave a mark on culture. It can be argued that the mark is not as wide but it is a mark nonetheless.

Video games help us to find friends from other regions. Through this, we get to know about their culture. How they behave.

Videogames have brought gamification everywhere.

In the same way as any other Entertainment.

It's good to for taking the work pressure out (1) By the representation of objects, people, societies, environments to portray events and tell stories (2) By allowing both immersion into these representations and yet allowing a user interaction/manipulation of the events that are portrayed (3) Social behaviour, intra-and-inter cultural relationships are thus represented and modulated (4) These in turn condition responses and cultural thought, and stimulates resistance or countercultural thought (5) Which in turn influences game making and gameplay, setting up a feedback loop with culture (6) As a result, the previous escapist, 'non-serious' space set up by games become more reflective, and achieves an increase in the porosity between the 'non-serious' and the 'serious'. (7) It thus integrates into a collective memory and is referenced in social behaviour and discourses across generations, just like any other narrative media: videogames 'become' (quotes for lack of italics) culture.

Which country are you from?
43 responses

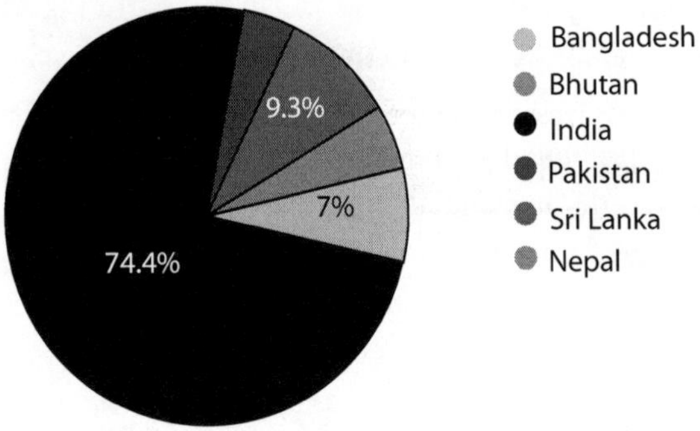

How do videogames influence your country's culture, if at all? 20 responses

I think they influence culture but they are not big enough yet to influence it at large. They influence it in niches. Until we come to games like *PubG* which have influenced a whole generation, but I'm not sure in what ways.

They don't influence, they're for entertainment and fun with friends.

Video games, especially online multiplayer ones, help people connect internationally. Not to mention, video gaming has become a growing market in the country. Indian themes in certain videogames, like *Raji*, also help in getting a glimpse into the variety of different cultures in the country via storytelling.

Can't say about the entire country but in my community gaming is frequently used as an activity in social bonding.

For us, gaming would have been a fatal future to the kinds even three years before. But now that we and the younger generation are growing up among gamers—even though parents know—it gives the future a slight bit of change. For the younger ones having idols such as Mortal, Scout, acue, shroud, all master class gamers should chase gaming as a career.

Friends in my neighborhood come together to play videogames in cybercafés, or phones, in the process making friends and socialising.

In our country, the inclination to play and recognise video games as a part of culture increases steadily up the age pyramid up to a certain point when it breaks off sharply and videogames become nothing but 'distractions' and 'tools of teaching violence'.

Both in positive ways and negative ways. Teenagers who used to go out, socialise and play cricket, climb trees have moved towards staying in a room, and playing games, as well as some of the teenagers who used to do drugs and all.

India is much more a base of consumers than a production hub. The dominant discourse here is still around it being an idle form of entertainment, or a desensitisation toward graphic violence. However, perhaps it is worth noting that videogames tangibly influence pop culture in terms of building friendships, events, etc.

People can get arrested for playing *PUBG*.

As per my knowledge, videogames are yet to penetrate Indian subcultures on a substantial level.

It has made us more violent but it helps us to express ourselves as well.

There has been a growing rise in esport enthusiasts in India over the past couple of years. With the advent of influencers sponsored by overseas teams and corporations such as Red Bull, Corsair, Alienware, etc, people are finding pathways to success in gaming too (I would highly recommend following Ankit Pant, also known as V3NOM, on Instagram and checking his Instagram stories to see how much of an influence a single person pursuing eSports in India has become). Beyond that, with games such as *Raji*, India has well seeped into the world market and has garnered quite a bit of attention and recognition.

It influences the youth's way of thinking and communication.

Video games are mainly played by 10–30-year-old people. So we can say the youth of our country mainly play video games. By playing video games they make friends from other countries and they get to about other countries' cultures. Sometimes they adopt some good things from other countries and also bad things. Like they adopt clothing styles and sometimes they adopt slang.

Videogames are slowly becoming a massive source of entertainment, especially among young adults.

Not in my country, not yet.

It has made us more open to other people and cultures, I guess.

It links Indian audiences to a global gaming audience and thus is a major source of cosmopolitanism in Indian culture. Game mechanics and questions of prices stimulate discussions on late capitalism and technological modernity. Depictions of India in videogames made by international game makers invite celebrations or criticism depending on colonial, Islamic and Hindu past. The expanding Indian gaming industry takes these things into consideration, along with geopolitics, in making its videogames. Nationalist sentiment and the still-independent nature of diverse gamemaking studios in India results in increasing numbers of Indian gamers, and speaks to Indian ethnic, religious and cultural tensions, along with discourses of sovereignty, modernity and history, not to mention how Indian audiences imagine themselves politically in the world. A rise in popularity of multiplayer shooter games might echo the recent worrying rise of majoritarian mob violence and troubling political cultivation of discourses of victimization and misdirected socio-economic-political frustration.

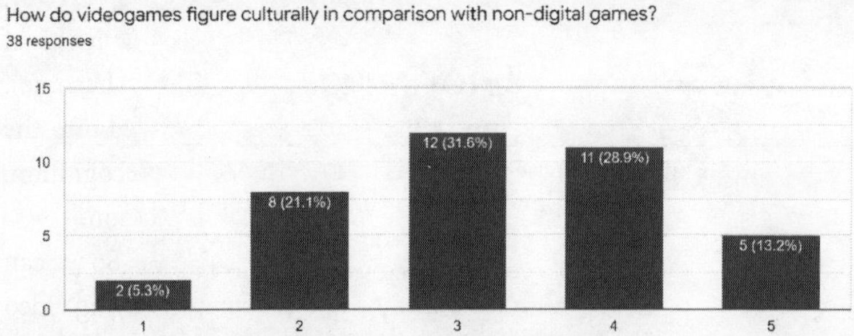

(This is a Likert scale on which 1 = very poorly and 5 = as popular as older games, culturally.)

Glossary

8-bit and 16-bit	These were terms that referred to the processor size necessary to run games. These refer to the retro games that ran on the early platforms and allowed the developer limited colour tiles to work with. One bit, of the unit of computer data-processing, has two states—one or zero or 'true or false' or 'on or off'. Computers encode data in binary units to be able to move data around. Today, there are games 'inspired' by the retro-look of the 8-bit and 16-bit games. The original games would look like they did not out of artistic choice but a technical necessity.
Battle Royale Game	*Battle Royale* games are multiplayer videogames that involve a last-man-standing style game that combines survival and exploitation. Players start with minimal equipment and must eliminate all opponents as they fight from within a shrinking 'safe area' with the winner being the last player or team alive. These games take their name from the 2000 Japanese film *Battle Royale* directed by Kinji Fukasaku.
Bodyshopping	Bodyshopping is an IT industry term that describes the process of subcontracting employees to another company for a limited period. This is connected to outsourcing.
Business process outsourcing (BPO)	Business process outsourcing (BPO) is the contracting of business activities and functions to a third-party provider.
eSports	eSports (or electronic sports) is a term used to describe competitive videogaming. eSports tournaments usually consist of amateur or professional gamers competing against one another for cash prizes.
First-Person Shooter	A first-person shooter (FPS) is a genre of action video game that is played from the point of view of the protagonist. FPS games typically map the gamer's movements and provide a view of what an actual person would see and do in the game.

Floppy disks	A floppy disk is a magnetic data storage device that is composed of a disk of thin, flexible ('floppy') encased in a square or rectangular plastic shell. Initially available as 5.25-inch disks, the standard floppy disks were 3.5 inches and had a memory of 1.44 MB.
Gamer	A person who plays interactive games such as videogames. Adrienne Shaw notes that there is no equivalent in Hindi and other Indian languages; the same possibly holds across the Subcontinent.
Games process outsourcing (GPO)	See Business process outsourcing. The same process when applies to the videogame industry.
Global South	The phrase broadly refers to the regions of Latin America, Asia, Africa, and some parts of Oceania. It denotes mostly (though not all) low-income and often politically or culturally marginalised countries. The use of the phrase marks a shift from a central focus on development ('developing' or 'third world') or cultural difference toward an emphasis on geopolitical relations of power.
Glocalisation	Glocalisation is a combination of the words 'globalisation' and 'localisation.' The word describes a global product that can accommodate consumers in a local market.
Homebrew	When proprietary videogame and computer systems are used by hobbyists to make games that they were not originally intended for. Often, these are accompanied by adaptations of the hardware.
Indie	Independent or 'indie games' are games made by small teams or individual designers who are usually on a low budget.
Jugaad	Jugaad is a North Indian term that may mean something like DIY (do-it-yourself), homebrew or hack or even combinations of these. Jugaad, which signifies a quick fix in general, has both its champions and detractors.
License Raj	Between 1947 and 1990, India had a complex system of obtaining licenses to start a business that slowed its growth considerably. This is commonly called 'License Raj.'
Localisation	Videogame localisation is the process of producing/adding content for a specific region to make it seem that it was originally made for that region.

Ludification	Ludification is the process that inserts playfulness into quotidian activities and traditional media.
Ludology	Ludology is a school of thinking in Games Studies, where videogame researchers concentrate on rules and the formal features of games. The term was first used by Gonzalo Frasca. Espen Aarseth, Markku Eskelinen and Jesper Juul are some well-known scholars who associated their work with Ludology.
Magic circle	Johan Huizinga described a special space where all play takes place as 'magic circle'. The 'magic circle' later became a key theme in videogame studies Katie Salen (Tekinbas) and Eric Zimmerman popularised it in their book *Rules of Play* in 2003.
Narratology	This was the term used by the Ludologist group to describe all those who proposed that videogames tell stories. This application of the term is quite different from that in literary theory.
Online gaming	Playing videogames online is referred to as online gaming. Gaming, in this case, does not refer to gambling as in its traditional meaning.
PS, PS2, PS3, PS4 and PS5	This is an abbreviation for the Sony videogame console PlayStation. The name is the opposite of a 'work station' and the console is now in its fifth version. The numbers after 'PS' indicate the version.
RPG or Role-Playing Game	Role-playing games are a genre of electronic games and board games in which players follow a story quest as well as side quests, for which their character or party of characters gain experience that improves various attributes and abilities.
Third-person games	Third-person games are videogames that use a third-person point-of-view, i.e. have the camera focus from behind the player character.
Transculturation	Transculturation is a term coined by the South American anthropologist Fernando Ortiz to describe cultural exchange as a combination of acculturation, deculturation and neoculturation in his book *Cuban Counterpoint*.
Triple-A Games (or AAA games)	AAA games (pronounced triple-A games) are videogames that are distinguished by their huge development and marketing budgets.

Ludography

Alexei Pajitnov. *Tetris*. Alexei Pajitnov, 1984.

Arcils. *Thakuru Wars*. Arcils, 2020.

Arcube. *Polytricks*. Arcube, 2016.

Arimac. *Kanchayudha*. Colombo: N.p., 2017.

———. *Nero*. Arimac, 2021.

Atari. *Missile Command*. Atari, 1980.

Attrito. *Agontuk*. M7 Productions, 2019.

Audiogenic. *Brian Lara's Cricket*. Codemasters, 1994.

Aurona Technologies. *Hanuman: Boy Warrior*. Sony Computer Entertainment Europe, 2009.

Beam Software. *EA Sports Cricket 1997*. Electronic Arts, 1997.

Capcom. *Cadillacs and Dinosaurs*. Capcom, 1993.

———.*Streetfighter II*. Capcom, 1991.

CD Projekt. *Cyberpunk 2077*. CD Projekt, 2020.

Chakraborty, Satyajit. *Missing: A Game for a Cause*. Flying Robot Studios, 2016.

Church, Doug. *Tomb Raider: Legend*. Crystal Dynamics, 2006.

Core Design. *Tomb Raider 3*. Eidos, 1998.

Daisy Ale Soundworks. *Lost and Hound*. Daisy Ale Soundworks, 2020.

Danger Close Games. *Medal of Honor: Warfighter*. Electronic Arts, 2012.

Dhruva. *Kaun Banega Crorepati*. Dhruva, 2001.

Dowino. *A Blind Legend*. Dowino, 2015.

Electronic Arts. *Star Wars: Rogue One - Scarif*. Electronic Arts, 2017.

Ensemble Studios. *Age of Empires*. Microsoft Game Studios, 1997.

eSophers. *Dhaka Racing*. eSophers, 2003.

Flying Robots Studio. *Durga Puja Mystery*. University of Helsinki, 2020.

———. *Two Leaves and a Bud: Tea Garden Simulator*. Flying Robot Studios, 2021.

Frostwood Interactive. *Forgotten Fields*. Dino Digital, 2021.

FX Labs. *Dhoom 2*. FX Labs, 2008.

FX Labs and Geetha Arts. *Ghajini - The Game*. FX Labs and Geetha Arts, 2008.

Gamos Technology Solutions. *The Colombo Ride*. Colombo: Gamos Technology Solutions, 2007.

Garena. *Garena Freefire*. Garena, 2017.

Gearbox Software. *Borderlands 3*. 2K Games, 2019.

Gondal, Vishal, and Ninad Chhaya. *Yoddha: The Warrior*. Indiagames, 2000.

Halfbrick Studios. *Fruit Ninja*. Halfbrick Studios, 2010.

ID Software. *Doom*. ID Software, 1993.

———.*Quake*. ID Software, 1996.

———. *Wolfenstein 3d*. ID Software, 1993.

Imangi Studios. *Temple Run*. Imangi Studios, 2011.

Immersive Games. *Chandragupta - Warrior Prince*. Sony Computer Entertainment, 2009.

Infinity Ward. *Call of Duty: Modern Warfare 3*. Activision, 2011.

Ironcode Software. *Pahelika: Secret Legends*. Ironcode Software, 2009.

Iwatani, Toru. *Pacman*. Namco, 1980.

Kailash Satyarthi Children's Foundation. *(Un)Trafficked*. Kailash Satyarthi Children's Foundation.

Kain, K.V. Ketan, knyghtro, and praymurray. *Darshan Diversion*. A Local Game for Local People, 2016.

Krafton. *Battlegrounds India Mobile*. Krafton, 2021.

Mindstorm Studios. *Cricket Revolution*. Mindstorm Studios, 2009.

———. *Whacksy Taxi*. Mindstorm Studios, 2010.

Monolith Productions. *Middle Earth: Shadow of War*. Warner Brothers, 2017.

Namco. *Digdug*. Namco, 1982.

———. *Tekken 3*. Namco, 1997.

Naughty Dog, *Uncharted: A Thief's End*. Sony Interactive Entertainment. 2016.

Naughty Dog, *Uncharted: The Lost Legacy*. Sony Interactive Entertainment. 2017.

Niantic. *Pokemon Go*. Niantic, 2016.

Nishikado, Tomohiro. *Space Invaders*. Taito, 1978.

Nodding Heads. *Raji: An Ancient Epic*. Nodding Heads, 2020.

Portbliss. *Heroes of '71*. Portbliss, 2017.

Prabhu, Shailesh. *Huebrix*. Yellow Monkeys Studio, 2012.

Prodigi Interactive. *Threta*. Prodigi Interactive, n.d.

PUBG Corporation. *PlayerUnknown's Battlegrounds*. PUBG Corporation, 2017.

Punjab Information Technology Board. *Pakistan Army Retribution*. Punjab Information Technology Board, 2015.

Pyrodactyl Games. *Unrest*. Pyrodactyl Games, 2014.

Quicksand. *Antariksha Sanchar*. Quicksand.

Quicksand Labs. *Antariksha Sanchar: Transmissions in Space*. Quicksand Labs.

Rare. *Sea of Thieves*. XBox Game Studios, 2018.

Rockstar North. *Grand Theft Auto V*. Rockstar, 2013.

———.*Red Dead Rdemption*. Rockstar Games, 2018.

Rovio Entertainment. *Angry Birds*. Rovio Entertainment, 2009.

Sega. *Michael Jackson's Moonwalker*. Sega, 1989.

———.*Sonic the Hedgehog*. Sega, 1991.

Steve Russell. *Spacewar*. N.p., 1962.

Studio nCore. *FAU-G Fearless and United Guards*. Studio nCore, 2021.

Studio Oleomingus. *Somewhere*. Studio Oleomingus, 2014.

Tapstar Interactive. *Ludu Friends*. Tapstar Interactive, 2014.

The Collective. *Indiana Jones and the Emperor's Tomb*. Lucas Arts, 2003.

Treyarch. *Call of Duty: Balck Ops 2*. Activision, 2012.

Trimatrik Interactive. *Arunodoyer Agnisikha (Flame of the Sunrise)*. Shom Computers, 2004.

Trine. *Ra.One The Game*. Sony Computer Entertainment, 2011.

———.*Street Cricket Champions 2*. Trine, 2010.

Ubisoft Montreal. *Far Cry 4*. Ubisoft, 2014.

Undead Labs. *State of Decay 2*. XBox Game Studios, 2013.

Underdogs. *Mukti*. Underdogs, TBA.

United Front Games. *Sleeping Dogs*. Square Enix, 2012.

Valve Software. *Counter-Strike*. Valve Software, 2000.

Visai Games. *Venba*. Visai Games, TBA.

Willy Higginbotham. *Tennis for Two*. N.p., 1958.

Windmill Software. *Digger*. Windmill Software, 1983.

Wozniak, Steve, and Steve Jobs. *Breakout*. Atari, 1976.

Yellow Monkey Studios. *It's Just a Thought*. Yellow Monkeys Studio, 2011.

Zapak Games. *Sleeping at the Meeting*. Zapak Games.

———. *Yoga Teacher*. Zapak Games.

———.*Zombie Pirate*. Zapak Games.

Zia, Bisma, and Anam Sajid. *Trying to Fly*. N.p., 2020.

Index

About the Author

Dr Souvik Mukherjee is assistant professor of Cultural Studies at the Centre for Studies in Social Sciences Calcutta, India and a pioneering games studies scholar from the Indian Subcontinent. In his research spanning two decades, he looks at a diversity of topics starting with a poststructuralist reading of videogames as storytelling media, videogames as colonial and postcolonial media, videogame production studies in the Indian Subcontinent and currently, Indian boardgames and their colonial avatars. Souvik is the author of two monographs, *Videogames and Storytelling: Reading Games and Playing Books* and *Videogames and Postcolonialism: Empire Plays Back* as well as many articles and book chapters in national and international publications.

Souvik has been a board-member of the Digital Games Research Association (DiGRA) and a founder-member of DiGRA India and DHARTI, the Digital Humanities group in India. Souvik has been named a 'DiGRA Distinguished Scholar' in 2019. He is also an affiliated senior research fellow at the Centre of Excellence, Game Studies at Tampere University.

His other interests are (the) Digital Humanities, Poststructuralist theory, Posthumanism and Early Modern Literature. His databases on the Dutch Cemetery at Chinsurah, the Scottish Cemetery in Kolkata and the 19th-century Bengali industrialist, Mutty Lall Seal are all available open-access. He had been recently nominated a HEVGA (Higher Education Video Game Alliance) fellow.